W9-BLJ-770

Violence Unveiled

Violence Unveiled

Humanity at the Crossroads

GIL BAILIE

CROSSROAD · NEW YORK

1995

The Crossroad Publishing Company
370 Lexington Avenue, New York, NY 10017

Printed in the United States of America

Library of Congress Cataloging-in-Publication Data

Bailie, Gil.
Violence unveiled : humanity at the crossroads / Gil Bailie.
p. cm.
Includes bibliographical references and index.
ISBN 0-8245-1464-5
1. Apologetics—20th century. 2. Violence—Religious aspects. 3. Victims. 4. Myth. 5. Christianity and literature. I. Title.
BT1102.B215 1995
261.8–dc20 94-48633
CIP

To my mother for her enduring faith,
my father for his extraordinary example,
and to Kaeti, Allyson, Hunt, and Aña,
for their love, friendship, and trust.

At that, the veil of the Temple was torn in two from top to bottom...

—Matthew 27:51

...the Devil has landed in a furious rage;
he knows his time is up.

—Revelation 12:12

Things fall apart; the centre cannot hold;
Mere anarchy is loosed upon the world...
Surely some revelation is at hand...

—William Butler Yeats

Ring the bells that still can ring.
Forget your perfect offering.
There is a crack in everything.
That's how the light gets in.

—Leonard Cohen

Contents

Foreword

Violence Unveiled is about the spiritual crisis of our time. It is also a literary work, an often miraculous interplay between cultural documents and historical periods so distant from each other that they should not blend well, or so we think, until we find that, in this book, they harmonize perfectly. Such is the talent of Gil Bailie and the power of his analyses that he can bring together Bob Dylan and the Aztec myth of Tezcatlipoca without giving an impression of disharmony or discontinuity.

I would mislead the reader, however, if I gave the impression that *Violence Unveiled,* readable as it is, is a work of vulgarization. It is a most significant achievement in an intellectual and spiritual battle of great significance for our future. I feel very much involved myself because I have worked for many years on some of the ideas developed in this book. They have never looked better than they do here, and they have never been so accessible to readers of all kinds.

This impression is due, I believe, to the essential role of contemporary examples that Bailie handles masterfully and gracefully. When writers deal with current events, it is difficult for their style not to reflect the superficial and vulgar channels through which the information reached them. Bailie is different. He can discuss these events in the context of Greek tragedy and the Jewish prophets. He can illuminate the one with the others and vice versa. He can make Aeschylus accessible through Rodney King and purify Rodney King of journalistic clichés by placing his affair in an Aeschylian light. He can deal with even the tritest of current events without compromising the integrity of his analyses. He lifts us effortlessly to a level far superior to what most writers think the average reader is able to absorb.

Our world is in the midst of a great religious and cultural crisis. Many Christians have been won over to the view that insofar as our religion influences the world it does not make it better but worse. Above all, Christianity is supposed to leave the world unchanged because it is irrelevant, insignificant. It is one more *myth*.

Christianity resembles myth too closely, many people believe, not to be mythical itself. Once upon a time, just like Jesus, many divinities died a violent death after which they were reborn and resurrected, just like Jesus. The Christian narrative can only be a late version of some universal resurrection myth. What else could it be?

The book you are about to read powerfully contradicts this nihilistic consensus. It is an apology of Christianity but a most unconventional one. Instead of eluding or minimizing the similarities between myth and gospel, it is based on them, on the very data that seem to make relativism the only sensible belief in the modern world. In this book, the close relatedness of gospel and myth is the means through which the uniqueness of the Judeo-Christian tradition is vindicated, not the means through which it is denied.

How is this possible? This is what you will find out when you read this book. Gil Bailie achieves his purpose with such clarity, dramatic power, and simplicity that his book should cure the "inferiority complex" that many Christians have vis-à-vis the philosophical and pseudo-scientific dismissals of their religion. The problem with Christians is that they have lost all confidence in their Scriptures. If they listen to this book, they will understand that the Gospels contain an anthropology of religion far superior to anything the social sciences can provide and they will see the shallowness of religious relativism.

In this book, the Christian Cross is revealed as the most powerful instrument not only for understanding mythology and ritual but for interpreting the simultaneously frightening, horrible, and admirable developments in our contemporary world. The importance of *Violence Unveiled* is that it participates in the discovery of a most neglected dimension of the Gospels, their anthropology, which too exclusive an emphasis on theology has obscured. It should be noted however, that the discovery of this evangelical anthropology in no way contradicts traditional theology. On the contrary, it reinforces its now threatened credibility.

Next to the revelatory power of Scripture the most enlightening texts in our culture are not philosophical, psychological, or sociological but poetic and literary. This is why, in addition to being a great book about Christianity and modern culture, *Violence Unveiled* is also a remarkable work of literary interpretation. Gil Bailie surrounds himself with some of the greatest Western writers, notably modern English poets, showing as he goes that their most striking insights often anticipate uncannily what he himself has to say. I have always believed that the great Western writers, Christian or not, from Greek tragedy to Dante, Shakespeare, Cervantes, Pascal, down to the great novelists and poets of our own age, are more relevant to our modern predicament than all the philosophers and scientists in our universities. The marvelous analyses of this book strengthen this belief.

Above all *Violence Unveiled* is a book of hope. The worst thing about our intellectual life nowadays is its implicit or explicit agreement with the famous Shakespearean phrase about "the sound and the fury *signifying nothing*." This is the message that the fashionable trends in contemporary culture have been drilling into us for decades. Whatever we do to increase the din, the sound and the fury will still signify something and this something will be Christian. This, I believe, is the most important message of this most important book.

RENÉ GIRARD
Stanford University
November 1994

In Gratitude

Once, when I was seeking the advice of Howard Thurman and talking to him at some length about what needed to be done in the world, he interrupted me and said: "Don't ask yourself what the world needs. Ask yourself what makes you come alive, and go do that, because what the world needs is people who have come alive."

In trying to follow that advice, I found my way back into the rich treasure trove of the Western religious and literary tradition. In due course, I began to teach classes at a small institute I started largely on the strength of Dr. Thurman's admonition.

In the intervening twenty years, it has been my immense good fortune to teach classes on the literary and religious themes that excite me the most and to have been joined in those classes by men and women as excited by these themes as I have been. Eventually, our circle expanded to a larger group of people who began subscribing to weekly cassette tapes of the classes. Over the years, enduring friendships were formed, for which I am deeply grateful. This book is a product of both those classes and the friendships that developed in them.

Though I cannot here acknowledge by name all those who have helped make this book possible, there are a few people I especially want to thank. For their friendship and support over the years: Russ and Judy Dieter, Jim and Elizabeth Kemp, Salty Allen, Randy Coleman-Riese, Sally Grimshaw, Tom Richards, John and Nancy Boettiger, David and Joyce Bock, Jim and Jennifer Steinwedell, Jack Noble, James Jereb, Don Eddy, and McGregor Smith. For serving as an unerring compass in matters of the spirit: Dunstan Morrissey. For their many kindnesses and encouragements: Jack Gardner, Mary Leu McPherson, and Mark Uzzo. For their editorial suggestions: Nancy Reynes and Judith Stephenson.

The debt I owe to René Girard and to Robert Hamerton-Kelly and James G. Williams is, alas, too great to be paid in textual citations. Were I to trace the origin of my thinking back to those whose insights nurtured it, the notes would quickly fill the pages of this book and put the text to shame. For both their scholarship and their friendship, I am likewise grateful to Cesáreo Bandera, Byron Bland, Diana Culbertson,

Roel Kaptein, Andrew McKenna, Wolfgang Palaver, Father Raymund Schwager, S.J., and many other members of the Colloquium on Violence and Religion.

Most especially, of course, my greatest gratitude goes to my wife, Kaeti, and our children, Allyson, Hunt, and Aña, whose love and laughter sustain me.

Gil Bailie
Sonoma, California
August 1994

Acknowledgments

Permission is gratefully acknowledged to quote the following excerpts:

From "A Hole in the Floor" in *Advice to a Prophet and Other Poems,* copyright © 1961 and renewed 1989 by Richard Wilbur, reprinted by permission of Harcourt Brace & Company; and from *New and Collected Poems* by Richard Wilbur, reprinted by permission of Faber and Faber Ltd.

From "The Waste Land" and "Ash Wednesday" in *Collected Poems 1909–1962* by T. S. Eliot, copyright 1936 by Harcourt Brace & Company, copyright 1964, 1963 by T. S. Eliot, reprinted by permission of Harcourt Brace & Company and Faber and Faber Ltd.

From "Little Gidding" in *Four Quartets,* copyright 1943 by T. S. Eliot and renewed 1971 by Esme Valerie Eliot, reprinted by permission of Harcourt Brace & Company; in *Collected Poems 1909–1962,* reprinted by permission of Faber and Faber Ltd.

From "Devotions" in *Collected Poems,* copyright 1971 by James Wright, Wesleyan University Press by permission of the University Press of New England.

From "Bearded Oaks" in *Selected Poems 1923–1975* by Robert Penn Warren, copyright © 1942 and renewed 1970 by Robert Penn Warren. Reprinted by permission of Random House, Inc.

From "To Clio, Muse of History" in *The Collected Poems of Howard Nemerov* by Howard Nemerov (Chicago: University of Chicago Press, 1977).

From *Stranger Music: Selected Poems and Songs,* by Leonard Cohen, copyright © 1993 by Leonard Cohen and Leonard Cohen Stranger Music, Inc. Reprinted by permission of Pantheon Books, a division of Random House, Inc.

From "Diaspora" in *W. H. Auden: Collected Poems* by W. H. Auden, edited by Edward Mendelson, copyright © 1976 by Edward Mendelson, William Meredith and Monroe K. Spears, Executors of the Estate of W. H. Auden. Reprinted by permission of Random House, Inc.

From "The Rock" in *Wallace Stevens: The Collected Poems* by Wallace Stevens, copyright © 1954 by Wallace Stevens. Reprinted by permission of Alfred A. Knopf, Inc.

Violence
Unveiled

Introduction

The Hole in the Parlor Floor

> The carpenter's made a hole
> In the parlor floor, and I'm standing
> Staring down into it now
> At four o'clock in the evening,
> As Schliemann stood when his shovel
> Knocked on the crowns of Troy....[1]
>
> RICHARD WILBUR

The carpenter's work is unfinished. The poet says nothing about the renovations that are under way. Whatever the future outcome of these renovations, it is safe to assume that they will disrupt the household routines in the meantime. The poet is not complaining. For him, the carpenter's work-in-progress is a welcomed opportunity to explore the house's foundations, to look back to "the time when the floor was laid." He is pleased to have happened on the scene when he did. He kneels to get a better look.

The poet says he feels like Heinrich Schliemann, the nineteenth-century merchant-turned-archaeologist who, defying the scholarly consensus that the Troy of Homer's epics was a myth, discovered the ruins of the Trojan citadel. Like Schliemann, the poet senses that he, too, may discover something that others dismiss as fanciful.

These lines from Richard Wilbur come now to mind because they bear somewhat on the intellectual and spiritual journey that has led to this book. Some years ago, while I was browsing at the University of California bookstore, I happened upon a book with the intriguing title of *Violence and the Sacred* by René Girard.[2] I had seen references to Girard, but I had not read his work and knew little about it. I bought the book. The next morning, I opened it and within a few minutes I felt as Schliemann must have felt when he discovered that beneath the myth of the Trojan War was concrete reality. I felt like Richard Wilbur when he found himself staring down into a hole in the parlor floor.

There is another link with Homer. I discovered *Violence and the Sacred* at the same time that I was starting to teach a course on Homer's *Iliad* and *Odyssey.* Just as one of Keats's famous sonnets describes how he discovered Homer anew when he read Chapman's translation for the first time, I discovered Homer anew by reading his epics in the light of Girard's theory of culture, religion, and violence. Since then, I have found the interpretive range of Girard's theory to be astonishing. Whether I have tried to understand a piece of literature, an ancient myth, a historical event, or the morning newspaper, I have found Girard's insights invaluable. By turns, I have been inspired by the breadth and depth of his discovery and sobered by its immediate cultural implications. In my view, Girard has made the most sweeping and significant intellectual breakthrough of the modern age. He has formulated something like the unified field theory for the humanities, one, for instance, that can lead to a resolution of the nature-nurture quandary that has for so long kept the social sciences off balance and hampered their progress.

This is no time to be hampering the progress of the social sciences. Our cities are collapsing, our political processes are frayed and fragmented, our sense of historical responsibility has virtually disappeared, and, most seriously of all, our social and psychological stability now seems imperiled. At the end of the 1980s, the Cold War ended abruptly — a miracle no one thought possible — and, just as abruptly, the world that had been stabilized by cold war doctrines began to fall into confusion, animosity, and violence. Our world is now convulsing with disorder and violence, vivid scenes of which are beamed into our living rooms and burned into our sensibilities every day. The reassuring sense that progress is being made in social and political affairs is being replaced by an increasingly anxious concern for maintaining at least a minimum level of social decorum. Essential social institutions are reeling in the face of a cultural meltdown the real nature of which remains a mystery.

The epidemic of crime, drugs, and violence we are now experiencing is just the most conspicuous manifestation of a broader and deeper disintegration. The family, as an institution, is in such disarray that sitcoms have to redefine it each fall in order to appear relevant. The dismantling of sturdy, stable, and lifelong loyalties in the interest of increasingly fragile and fickle forms of selfhood is proceeding at a dizzying pace. For the most part, those on whom this process takes its greatest toll turn for help and solace to a psychological establishment still wedded to the theoretical misconceptions that helped foster the crisis in the first place. Meanwhile, the number of those soon to be in need of such help and solace is vastly increasing, as young people experiment with ways of adapting to the social and moral whirlwind in which they find themselves. Until we better understand the nature of the crisis of which all these things are symptoms, our attempts to solve social problems will continue to rely on assumptions that are intellectual symptoms of the same crisis.

Of course, there is a general consensus among those concerned with the present crisis that cultural, religious, psychological, and moral issues are linked, but the exact nature of their interrelationship has remained largely unexplored. The hope that some intelligible link might be found is itself in short supply. The unedifying spectacle of Marxist and Freudian doctrine collapsing in intellectual and spiritual exhaustion has left the human sciences understandably wary of unifying theories. In a desire to avoid further embarrassment, modest goals and modest hopes have been the order of the day. About the only sweeping theory that has recently found favor is one that holds that sweeping theories are no longer possible. When, in this milieu, René Girard proposed a sweeping new theory and argued for its universal applicability, it seemed almost a nuisance to have to reckon with it.

What is happening in our world, Girard argues, is nothing less than the disintegration of conventional culture, a process that is irreversible and one that constitutes humanity's moment of truth. We grow dizzy from an avalanche of change and risk losing our way in history, because we remain unclear about the underlying dynamic of history and oblivious of its determining forces. Unless we better understand what is happening to us, we will continue to be buffeted by wave after wave of this disintegration, reluctant to recognize its scope, unable to appreciate its spiritual meaning, and unprepared to meet its historical challenges. Coming to grips with the depth of the crisis is a daunting task, but it is also one that is full of promise, and the price to be paid for shrinking from it is too horrendous to seriously contemplate.

Violence and the Sacred was first published in France in 1972. The French newspaper *Le Monde* announced: "The year 1972 should be marked with an asterisk in the annals of the humanities. *La violence et le sacré* is not only a great book, it is also unique and profoundly contemporary."[3] A year later, writing in the French periodical *Esprit,* Eric Gans declared that Girard's research in anthropology had given the world an "Archimedean point" from which it would now be possible to rethink the human sciences. Some years later, Sandor Goodhart referred to Gans's comment as an understatement, noting the relevance of Girard's work to the study of economics, political science, and even the hard sciences.[4] At a 1983 symposium on Girard's work, the philosopher Paul Dumouchel summed up the situation this way:

> Beginning from literary criticism and ending with a general theory of culture, through an explanation of the role of religion in primitive societies and a radical reinterpretation of Christianity, René Girard has completely modified the landscape in the social sciences. Ethnology, history of religion, philosophy, psychoanalysis, psychology and literary criticism are explicitly mobilized in this enterprise. Theology, economics and political sciences, history and sociology—in short, all the social sciences, and those that used to be called moral sciences—are influenced by it.[5]

No summary brief enough for an introduction could convey the subtlety of the Girardian theory, and an oversimplified presentation of it would lead to misconceptions, defeating the very purpose of an introduction. Suffice it to say that Girard has uncovered the role violence plays in archaic religion and the role these religious systems play in human culture. Human history is the relentless chronicle of violence that it is because when cultures fall apart they fall into violence, and when they revive themselves they do so violently. Primitive religion is the institution that remembers the reviving violence mythologically and ritually reenacts its spellbinding climax. Primitive religion grants one form of violence a moral monopoly, endowing it with enough power and prestige to preempt other forms of violence and restore order. The famous distinction between "sacred" and "profane" is born as the culture glorifies the decisive violence (sacred) that brought an episode of chaotic violence (profane) to an end and made warriors into worshipers. Distinguishing these two forms of violence is always an extremely arbitrary affair, but that does not keep the distinction from having beneficial effects. Religion makes possible these benefits by bestowing sacred status on a socially tolerable form of violence to which the culture can resort as an alternative to greater and more catastrophic violence. "It is better that one man should die," said Caiaphas of Jesus, "than that the whole nation be destroyed."

Caiaphas was invoking a mechanism for preserving culture that is as old as culture itself. Whether it is the Assyro-Babylonian myth declaring that Marduk created the world by killing the monster Tiamat; or the Teutonic myth telling how Odin formed the world by raising the corpse of Ymir from the sea of Ymir's own blood; or Pope Urban II declaring that God willed the first Crusade; or Thomas Jefferson saying that the tree of liberty must be periodically watered with the blood of patriots and tyrants; or Lenin saying you can't make an omelet without breaking eggs — cultures have forever commemorated some form of sacred violence at their origins and considered it a sacred duty to reenact it in times of crisis. The logic of sacred violence is nowhere expressed more succinctly nor repudiated more completely than in the New Testament, where the high priest solemnly announces its benefits and the crucifixion straightaway reveals its arbitrariness and horror. The New Testament account of the crucifixion reproduces the myths and mechanisms of primitive religion only to explode them, reveal their perversities, and declare allegiance to the Victim of them. As the theologian Robert Hamerton-Kelly, one of Girard's most astute interpreters, puts it: "Christian theology provides a trenchant critique of religion."[6]

There was, however, something profoundly true about what Caiaphas said. Up to this very day, cultures rely on scapegoating violence to a far greater degree than we realize.[7] The reason culture is now in such disarray, however, is that this ancient recipe for generating social solidarity has ceased to have its once reliable effects. It has been gradually shorn of its religious mystifications, and, as a result, its ability to promote cultural order has waned. By mystifying human violence and attributing it to the gods, archaic religion endowed a certain form of physical might — usually the most powerful form — with metaphysical significance. As long as the myths that mythologized certain human violence remained in effect, this sacralized violence was able to ward off other violence or crush it with religious conviction when it arose. As the myths that divinized the violence were weakened, the difference between order-destroying violence and order-restoring violence likewise began to break down.

Which brings me back to the hole in the parlor floor. As Girard explained in his next book — *Things Hidden since the Foundation of the World* — the hole in the parlor floor into which he had peered in *Violence and the Sacred* was made by the Galilean Carpenter who was publicly executed outside Jerusalem two thousand years ago. As profoundly novel as Girard's insights seem, he insists that they simply clarify and explicate a revelation of sacred violence that has its seeds in the Hebrew Scriptures and its stunning climax in the New Testament passion story. The Carpenter made a hole in the parlor floor and Girard simply looked into it and saw there things hidden since the foundation of the world. "Thus," writes Robert Hamerton-Kelly, "Girard points us to a possible restatement of biblical faith that places it at the center of the struggle for a culture beyond violence."[8]

According to the currently fashionable school of literary deconstruction, literary criticism is in a tailspin that is too momentous to be interrupted. There is nothing but the text. One reading is as good as another. Girard's work, however, articulates the terms under which the critical work might be revived, grounded once again in historical reality and made both anthropologically and spiritually significant. As the criteria for assessing cultural arrangements generally, and literary traditions specifically, Girard has proposed the victim and the truth about the victim. He has suggested that the real task of literary criticism has just begun, and that at its center is the Cross. With the Cross as his hermeneutic principle, Girard's work deconstructs literary deconstruction and replaces its purely literary vertigo with intellectual and moral vigor.

The phrase "things hidden since the foundation of the world" is taken from the Gospel of Matthew. In the passage from which it is taken, Matthew says that Jesus' use of parables was linked to his mission to reveal those things hidden since the foundation of the world. The implication is that the practical meaning of revolutionary and "counter-intuitive" truths is more likely to be conveyed by anecdotes than by an abstract statement of the truths themselves. I hope that is the case, for in the pages to follow I have tried to report on what lies beneath the parlor floor and what the hole in that floor means by relying heavily on anecdotes—anecdotes drawn from history, anthropology, literature, the Bible, and contemporary public affairs.

Though literary and scriptural references are plentiful enough, I have quoted rather extensively from contemporary newspaper articles in order to show what the unveiling of violence looks like in the world today. I hope in this way to make the relevance of Girard's insights palpable. I want to show that, once the basic features of Girard's hypothesis are understood, evidence of its validity is never far to seek. The newspaper provides a daily harvest of such references. Neither these stories nor my rather casual selection of them deserve to be called "research," and I make no scientific claims for them. I have rather tried to highlight these articles as "signs of the times." I haven't the slightest doubt that stories that are either structurally identical to the ones I have quoted or the historical extensions of them will be in the news and part of our daily experience for decades to come.

Since almost all of my literary anecdotes are taken from what we once called the Western tradition, a word may be in order about the issue of what constitutes the "Western" canon, an issue that has been such a contentious one in academic circles in recent years. There is nothing more distinctively "Western" than the current debate over multiculturalism. The debate is simply Western culture doing what it has always done. It is Western culture losing its life in order to find it, surrendering its cultural specificity in a specifically Western way.

The biblical empathy for the victims of social derision is the goose that laid multiculturalism's golden egg. Trying to avoid intolerance by presenting all possible points of view will be a boon to those suffering intolerance only if the various points of view presented express an equally robust empathy for the victims of intolerance. If the debate over multiculturalism results in a culture where fewer people are victimized or marginalized, it will be because the biblical empathy for victims is still the moral force at the heart of the debate.

Perhaps a metaphor may help. The life that Charles Darwin found on the Galapagos Islands was unique, but it was the key to his discovery of something universal. There is something comparably unique and at the same time universal about the Judeo-Christian tradition. If I insist on the uniqueness of this tradition, it is only to show that it discloses the universal human predicament in a uniquely powerful way, and it provides an equally unique prism through which to comprehend the cultural and spiritual issues of our time.

It is clear, I think, that our effort to comprehend the contemporary cultural crisis has been hampered by our tendency to analyze the various symptoms of the crisis in isolation from one another. In this regard, I feel it is especially important that we recognize the link between social and psychological instability. The subjective experience of psychological insubstantiality, and the myriad ways of compensating for it, is a growing problem, especially among the young. Not even a summary analysis of our present dilemma would be complete without addressing so significant a symptom of it. Where appropriate in the following pages, I briefly allude to the psychological repercussions of the crisis of culture. In order to retain the social and cultural focus of this book, however, I have chosen to devote a separate volume, now in preparation, to a more detailed discussion of the "crisis of the self," its psychological dynamics, its religious significance, and its relationship to the larger cultural crisis.

Chapter 1

"A Sort of Surreal Confusion"

The Revolutionary Tribunal went to work, and a steady slaughtering began.... The invention of the guillotine was opportune to this mood. The queen was guillotined, and most of Robespierre's antagonists were guillotined; atheists who argued that there was no Supreme Being were guillotined; Danton was guillotined because he thought there was too much guillotine; day by day, week by week, this infernal new machine chopped off heads and more heads and more. The reign of Robespierre lived, it seemed, on blood, and needed more and more, as an opium-taker needs more and more opium.[1]

H. G. WELLS

In the case of tens of millions killed and the lives of entire nations subverted, a catchword simply won't do.... "Communism" was the breakdown of humanity and not a political problem. It was a human problem, a problem of our species, and thus of a lingering nature.... Why don't we simply start by admitting that an extraordinary anthropological backslide has taken place in our century?[2]

JOSEPH BRODSKY

Will we actually allow [Auschwitz] to be the end point, the disruption which it really was, the catastrophe of our history, out of which we can find a way only through a radical change of direction achieved via new standards of action? Or will we see it only as a monstrous accident within this history but not affecting history's course?[3]

JOHANN BAPTIST METZ

"Every historical development," wrote the historian John Lukacs, "is inseparable from its recognition."[4] Almost by definition, a truly historic development is one that cannot be adequately assessed by the conventional wisdom and intellectual presuppositions whose historical relevance it is bringing to an end. The worldwide crisis of culture in the midst of which we now find ourselves is just such a historical development. If historical developments are inseparable from their recognition, and if the one we're living through is having some terrible consequences in part because we have failed to recognize its true significance, then it is our responsibility to try anew to recognize it. Those who come after us may be better able than we to recognize the nature of the present crisis, but they may not have a chance to do so unless we begin to recognize it better than we have so far.

It has been said that "the Nazi experience tests the limits of what history can explain."[5] Nor is the Nazi holocaust alone in defying explanation. Today, we are constantly confronted by news of horrendous acts of collective violence for which our familiar explanations seem inadequate. If we are no longer able to explain away the violence that is upon us, it is because almost all of the interpretive and explanatory tools with which we have tried to explain it are those bequeathed to us by the European Enlightenment. The Enlightenment came into being by expelling or marginalizing the religious perspective without which some of the oddest vagaries of the human drama become incomprehensible. For perfectly understandable reasons, the Enlightenment had hoped to rid the world of religious superstition and the religious passions that had proven so destructive. It proposed to do so by placing an empirical rationalism at the spiritual center of the West's cultural undertaking—a place once occupied by Christian moral and intellectual sensibilities, whose source of clarity remained unclear and whose historical and cultural effects were, shall we say, not uniformly edifying. In truth, however, what the Enlightenment did was to secularize a wariness about religion that has its roots in the Old Testament prophets, the Gospels, and the letters of Paul. For both the secularizing and rationalizing impulses it espoused were products of the Judeo-Christian tradition that the Enlightenment came into existence by underestimating and repudiating.

There may be no more urgent task today than that of renouncing religious superstition and freeing ourselves from its grip, but we're not likely to do so by abandoning the spiritual tradition that taught us to be wary of religious superstition in the first place. Things have changed. Today, one is more likely to find people who have renounced religious superstition in monasteries and in synagogues, in church-sponsored soup kitchens, and at morning Mass than at the shopping mall, the fitness gym, the stock exchange, or the faculty lounge. Those who think that disdain for religion is an antidote for religious superstition haven't sufficiently pondered the French Revolution or Madam Mao's cultural revolution or Pol Pot's bloody attempt at social engineering. On the other hand, if we could dispense with both the credulous forms of piety and the gullible forms of skepticism that combine to insulate the modern world from the biblical tradition, we might finally realize that the Hebrew prophets and the New Testament represent the world's mother lode of anti-superstition.

The European Enlightenment has been a cat with nine lives, but it is now a spent force and the optimism it fostered is sputtering out. Even the more thoughtful attempts to revive it, like Francis Fukuyama's *The End of History,* ring hollow. Who can still believe that self-governing political arrangements and self-regulating mechanisms of economic ambition are capable of stopping, much less reversing, the alarming rate of social disintegration that is occurring in our nations, cities, neighborhoods, and families? As these forms of community, intimacy, and commitment lose their binding power, societies all over the world are growing more socially volatile and the psychological stability of those living in them is declining. The situation is comparable in every respect to the deterioration of the ozone layer. In both cases, the effects of deterioration are both incremental and cumulative, and their consequences almost impossible to imagine.

As Girard's seminal work indicates, and as I will try to show, we are in the midst of perhaps the greatest anthropological challenge in history. It is a challenge that goes to the heart of culture itself. So much so, that in order to approximate its historical and anthropological significance, I, too, want to begin by referring to the epochal shift this challenge is precipitating as the end of "history." Let me stress that by "history" (in quotes) I do not mean the human enterprise on this planet, but rather one particular phase of that enterprise. By "history" (in quotes) I mean the stage in human history (without quotes) during which collective and cathartic acts of violence could be counted on to bring a period of social chaos to an end and, in doing so, to convince its participants and sympathetic observers of the truth of the myth that justified the violence. Since such rituals of collective violence have played a key role in generating the social solidarity necessary for ordinary cultural life "since the foundation of the world," the waning of their power confronts us with an anthropological dilemma of the first magnitude. And so I shall speak of it as the end of "history" in order to underscore its significance.

The irony, of course, is that this end of "history" is being brought about by the same moral force that gave rise to the specifically Western experience of history in the first place. In the West, due to the influence of the biblical tradition, the term "history" refers neither just to the recollection of events nor to the passage of time during which they occur. Rather it implies a journey toward truth. At its core, the Western sense of history assumes the gradual emergence of something that is both radically new and the fulfillment of what preceded it. Modernity's now-defunct notions of inevitable social "evolution" or historical "progress" were shallow and insubstantial ones, but the principle they misconstrued and underestimated is at the heart of Western civilization, and its roots are biblical. For the West, history is the *future* as much as it is the past, but it is also the mental and spiritual atmosphere in which we think about our lives. "Western civilization has now spread all over the world," wrote Lukacs "Neither the scientific method nor the professional study of history are any longer European and American intellectual monopolies. Yet historical consciousness is still something specifically 'Western.'"[6] As Lukacs and most other historians — both Western and non-Western — acknowledge, the West's historical consciousness is inextricably bound up with the historicity of the Judeo-Christian tradition. "Christianity is not one of the great things of history," wrote Henri de Lubac, "it is history that is one of the great things of Christianity."[7] The biblical sensibility that shaped Western cultures endowed them with a palpable sense that something new was happening in history and an insatiable curiosity for finding out what it was. Western historical consciousness is concerned not only with what actually happened in the past but also with trying to understand the direction history is taking and what forces are driving it. It is a worthy undertaking, and one which Girard's work allows us to take up with new zest.

Apocalypse

"Man creates what he calls history as a screen to conceal the workings of the apocalypse from himself," wrote the literary critic Northrop Frye.[8] This is a stunning insight. It cries out to be paired with the observation that the Nazi experience tests the limits of what "history" can explain. It implies that "history" pays a price in return for its explanatory power. It suggests that "history" conceals something in order to illuminate everything else. It implies what Cesáreo Bandera made explicit when he called attention to "what literal historical reality itself hides or disguises in order to constitute itself as such, as meaningful historical reality."[9] In other words, what makes "meaningful historical reality" meaningful is the concealing of something that might rob it of its meaning were it not concealed. If "the Nazi experience tests the limits of what history can explain," it is because the explanatory power of "history" begins and ends with its ability to explain away the victims and the violence vented against them.

Equally remarkable in Frye's lapidary statement is its implication that the end of "history" was inextricably bound up with the Bible, and that the biblical texts could not be fully comprehended if their apocalyptic features were neglected. Frye even went so far as to suggest that the "vision of the apocalypse is the vision of the total meaning of the Scriptures," though he erred when he took the next step, asserting that apocalyptic destruction "is what the Scripture is intended to achieve."[10] On the contrary, what Scripture is intended to achieve is a conversion of the human heart that will allow humanity to dispense with organized violence without sliding into the abyss of uncontrollable violence, the apocalyptic abyss.

The word "apocalypse" means "unveiling." What, then, is veiled, the unveiling of which can have apocalyptic consequences? The answer is: violence. Veiled violence is violence whose religious or historical justifications still provide it with an aura of respectability and give it a moral and religious monopoly over any "unofficial" violence whose claim to "official" status it preempts. Unveiled violence is apocalyptic violence precisely because, once shorn of its religious and historical justifications, it cannot sufficiently distinguish itself from the counter-violence it opposes. Without benefit of religious and cultural privilege, violence simply does what unveiled violence always does: it incites more violence. In such situations, the scope of violence grows while the ability of its perpetrators to reclaim that religious and moral privilege diminishes. The reciprocities of violence and counter-violence threaten to spin completely out of control.

The weakness of Frye's analysis was that he treated the apocalyptic phenomenon as though it were exclusively a literary or psychological one, and he ignored its historical and anthropological implications. The "vision of the apocalypse," he wrote, "may break in on anyone at any time."[11] For Frye, the apocalypse was ultimately a *vision* forming in the mind or psyche of the *reader.* Of course, Frye was right to reject the notion of the apocalypse as a lurid prophesy of God's final orgy of vengeance, but whether Frye's alternative — a purely literary and psychological apocalypse — better accounts for either the biblical texts or the historical events is doubtful.

The other literary critic who has argued for the unique relevance of the biblical tradition for our troubled times is, of course, René Girard. Like Frye, Girard has insisted that the apocalyptic language of the Bible cannot and should not be dismissed. "Apocalyptic prophecy," Girard argues, "means no more and no less than a rational anticipation of what men are likely to do to each other and to their environment, if they go on disregarding the [Gospel's] warning against revenge in a desacralized and sacrificially unprotected world."[12] "The idea of 'limitless' violence, long scorned by sophisticated Westerners, suddenly looms up before us,"[13] writes Girard. "For the first time," he says, humanity faces "a perfectly straightforward and even scientifically calculable choice between total destruction and the total renunciation of violence."[14]

For Girard, however, it was not "history" that humanity created to screen the workings of the apocalypse from itself. It was religion — archaic religion — that came into being in the first instance, Girard has argued, with the sacralization of a spontaneous act of scapegoating violence. In other words, archaic religion is humanity's astonishing instrument for turning murder and madness into a sacralized bulwark against madness and murder. More or less refined forms of this same recipe for generating social solidarity and lending it the requisite solemnity have played a part in cultural existence since the dawn of human culture. The social stability of these cultures was determined to a considerable degree by the success with which they were able to experience and interpret the violence which brought them into being as holy. And any given culture's attempt to endow its scapegoating violence with religious sanction depends on the degree of unanimity the violence inspires, and unanimity requires that all empathy for the victim or victims of the violence be extinguished. To use Frye's evocative imagery, the screen that we have used to conceal from ourselves the workings of the apocalypse is the screen that has kept us from recognizing the humanity of our victims and the truth about the violence inflicted on them.

The generic term for the systematic misrecognitions that have veiled the victim's face and silenced the victim's voice is "myth." If we live at a moment in human history when "history" is no longer able to screen us from the apocalypse, no longer able to explain away the violence it documents, it is because in our day "history" is exhausting the last vestige of its mythological power. In the *foreseeable* future, neither religious mystification nor the solemn and quasi-religious causes of "history" will sufficiently veil our violence from our own eyes nor keep us from seeing the faces of our victims.

A Place to Begin

In 1992, in response to pitiable scenes of starvation and wretched deprivation in Somalia, the United States accepted a major role in a United Nations military operation aimed at ending the factional fighting that had made it impossible to get Western aid to those suffering Somalis most in need of it. The popular support that made the mission politically feasible derived largely from the fact that in the months and weeks prior to the decision to send U.S. troops television newscasts regularly confronted viewers with scenes of the terrible suffering of Somali men, women, and children. Over time, however, the campaign to restore order in Somalia proved more difficult. And if pictures of the emaciated victims of Somalia's cultural disintegration played the major role in arousing the U.S. determination to aid the victims, it was pictures of another sort that brought a sharp decline in public support for American involvement. Amid an escalation of violence and vehemence on the part of both Somalis and U.N. forces, an American serviceman was killed by a Somali mob. The gleeful mob dragged the serviceman's body through the streets of Mogadishu in joyous triumph. Americans suddenly saw on their television screens *another* victim. Almost overnight, public sentiment for the operation reversed itself. A chorus of voices was raised — in Congress and elsewhere — for a withdrawal of U.S. troops.

I have chosen to begin this exploration of the contemporary crisis of culture with a mention of the U.S. effort to get relief to starving Somalis for two reasons. First, because the Somali effort was an instance of the moral double bind that Western culture faces at this critical moment in history. It will be the burden of this book to show that we face this double bind because we are the spiritual and moral heirs of a biblical tradition, the historical effect of which is the gradual awakening of a concern for the plight of victims. Second, the U.S. effort in Somali is a good place to begin because an astute social and political commentator has made remarks about the effort that are not only noteworthy, but which also contain undeveloped hints of many of the issues with which I will be dealing in the pages that follow. And so I want to reflect briefly on the dilemma presented by the Somali famine relief effort and ponder a few of the pregnant remarks about the U.S. effort made in the October 18, 1993, edition of *Time* magazine by Lance Morrow.

During the week when public opinion about the Somali operation was reversing itself, Morrow offered the following observation to his *Time* magazine readers:

> An advertent and sustained foreign policy uses a different part of the brain from the one engaged by horrifying images. If Americans had seen the battles of the Wilderness and Cold Harbor on TV screens in 1864, if they had witnessed the meat-grinding carnage of Ulysses Grant's warmaking, then public opinion would have demanded an end to the Civil War, and the Union might well have split into two countries, one of them farmed by black slaves.

With the combination of insight and common sense that typify his essays, Morrow glimpsed, not only the foreign policy complications of the Somali intervention, but the Western world's essential moral conundrum, a growing inability to subordinate its empathy for victims to more practical political and geopolitical concerns. It is true, of course, that a "sustained foreign policy uses a different part of the brain from the one engaged by horrifying images" — images, say, of starving children or murderous mobs — but in Western cultures the wall separating these two "parts of the brain" has been slowly crumbling for centuries. By comparison, the collapse of the Berlin Wall was a minor historical event.

Morrow's analogy underscores the moral paradox at the heart of the West's historical dilemma, namely, that efforts made to fulfill the moral imperative to aid victims — especially when these efforts involve violence — inevitably produce victims of their own. The point of Morrow's Civil War analogy is that our efforts to rescue victims would be seriously undermined if our empathy for victims were to be extended to those victimized by our own rescuing efforts. In other words, there is a line which our empathy for victims must not cross, lest our ability to aid victims be lost.

Morrow is no doubt right, but in his short essay he succeeded more in locating the underlying dilemma than in clarifying its complex implications. For one thing, he seems to have assumed that the key feature in the West's moral double bind was the wide dissemination of televised images of the horrors of violence or victimization. There is some truth to this, of course; what is historically significant, however, is not the technology of telecommunications, but the moral and spiritual impulse to put this technology to work showing the world the face of the victim. Unless we recognize the profound historical shift represented by the West's progressive concern for victims, we cannot really comprehend the historical crisis in the midst of which we now live.

The more interesting point of Morrow's analogy, however, is that, had the abolitionist North seen the real horrors of the Civil War, it might have lacked the resolve to end the real horrors of slavery. But suppose, for example, that the Civil War partisans had had television, and suppose they had chosen to use it to show, not just the atrocities of their enemies, but the horrors of war itself. Surely the moral imperative that would have inspired them to do so would have prompted them to show the horrors of slavery with equal determination. It is that *determination,* and not the technological instruments it employs, that is the defining impulse at the heart of what we call Western culture and, in fact, the true driving force of history in our world.

In one form or another, all of the world's great religions urge their faithful to exercise compassion and mercy, as does the Judeo-Christian tradition. But the empathy for victims — *as victims* — is specifically Western and quintessentially biblical. The burr under the saddle of "Western" culture, the source of its moral uneasiness and social restlessness, is precisely this growing empathy for victims. Most of the West's political innovations are linked to it, and our most deeply held social and moral sensibilities are suffused with it. Surely Morrow can't be faulted for omitting from his short magazine article an account of such things. I have chosen to begin my exploration of these issues with his brief comments, however, because I feel he has at least vaguely intuited our historical predicament. For example, Morrow observed:

> The Americans have ventured into Somalia in a sort of surreal confusion, first impersonating Mother Teresa and now John Wayne. It would help to clarify that self-image, for to do so would clarify the mission, and then to recast the rhetoric of the enterprise.

I would extend the implications of this remark, and apply it not just to American foreign policy, but to the history of Western civilization and, ultimately, to history itself. At the heart of the cultural world in which we live, and into whose orbit the whole world is being gradually drawn, is a *surreal confusion.* The impossible Mother Teresa–John Wayne antinomy Morrow has discerned in America's Somali operation is simply a contemporary manifestation of the tension that for centuries has hounded those cultures under biblical influence.

The more we *realize* that we have been alternately impersonating Mother Teresa and John Wayne, the less we will be able to avoid the moral dilemma we were once able to avoid by *alternately* impersonating them. We will have no choice except to "clarify the mission" and "recast the rhetoric of the enterprise." It will be a daunting task, one that will have to be taken up anew again and again. In its largest sense, the task is nothing less than an ongoing effort to discover the nature of the historical dynamic, to recognize its source, and to discern its implications. What follows is something far more modest: an *essay* in clarification, an attempt to understand our cultural and historical crisis by trying to locate its underlying moral and religious dynamics.

The Victim

There's plenty of truth in the revised picture of Western history that the young are now routinely taught, the picture of the West's swashbuckling appetite for power, wealth, and dominion. What's to be noted is that it is *we,* and not our cultural adversaries, who are teaching it to them. It is *we,* the spiritual beneficiaries of that less than always edifying history, who automatically empathize more with our ancestors' victims than with our ancestors themselves. If we are tempted to think that this amazing shift is the product of our own moral achievement, all we have to do is look around at how shamelessly we exploit it for a little power, wealth, and dominion of our own.

The fact is that the concern for victims has gradually become the principal moral gyroscope in the Western world. Even the most vicious campaigns of victimization — including, astonishingly, even Hitler's — have found it necessary to base their assertion of moral legitimacy on the claim that their goal was the protection or vindication of victims. However savagely we behave, and however wickedly and selectively we wield this moral gavel, protecting or rescuing innocent victims has become *the* cultural imperative everywhere the biblical influence has been felt. Both our Mother Teresa and our John Wayne impersonations are based on it. The "surreal confusion" we are now experiencing is the symptom of a momentous historical development, a historical development that, in the words of John Lukacs, is inseparable from its recognition.

Journalists can sometimes be a source of surreal confusion, but they can also be the first to chronicle the follies that result from it. In recent years, as the chorus of voices arose, each claiming for itself the status of victim, many journalists took the opportunity to mock the hypocrisy. Articles both whimsical and withering began to appear. "Like contestants on *Queen for a Day,*" wrote Wendy Haminer in an article typical of many, "Americans of various persuasions assert competing claims of victimhood, vying for attention and support." "Not only may victimization make you famous and the center of some small circle of attention," Haminer continues, "it offers absolution and no accountability and creates entitlements to sympathy, support and reparations."[15] In other words, once one's claim to victim status is established, one can use the moral swagger of that position to extort certain social, political, or material advantages from the ever-shrinking number of those who have yet to find a plausible premise on which to base their own claim to victim status.

The September 29, 1992, *Wall Street Journal,* carried an article on a related subject by Heather MacDonald. MacDonald reported on how rigorously the doctrine of multiculturalism was being enforced on today's college campuses. Her article began this way:

> It is never too soon to learn to identify yourself as a victim. Such, at least, is the philosophy of today's college freshman orientation, which has become a crash course in the strange new world of university politics. Within days of arrival on campus, "new students" (the euphemism of choice for "freshmen") learn the paramount role of gender, race, ethnicity, class and sexual orientation in determining their own and others' identity. Most important, they are provided with the most critical tool of their college career: the ability to recognize their own victimization.

Such things are so self-satirizing that journalistic satire seems wasted on them. What must not be missed, however, is that beneath all the buffoonery lies the most sweeping historical revolution in the world, namely, the emergence of an empathy for victims and a dawning realization that no event can be fully assessed until its victims have been heard from. Of course, the trivialization of this empathy for victims was virtually inevitable, and so was the attempt to exploit the victim's moral power for social, economic, and political advantage. But neither the trivialization nor the exploitation diminish in any way the historical and anthropological significance of the West's moral concern for victims.

A few years ago, another related story appeared in the fashion section of the *New York Times.* The story was largely a montage of photographs apparently taken on the streets of New York of people dressed in clothes with patches sewn prominently on them. The brief story ran beneath the headline: "Patches: In, Not Down and Out." It reads:

> All the patched clothes seen around town recently were not a result of the present recession, nor yet of nostalgia for the Great Depression of the 1930's, when patching clothes was a necessity. Today's patches are all about status and style.
>
> Christian Francis Roth's clothes have intricate patch inserts that are part of Mr. Roth's designs.
>
> Patched jeans have been around since the 1960's. The newer ones are imitating Mr. Roth's more expensive designs with appliquéd patches that don't cost as much.

> And not to be confused with those styles are the rap-style patches with fringed—or frayed—edges on denim clothes.[16]

This style came to be called "homeless chic," a name that is no less ironic and bizarre than the fashion contest to which the story alluded, a contest between those with designer patches, those with less expensive imitations, and those desperately hoping to distinguish themselves from the others by wearing "rap-style patches" with frayed edges. This is all very funny and very expensive and more than a little pathetic. If money can't buy happiness, maybe it can buy poverty, or at least catch clumsily at the moral distinction that adheres to social marginality in a world exposed for centuries to the Sermon on the Mount.

The fact that concern for victims is so ridiculously trivialized does not mean that it is a trivial concern—far from it. "Identification with the victim can be perverted," writes Andrew McKenna, "but this only authenticates the undisputed privilege of the victim as the site from which truth is determined in our era."[17] After the sniggers die down, the deeper issue raised by this new and widespread claim to victim status must be explored. For, as the Dutch theologian Edward Schillebeeckx argues, the historical conversation-partner of European culture is the victim.[18]

In recent years, skewering the politically correct and the political correctness of those mocking political correctness has become a thriving journalistic enterprise. One of the more interesting examples of the genre was a cover-story essay by Robert Hughes, which appeared in the February 3, 1992, edition of *Time* magazine. The essay was entitled "The Fraying of America."[19] In it, Hughes cast a cold eye on the American social landscape, and his assessment was summarized in the article's subtitle: "When a nation's diversity breaks into factions, demagogues rush in, false issues cloud debate, and everybody has a grievance."

Like others, Hughes found himself puzzling over how and why the status of "victim" had become *the* seal of moral rectitude in American society. He began his essay by quoting a passage from W. H. Auden's Christmas oratorio, *For the Time Being*. The lines he quoted were ones in which King Herod ruminates over whether the threat to civilization posed by the birth of Christ is serious enough to warrant murdering all the male children in one region of the empire. (The historical Herod may have been a vulgar and conniving Roman sycophant, but Auden's Herod, let's not forget, is watching the rough beast of the twentieth century slouching toward Bethlehem.) Weighing all the factors, Herod decides that the Christ child must be destroyed, even if to do so innocents must be slaughtered. For, he argues in the passage that Hughes quoted, should the Child survive:

> Reason will be replaced by Revelation. . . . Justice will be replaced by Pity as the cardinal virtue, and all fear of retribution will vanish. . . . The New Aristocracy will consist exclusively of hermits, bums and permanent invalids. The Rough Diamond, the Consumptive Whore, the bandit who is good to his mother, the epileptic girl who has a way with animals will be the heroes and heroines of the New Age, when the general, the statesman, and the philosopher have become the butt of every farce and satire.[20]

Hughes quoted this passage from Auden in order to point out that Auden's prophecy had come true. As Auden's Herod had predicted, American society was awash in what Hughes termed the "all-pervasive claim to victimhood." He noted that in virtually all the contemporary social, political, or moral debates, both sides were either claiming to be victims or claiming to speak on their behalf. It was clear to Hughes, however, that this was not a symptom of a moral victory over our scapegoating impulses. There can be no victims without victimizers. Even though virtually everyone seemed to be claiming the status of victim, the claims could be sustained only if some of the claims could be denied. (At this point, things become even murkier, for in the topsy-turvy world of victimology, a claimant denied can easily be mistaken for a victim scorned, the result being that denying someone's claim to victim status can have the same effect as granting it.) Nevertheless, the algebraic equation of victimhood requires victimizers, and so, for purely logical reasons, some claims have to be denied. Some, in Hughes's words, would have to remain "the butt of every farce and satire." Hughes argued that all those who claim victim status share one thing in common, "they have been denied parity with that Blond Beast of the sentimental imagination, the heterosexual, middle-class, white male."

Hughes realized that a hardy strain of envy and resentment toward this one, lone nonvictim continued to play an important role in the squabbles over who would be granted victim status. Those whose status as victim was secure were glaring at this last nonvictim with something of the vigilante's narrow squint. Understandably, the culprit was anxious to remove his blemish. "Since our new found sensitivity decrees that only the victim shall be the hero," Hughes wrote, "the white American male starts bawling for victim status too."

Hughes's essay was both insightful and entertaining, and yet he never returned to the most important point of all. He never took seriously the words from Auden with which his essay began. Auden's Herod had sanctioned the slaughter of the innocents in order to keep the events depicted in the New Testament from happening and to prevent these events from having the effect on culture that Hughes and his fellow journalists were lampooning. Hughes never addressed the explicit inference of the Auden quotation from which his whole essay hung like an unripe fruit. He flatly acknowledged that "what Herod saw was America in the late 1980s and early '90s," and he strongly implied that the confusion of these years was *somehow* bound up with an ill-defined and selectively applied empathy for victims. And yet, he never asked why Auden's Herod had said what he said. He never asked what might have been the role of Christianity in awakening an empathy for victims. Nor did he ponder openly how this empathy might have had the disturbing effects he describes in his article, nor what its larger historical implications might be. This book is an attempt to ponder just those things.

Auden had an anthropological sensibility, and it made him aware of features of the Christian revelation to which conventional Christian piety has yet to fully awaken. Many of Auden's most important poems toy with insights that René Girard has since formulated explicitly. "The victim has the last word in the Bible," Girard writes, and "we are influenced by this even though we do not want to pay the Bible the homage it deserves."[21] The victim's "last *word*" in the Christian Bible is the Crucified *Logos* of the gospel. Like Girard, Auden seems to have sensed what troubling consequences the worldwide proclamation of the victim as "Lord" would eventually have for cultures that still rely for their social solidarity on periodic episodes of solemnly sanctioned righteous violence.

Disruptive Empathy

At first blush, it would seem that the awakening of an empathy for victims would have the effect of reducing both victimization and violence. On the contrary, by arousing empathy for victims, the biblical tradition has destroyed the kind of peace and social consensus that conventional cultures were once able to achieve at the victim's expense. In clogging the gears of the scapegoating machinery, the gospel revelation brings not peace but a sword. This is purely and simply because it interrupts the only kind of peace that "the world" — the world of conventional culture — understands. The only kind of violence that can end violence effectively is sacred violence, and, over time, the gospel revelation gradually destroys the ability to sacralize violence. Sacred violence is at the heart of primitive religion, and vestiges of it are at the heart of all "the kingdoms of this world." It is the sacred violence hidden at the core of archaic religion, therefore, that screens us from the apocalypse. The amalgam of religious awe and violence that primitive religion exists to hallow made it possible for archaic societies to endow certain acts of violence with religious significance and thereby to put an end to the relentless reciprocity into which all violence otherwise tends to collapse. The apocalypse is what happens when cultures continue to be breeding grounds for violence, but when not even the most solemnly sanctioned violence can acquire genuinely religious status, and when even its perpetrators and advocates are less and less able to regard it as *absolutely* distinct from the violence it strives to suppress. Ultimately, there are only two alternatives to apocalyptic violence: the sacred violence and scapegoating of conventional culture and religion, on the one hand, and forgiveness and the renunciation of violence and vengeance, on the other. That the former is now impossible, and that the latter seems hardly less so, doesn't change the facts.

Try as we might, we can no longer generate lasting cultural enterprises by enflaming national, tribal, ethnic, racial, and ideological passions, and with each new effort to do so we move closer to the abyss of uncontrollable violence. Belligerents caught in orgies of mob violence may still succumb to the momentary intoxication of the primitive sacred, but the age when it was possible for cultures under biblical influence to turn these delusions into cultural legitimacy has passed. Fortunately, of course, the societies whose sacrificial structures have been undermined the most are those that have fallen *directly* under the influence of the New Testament. In these societies, the peril of having to function with weakened and morally problematic sacrificial systems has been partially offset by the fact that the moral admonitions of the gospel — loving one's enemies, forgiving one's persecutors, turning the other cheek, renouncing vengeance, and so on — have helped foster the kind of human relationships that are less likely to lead to violence or more likely to prevent its contagious spread. I am not, of course, saying that the Western world has been either peaceful or a paragon of Christian virtue. I am saying that had its exposure to the Gospels not jeopardized its conventional apparatus for turning social discord into camaraderie at the victim's expense, it would no doubt have been more peaceful. On the other hand, given the gospel's gradual erosion of the West's sacrificial mythology, had the gospel's moral admonitions not had some effect, Western history would have been far more violent than it was.

In those cultures under the gospel influence, moral misgivings about scapegoating or sacrificial violence gradually arose and almost imperceptibly became their driving cultural and historical thrust. These societies are conspicuous for the degree to which a demand for social reforms arose within them. This never-ending parade of social innovations and political correctives is the defining characteristic of Western civilization, and at its core lies the biblical sympathy for victims. The moral discomfort that led to such reforms is a symptom of the weakening of the sacrificial system and its justifying myths. No such moral misgivings arise when a culture's sacrificial mechanisms are operating with their original mystifying power. On the other hand, the very act of undertaking moral reforms has the effect of further awakening the moral acuity that led to the demand for reforms in the first place. In other words, the social reforms to which the empathy for victims gives rise have a progressively destabilizing effect on culture, arousing an empathy for the culture's victims, bringing the plight of victims and the fact of victimization into sharper focus, undermining the moral legitimacy of the culture's sacrificial rituals for restoring social solidarity, and insuring that eventually the reformed system will arouse more moral misgivings in later generations than did the unreformed system in earlier periods. The result of this, of course, is that new reforms will be required, and their implementation will have the same effect. As the modern world is finding out to its dismay, the process is inexorable.

Perhaps the first modern to sense the full significance of the empathy for victims the gospel revelation was awakening was Friedrich Nietzsche, the German philosopher who has had such an enormous impact on our time. He reacted with horror as he saw moral authority shifting from the powerful to the weak, the downtrodden, and the outcast. The West was becoming ambivalent about performing cultural routines that involved no moral dilemma for societies not under the influence of the gospel tradition. As Nietzsche saw so well, this cultural equivocation was a product of Christianity. "I *condemn* Christianity," he declared.

> I raise against the Christian church the most terrible of all accusations that any accuser ever uttered.... The Christian church has left nothing untouched by its corruption.... The "equality of souls before God," this falsehood, this *pretext* for the rancor of all the base-minded, this explosive of a concept which eventually became revolution, modern idea, and the principle of decline of the whole order of society — is *Christian* dynamite.[22]

In his characteristically truculent way, Nietzsche recognized how the Gospels were awakening an empathy for victims and outcasts, and he was appalled by what he felt that empathy was doing to the ancient heroic virtues. He condemned Christianity as a religion of pity. "Christianity has sided with all that is weak and base," Nietzsche wrote in *The Antichrist.* "Pity stands opposed to the tonic emotions which heighten our vitality," he inveighed. "We are deprived of strength when we feel pity.... Some have dared to call pity a virtue (in every *noble* ethic it is considered a weakness); and as if this were not enough, it has been made *the* virtue, the basis and source of all virtues."[23]

Nietzsche's contempt for the idea of the conscience and its moral pangs, on one hand, and his romance with "the will to power," on the other, are two aspects of one of his most brilliant and sinister realizations. Nietzsche understood that violence and sacrificial bloodletting had always been a part of humanity's cultural existence. It was his realization that the world no longer had myths capable of endowing these bloody rituals with moral respectability that led him to oppose the "conscience" that harbored the moral misgivings, and to castigate Christianity for bringing this "conscience" into being. He proposed to replace it with a will-to-power that would carry out its sacrificial duties, moral qualms notwithstanding.

It was both perfectly natural and poetically brilliant for Auden, in his Christmas oratorio, to place a variation of Nietzsche's tirade on Christian pity into the mouth of Herod. Like Nietzsche, Auden's Herod recoils from the thought of a world in which pity — for Nietzsche *the* Christian virtue — would replace Roman justice. "Pity" is hardly *the* Christian virtue, but at least in terms of its historical effects, empathy for victims *is* Christianity's cardinal virtue. This is so, not because Christianity is solely or even primarily concerned with making social or political improvements, but because it carries to its conclusion the biblical aversion for idolatry, and because idolatry's core illusion — humanity's oldest and most tenacious illusion — is the one that makes victimizers proud of what they've done. All human delusions lead to, or flow from, that one. Biblical revelation, especially the New Testament story of the crucifixion, challenges that primary illusion. It invites those it confronts to see scapegoating violence for what it is and to recognize their own complicity in it. By acclaiming the victim as Lord, the Gospels slowly begin to awaken an empathy for victims everywhere.

Again, this does not mean the world became, or is becoming, suddenly more virtuous, or that we have been cured of our scapegoating predilections. Rather it means that increasingly we can only lustily vent our violence against victims whom we can confidently regard as victimizers. Today, what is often called the "culture wars" is a struggle over which political or ideological or intellectual or religious camp can best claim to have been victimized in the past, or to have championed the cause of victims and outcasts, or to be the rightful heirs of those who did. In his *Time* magazine essay, Hughes alluded to this contest when he discussed the controversy, typical of so many, between those who laud and those who scorn the landing of Columbus in the Americas. Was Columbus, Hughes asked, "Manifest Destiny in tights" or a "Hitler in a caravel, landing like a virus among the innocent people of the New World?" In a marvelous phrase, Hughes described the historians on either side of this debate standing "with tarbrush and gold leaf," ready to vilify and valorize according to which myth they choose to champion.

Tarbrush and Gold Leaf

As I will try to show in more detail in a later chapter, human culture as we know it begins when an act of unanimous violence brings the violence that preceded it to an end in such a breathtaking way that it gives birth to primitive religion. *Myth* remembers this strange event and its dramatic resolution from the point of view of those who derived social benefits from it, namely, those who discovered their first social solidarity when they joined in the common cause of expelling or eliminating their scapegoat. Myth camouflages the violence and recalls it in ways that make it seem valiant and divinely ordained. Here, as hereafter, I use the term "myth," neither as a synonym for fiction nor as the pure figment of the primitive imagination. Rather I use "myth" to refer to a special combination of fact and fantasy, one that tells of an actual violent event, but that tells of it from the perspective of the society which benefited from the violence and that therefore veils and vindicates the actual violence. All mythological pictures of the world are painted with tarbrush and gold leaf, but no one in a society where the mythological system is still functioning is aware that any such tampering with the facts has taken place. Primitive peoples were not hypocrites. Once the myth can no longer effectively veil the reality of the violence — as is the case in cultures that have fallen under biblical influence — then even the culture's solemnly sanctioned violence becomes morally problematic, and the moral authority of the culture is undermined.

Myth is like a stone that has been tossed by innumerable waves of the sea and that now lies glistening in the surf. Those who live in cultures still under the sway of such myths know better than to pick it up and examine it. As we in the West are now realizing, if you pick the stone up, scrutinize it, and put it in your pocket, it loses its luster. It looks like so many other stones. To understand why it shimmers in the surf is to realize how circumstantial is its mesmerizing power. When that power begins to wane, as it has in our world, we turn almost instinctively to gold leaf and the tarbrush in an effort to restore luster to our myths and righteousness to our causes, extending thereby for a little while longer our "ceremony of innocence." As skillfully as partisans and propagandists have often applied the tarbrush and gold leaf, however, their task has been profoundly complicated by the fact that as the moral valence has shifted in the victim's favor, the social distinction the gold leaf is meant to bestow has tended to be reserved almost exclusively for the *past* victims of the tarbrush. To be sure, few are eager to be tarbrushed, but to *have been* tarbrushed is to enjoy a social status that buckets of gold leaf could not hope to bestow. All of this is part of what Lance Morrow called the surreal confusion of the world in which we now live. The quirkiness and perversity aside, what is underway is the most astonishing reversal of values in human history. Today the victim occupies the moral high ground everywhere in the Western world. The cultural and historical force that caused this reversal is the gospel. Nietzsche was right at least about that.

Chapter 2

"Jesus Thrown Everything Off..."

> The Gospels set in motion the only textual mechanism that can put an end to humanity's imprisonment in the system of mythological representation.[1]
>
> RENÉ GIRARD

> Christians stubbornly clung to their language even when it could be said they really didn't understand it. (And the sad thing is that, now when we are about to acquire the intellectual means for understanding the terminology, a failure of nerve has set in and many Christians are abandoning the terminology.)[2]
>
> JOHN W. DIXON, JR.

The Victim's Voice

Participants in Western culture have lived for so long under the influence of the biblical ethos that it is difficult for us to fully appreciate its uniqueness. So pervasive is the concern for victims it arouses that there is a tendency for us to think of it as either a natural, universal emotion or a personal moral achievement for which the individual can take credit. Were either of those assumptions the case, Nietzsche would have been simply wrong about Christianity. He wasn't simply wrong. He was mad. He was *totally* wrong, but he wasn't *simply* wrong. The Christian Gospels *have* done what Nietzsche accused Christianity of doing, though not for the reasons he alleged.

Whatever "natural" empathy for one another we may have under any given set of circumstances, an empathy specifically for victims *as victims* is a cultural and not a natural phenomenon. Not only is it not a natural emotion; in many cases it is not even a welcomed one. Those in whom this empathy awakens often try to suppress it in favor of more practical and conventional loyalties. Nietzsche was able to see that in those cultures influenced by the biblical tradition this empathy for the victim had gradually become a major historical force, one that was throwing conventional culture into disarray. Girard saw exactly what Nietzsche saw, and he recognized as keenly as did Nietzsche the perilousness of the situation. Whereas Nietzsche's response was to expel the Gospels and try to revive the sacrificial structures they vitiated, Girard recognized the anthropological and moral significance of what was happening. He realized that, as trivialized as it so often is, the empathy for victims is driven by the most irrepressible cultural force in the world today—the revelation of the Cross. The moral by-product of that revelation is the Christian "conscience" that Nietzsche so loathed. However poorly Christians may have lived up to the dictates of that conscience, the world would be an infinitely more brutal place without it. One can catch a glimpse of what the world might look like without this "conscience" by observing the use to which Hitler's National Socialism put Nietzsche's condemnation of it.

We have been unable to recognize the clumsy attempts to revive the sacrificial ethos of pagan antiquity in our world because we haven't fully understood the anthropological patterns to which these attempts conform. When we catch glimpses of these anthropological patterns, we blink in incredulity or we think them the product of the rich imagination of archaic peoples. What do we make of the rituals of human and animal sacrifice that are found everywhere in the ancient world? What do we make of even the most sophisticated and brilliant reformulations of these things? What do we make, for instance, of Aeschylus's *Agamemnon?*

Aeschylus recounts how the goddess Artemis cursed Agamemnon by calming the winds and stranding his fleet at Aulis. The seer Calchas was consulted, and he announced that only by sacrificing his own daughter, Iphigenia, could Agamemnon lift the curse of Artemis and proceed to Troy, where both the war and the glory he could win in fighting it awaited him. Aeschylus tells us that the rites of animal sacrifice had failed, and in response to the emergency that followed their failure, it was necessary to return to the more ancient and more reliably cathartic form of the ritual: human sacrifice. Preparations for the grim ritual began. The unique circumstances required special precautions.

> Her father spoke again, to bid
> One bring a gag, and press
> Her sweet mouth tightly with a cord,
> Lest Atreus' house be cursed by some ill-omened cry.

Through the Greek chorus, Aeschylus tells us that the victim's voice must not be heard lest the ritual sacrifice go awry and lead to cultural disaster. Furthermore, the victim's glance must not be allowed to awaken sympathies in those whose role in the ritual is essential.

> Rough hands tear at her girdle, cast
> Her saffron silks to earth. Her eyes
> Search for her slaughterers; and each,
> Seeing her beauty, that surpassed
> A painter's vision, yet denies
> The pity her dumb looks beseech,
> Struggling for voice; for often in old days,
> When brave men feasted in her father's hall,
> With simple skill and pious praise
> Linked to the flute's pure tone
> Her virgin voice would melt the hearts of all.[3]

The victim is "struggling for voice." The sacrificial community struggles to gag the mouth from which it might come. The victim is neither a prisoner of war, nor a wretched outcast, nor a certified culprit. She knows her executioners well, and she is known to them. Were she able to speak, she would call them by their names. She would plead for them to come to their senses. Were her voice to be heard, it would be recognized. Even as she is gagged, they hear it in their memories. They remember intimacies they have shared with the one they are now murdering. With the help of a physical gag, they are able to muster the will to carry out the sacrifice. So intense is the actual moment of the killing, however, that the chorus reports it in a stammering and halting way. Speaking with one voice the chorus says:

> The rest I did not see,
> Nor do I speak of it.

Herein lies the difference between the greatest Greek tragedies, on one hand, and the writings of the Hebrew prophets and the Gospels, on the other. The Greek tragedians caught a vivid glimpse of the sacrificial reality upon which their culture was based, but, unlike the Hebrew prophets, they had no religiously significant prospects for ordering their lives otherwise. They were capable of artistically revealing the hidden sacrificial realities, but they knew of no alternative reality toward which to begin a journey. The revelatory power of Greek tragedy, therefore, came and went, leaving only a literary residue, and not a religious and cultural one. The true tragic spirit, Girard observes, is "never widespread even in periods of crisis," and it "vanishes without a trace during periods of cultural stability."[4] The insight of the Greek tragedians rises like a plaintive cry only to be absorbed again in the mythological thought from which it was never able to fully extricate itself. "The rest I did not see, nor do I speak of it."

Myth

When the chorus in *Agamemnon* says, "The rest I did not see, nor do I speak of it," it virtually defines myth. The root of the Greek word for myth, *muthos,* is *mu,* which means "to close" or "keep secret." *Muo* means to close one's eyes or mouth, to mute the voice, or to remain mute. Myth remembers discretely and selectively. Myth closes its eyes to certain events and closes its mouth. The agencies for the muting and transmuting of the remembered past are the Muses, and the term "muse" is derived from the same root as the word "myth." In Greek mythology the Muses are the daughters of Memory (Mnemosyne). The Muses make it possible to remember the past fondly or heroically, but they do so with fog filters. (The Latin verb *mutare* means "to change.") The Muses bring into being *mu*sic and *mu*seums, but not, in the first instance, for purely aesthetic or merely archival purposes. The cultural archive and anthems that the Muses preserve represent the mythological remembrance of things past. The poet Hesiod says of the Muses that "they are all of one mind." As widely varying as the Muses' artistic interests may be, beneath this variety, and behind it, lies something about which they are "all of one mind." The Muses inspire poetry, epic, sacred music, tragedy, comedy, erotic verse, and history, but all these are per*mu*tations of the past events that, if Hesiod is to be trusted, they memorialize with one purpose. That purpose is buried in the etymology of their name. The Muses make culture possible by providing it with its myth — an enchanting story of its founding violence. But most myths contain at least faint traces of the violence they otherwise mask. By paying more careful attention to these traces, things mythologically remembered can be recollected with greater clarity.

In the New Testament, *mythos* is juxtaposed both to *Logos* — the revelation of that about which myth refuses to speak — and to *aletheia* — the Greek word for truth. *Aletheia* comes from the root *letho,* which is the verb "to forget." The prefix *a* is the negative. The literal meaning, then, of the Greek word for truth, *aletheia,* is "to stop forgetting." It is etymologically the opposite of myth. The Gospels tell of a perfectly typical story of victimization with astonishing insight into the role religious zeal and mob psychology played in it. Most importantly, and contrary to all myth, the story is told from the point of view of the victim and not that of the righteous community of persecutors. Thus the passion story breaks decisively with the silence and circumspection of the mythological thought. The gospel *truth* gradually makes it impossible for us to keep forgetting what myth exists to help us forget. It thereby sets up a struggle between the impulse to sacralize, justify, or romanticize the violence that generates and regenerates conventional culture and the impulse to reveal that violence and strip away its mythic justifications. Fundamentally, human history is a struggle between myth and gospel. Literature, as it has developed in Western culture, is neither myth (*muthos*) nor truth (*aletheia*); it is the textual arena in which the two struggle for the upper hand. What myth conceals, what literature alternately conceals and reveals, and what the gospel decisively reveals are the social dynamics that produce what Girard calls "the essential complicity between violence and human culture."[5]

Those present at the sacrifice of Iphigenia turned their faces at the last moment, struggling against the human sympathies they had only partially suppressed. Because they were not entirely successful in denying "the pity her dumb looks beseech," the sacrifice succeeded in the short term only to rebound on its perpetrators in the long term. Eventually it set in motion a series of reciprocal acts of violence that finally brought down the house of Atreus.

> Bloodshed bringing in its train
> Kindred blood that flows again,
> Anger still unreconciled
> Poisoning a house's life
> With darkness, treachery and strife,
> Wreaking vengeance for a murdered child.[6]

In Aeschylus's Oresteian trilogy, the House of Atreus was a synonym for culture itself. The culture collapsed because it tried to perform a sacrificial ritual it was incapable of fully mythologizing. It could not fully mythologize its blood rituals because it could not sufficiently silence the victim's voice and veil the victim's pitiable face.

Myth — and the primitive religious cosmology it narrates — mutes the victim's voice. It fills the eyes and nose with incense and the ears with incantations. When the myth is firmly in place, even those closest to the victims, the ones most likely to resist the myth's intoxications, concur in the ritual. While the myth holds sway, those under its spell are unwilling or unable to recognize what they are doing. "The rest I did not see," they say, "nor do I speak of it." In return for making conventional culture possible, myth silences the victim's voice and veils the victim's face. In his book on crowd behavior Gustave Le Bon says this of the Jacobin ideologues of the French Revolution:

> Dogmatic and logical to a man, and their brains full of vague generalities, they busied themselves with the application of fixed principles without concerning themselves with events. It has been said of them, with reason, that they went through the Revolution without witnessing it.[7]

This is what myth and the associated structures of what Girard calls the primitive sacred do. They make it possible to participate in, observe, or recollect certain violent events without having to actually *witness* them in any morally significant sense.

One could argue, I suppose, that the autobiography of Whittaker Chambers is a curious place to turn for insights into the collapse of the world's scapegoating and sacrificial apparatus. In Chambers's autobiography, however, there is an anecdote followed by a comment by Chambers that summarizes profoundly the problem that I will be exploring in the chapters to follow. Chambers recounts a conversation he had with the daughter of a former German diplomat in Moscow who tried to explain why her father, once extremely pro-Communist, had become deeply disillusioned with Stalin's regime. "She loved her father," Chambers writes, "and the irrationality of his defection embarrassed her. 'He was immensely pro-Soviet,' she said, 'and then — you will laugh at me — but you must not laugh at my father — and then — one night — in Moscow — he heard screams. That's all. Simply one night he heard screams.' "[8] Chambers remarked:

> She did not know at all that she had swept away the logic of the mind, the logic of history, the logic of politics, the myth of the 20th century, with five annihilating words: one night he heard screams.[9]

Could this be true? Could something as seemingly powerless as the screams of a victim actually annihilate the logic of the mind, the logic of history, the logic of politics, and the myth of the twentieth century? There is a haunting echo of this in Masao Yamaguchi's insistence that not only does "the scapegoat constitute a mechanism which assures culture of its basic vitality," but that it also "breathes vitality into cultural domains as varied as individual mentality, politics, morals, the history of ideas and aesthetics." [10] How profoundly might the world have to change if the mechanism for breathing vitality into these essential things were to break down? What would the world look like if the logic of the mind, the logic of history, the logic of politics, and the myth of the twentieth century were to be called into question? Look around.

"Jesus Thrown Everything Off Balance"

In Flannery O'Connor's short story "A Good Man Is Hard to Find," a psychopathic killer called the "Misfit" stands over the trembling old grandmother he will soon murder in cold blood. Almost speechless with terror, the old woman appeals to him:

> "Jesus, Jesus," meaning, Jesus will help you, but the way she was saying it, it sounded as if she might be cursing.
>
> "Yes'm," the Misfit said as if he agreed. "Jesus thrown everything off balance."[11]

Flannery O'Connor was fond of carving literary jack-o'-lanterns, but the light behind their fierce eyes and frozen grins was the incandescent radiance of the Gospels. Her Misfit was a psychopath and a moral cripple, but his madness is a vehicle for O'Connor's lucidity. When he says that Jesus "thrown everything off balance," the Misfit is expressing something embedded in Christian creeds since before the New Testament was written. What had been thrown off by the crucifixion was the mechanism for maintaining cultural order and psychological stability, "the infrastructure of all religions and all cultures," as Girard put it.

As vulgar and maniacal as the historical Herod might have been, as psycho-pathological as O'Connor's Misfit is, and as mad as Nietzsche was, they all share the suspicion that "Jesus thrown everything off balance," or, put another way, that his public execution has a prejudicial effect on the routines upon which cultural and psychological life depends. This same assessment is embedded in the New Testament's audacious assertion about the meaning and historical significance of the crucifixion. As the earliest New Testament writings make perfectly clear, *the* decisive event for those who later gave Christianity its charter documents was the crucifixion of Jesus. The events of this extraordinary man's life were initially of interest in direct proportion to their proximity to or relevance for the crucifixion. Paul, the author of the earliest New Testament texts, virtually never mentions details about the life or ministry of Jesus. His gospel centers entirely on the crucifixion. Moreover, anticipating what was to become the exegetical fixation of many modern biblical scholars, Paul warned against those whose fascination with the biographical details of the historical Jesus threatened to obscure the supreme centrality of the Cross in Christian revelation. Similarly, the first Gospel proper, the Gospel of Mark, has rightly been called the passion story with a long prologue. As the New Testament writers came to view it, the crucifixion, and its aftermath in the lives of those most devastated by it, represented the decisive culmination of everything that had preceded it in the scriptural tradition of the Jewish people. In other words, it was neither Friedrich Wilhelm Nietzsche, nor Auden's Herod, nor O'Connor's Misfit who first announced that "Jesus thrown everything off balance." It was Paul. It was Matthew, Mark, Luke, and John. What they asserted about the meaning and eventual consequences of the crucifixion is only now being placed in an anthropological context. We are only now beginning to recognize what Nietzsche glimpsed at the end of the nineteenth century. Only now are we realizing that the New Testament is, in Girard's words, "the essential text in the cultural upheaval of the modern world."[12]

Both Christianity's scriptural sources and its creedal formulae pivot around a public execution, an act of official violence regarded as legally righteous by the political authorities and as a sacred duty by the religionists. This simple and obvious fact is the most overlooked aspect of the colossal historical phenomenon we call Christianity. The Christian Scriptures and creeds make the outlandish assertion that because of this public execution the grip of sin has been broken, the human race has been offered a new lease on life and, at the same time, placed in grave peril if it refuses the offer. The Christian movement has pondered these weighty claims for two millennia with mixed results. How could a public execution have liberated the human race? Why was a public execution the necessary form that this liberation had to take? In answering this question, Christian doctrine has sometimes turned itself inside out. The most familiar form of the atonement doctrine, for instance, supposes that a wrathful God demanded that a victim pay in blood for human sin—like the animals that died in the atonement sacrifices at the Jewish Temple—and that God chose to take a human form and pay for the sin "Himself." It is an understandable doctrine, given the religious and cultic backdrop against which early Christian thought was first forming. But the doctrine is not only logically incoherent; it is morally and theologically inadequate as well.

Is it even remotely plausible, then, that the "grip of sin" was broken by a public execution and that a new humanity was made possible and even necessary as a result? If so, how so? If there is one comment that breaks through the countless layers of theological and doctrinal convolution, it is Victor White's: "Certainly," he wrote, "the remedy explains the disease as well as the disease explains the remedy."[13] If the Cross is *the* cure, could the kind of contagious scapegoating that led to it be *the* disease?

It has taken us this long to realize the gospel's anthropological implications in part because the moral, intellectual, and epistemological effects of the gospel revelation have of necessity developed gradually. The nascent anthropological sensibility of Paul and the early Christian writers stands out even in comparison to that of their closest biblical precursors, the Hebrew prophets, but the historical ferment unleashed by the Gospels didn't give rise to a full-fledged science of anthropology until the middle of the nineteenth century. Anthropology has rightly been recognized as Western civilization's quintessential science. Anthropology can, of course, explain many things, but, until it acknowledges its debt to the biblical tradition, it cannot adequately explain itself. The prerequisite for the development of the science of anthropology was the kind of cultural objectivity that arises only after a moral dissonance has been set up between the individual and the sanctioned structures of that individual's own culture. Perhaps St. Paul best qualifies as the first anthropologist, and his anthropological insights began when he discovered, with a moral shudder, how murderous he had become in the name of his own culture. Anthropology is simply the study of culture by people who are no longer *entirely* contained within one, and Paul, along with the Hebrew prophets before him, is its originator. Anthropology was invented in those cultures that had fallen under biblical influence because it was in these cultures that the moral problem of culture itself first surfaced.

By its very nature, the discipline of anthropology is an attempt to investigate human cultural phenomena by remaining independent of the cultic and mythic structures that exist to foreclose investigation. The science of anthropology is caught in a contradiction that is symptomatic of the contradictions that plague cultures under biblical influence. As Leszek Kolakowski put it:

> On one hand, we have managed to assimilate the kind of universalism which refuses to make value judgments about different civilizations, proclaiming their intrinsic equality; on the other hand, by affirming this equality we also affirm the exclusivity and intolerance of every culture — the very things we claim to have risen above in making that same affirmation.[14]

Many who focus the West's aversion for ethnocentricity like a laser on Western culture itself choose to view non-Western cultures through a fog filter and regard their conspicuous forms of ethnocentricity as signs of cultural confidence and vitality. If we regard our mental independence from our own culture as an intellectual and even a moral virtue, then our cooing admiration of cultures where no such mental independence exists is at least ironic. Whether we know it or not, and even when our attitude toward traditional cultures is explicitly preservationist, our mental equipment is infected with the demythologizing virus the gospel has let loose on the world. The culturally independent and even skeptical thought forms that make our anthropological open-mindedness possible are intellectual derivatives of the Bible's demythologizing impulse, and, as such, even scientific anthropology's secular versions of them are anathema to mythological existence.

In part, what makes the elimination of myth by gospel so inevitable is the radical difference between the mental horizons in which myth and gospel operate. Our social and psychological habits strongly favor the scapegoating phenomenon, but the myths that give moral or religious sanction to such violence are fragile. The reason archaic societies are as highly structured and as horrified by deviation from ritual and social norm as they are is because their whole cultural enterprise depends upon delicate mythological maneuvers of which they themselves must remain ignorant if the myths are to have their full effect. The intrusion of the slightest ritual irregularity or the presence of anyone not under the spell of the prevailing myth might destroy the mental shell game upon which mythological consciousness depends.

What is distinctive about the contest between myth and gospel, therefore, is that myth is fragile and survives only when its premises are accepted uncritically, while the gospel can be trashed and betrayed and corrupted almost beyond recognition without fatally compromising its inherent demythologizing power. Time and again, the gospel has been turned into a bludgeon or a religious emporium for generations or even centuries at a time, only to break its bonds and reveal itself anew just as its official obituary is being readied. Idle infatuation with myth may become fashionable, as it has in recent years in our society, but that infatuation is a symptom of spiritual weariness. In the way that I am using the term "myth," to believe in a myth as a result of a critical evaluation is to be expelled from a genuinely mythological world as decisively as if the critical evaluation had produced the opposite results. One cannot *prove* a myth true or valid and still retain a mythic attitude toward it. Verification is incompatible with the mental nonchalance of mythological existence.

It goes without saying that the gospel has often enough had to contend against the scapegoating and mythologizing predilections of Christians and institutional Christianity, but the fact that Christians fall under the judgment of the tradition they transmit should confirm rather than discredit the claims made by and for the gospel texts. We look back on those living in earlier periods of the gospel's cultural penetration and see the glaring moral oversights committed by our predecessors. Nothing makes these shortcomings more morally conspicuous than the fact that they were committed by those who professed fidelity to the gospel. Upon discovering these moral incongruities, there are two typically modern assumptions that we make. The first is that historical Christianity is a moral failure because its Scriptures have failed to instantly bring about the complete moral rehabilitation of those who read them. The second assumption we make is that, since we find the behavior or beliefs of our ancestors morally questionable, we must be their moral superiors. Jefferson, after all, had slaves; missionaries sometimes mistreated the people they converted; our ancestors were racists; our grandfathers were male supremacists; and so on.

Amazingly, we hardly ever turn the underlying assumptions around and look to the future. If we did, we would realize that our grandchildren will find incongruities between our behavior and the gospel principles we espouse. We who dare to aspire to the Christian vocation must know that our spiritual heirs will be able to see in our lives, not to mention our books, things that they will see — rightly — as morally dubious and that we cannot see at all. We must be prepared to repent of our literary as well as personal and historical betrayals of the revelation we have tried to transmit. This is simply the precondition of participating in the Christian revelation. Were there to be a generation of Christians that did not suddenly discover that it had been betraying the Gospels, it would *ipso facto* be betraying it in the worst way. Only in contrition does the Christian believer or the Christian community achieve lucidity. Only in repentance is either truly faithful. To measure the spiritual vitality of the Christian movement by any other standard is to miss its astonishing uniqueness. Contrition is the specifically Christian form of lucidity.

The gospel revelation could not overturn conventional culture abruptly, and mercifully it has not. As we will see in the chapters to follow, attempts to destroy the sacrificial or scapegoating structures of culture always proceed in a scapegoating and sacrificial manner. To put it in New Testament terms, Satan is always casting out Satan. The gospel revelation, on the contrary, undermines these structures by "deconstructing" their justifying myths and awakening a concern for their victims that gradually renders these structures morally unacceptable and socially counterproductive. For obvious reasons, societies trying to operate morally problematic and socially counterproductive cultural mechanisms are not likely to be the most stable and peaceful societies, the more so since the source of their former peace and stability was precisely those mechanisms that the gospel revelation jeopardizes. Those living closer to the gospel's epicenter — beginning with Christianity itself — are more likely to experience its cultural destabilizing effects than those at a greater distance from it. Christianity no more owns the Gospels than do multinational corporations own the earth, a point that the Gospels and the earth will make clear enough in due course. As the cultural and historical convolutions continue, Christians will have abundant reasons for entering into serious dialogue with the religions of the world. While the historical record of institutional Christianity is hardly the sordid affair its modern detractors seem to think, it is reason enough to enter the dialogue with others in a spirit of humility. In the dialogue itself, there is much that Christianity stands to learn from others, but there is one thing that it will have both to learn better itself and to convey more coherently to the world, and that is the staggering historical and anthropological significance of the Cross.

Chapter 3

"The Ceremony of Innocence Is Drowned"

> ... Things fall apart; the centre cannot hold;
> Mere anarchy is loosed upon the world,
> The blood-dimmed tide is loosed, and everywhere
> The ceremony of innocence is drowned ...[1]
>
> WILLIAM BUTLER YEATS,
> *The Second Coming*

> Christianity's impact on the West is a tribute to the power of its basic conception, which is the absolute centrality of the position of the victim.... The moral significance of this position is enormous.[2]
>
> ERIC GANS

> The hidden infrastructure of all religions and all cultures is in the process of declaring itself.[3]
>
> RENÉ GIRARD

There is a New Testament story that exemplifies how those in closest historical proximity to the crucifixion experienced its astonishing revelatory power. The story, recounted in the Acts of the Apostles, tells of an encounter between Philip and an Ethiopian eunuch on his way home from a pilgrimage to Jerusalem. The story is written by Luke, the evangelist most familiar with the Greek culture that was dominant in the first century and most aware of the confusion those with Greek cultural sensibilities felt when confronted with the Christian proclamation that the messiah — in Greek terms, the savior of the world — was a man condemned by Jewish authorities and executed on a Roman gallows. For Luke, the story of the encounter between Philip and the Ethiopian is a parable about the interpretative power of the gospel in resolving that confusion.

The story takes place in the aftermath of Jesus' crucifixion. Philip is one of the members of the fledgling community of Jesus' followers in Jerusalem. On the occasion in question, he is inspired to approach an Ethiopian traveling on the desert road from Jerusalem to Gaza. The Ethiopian is reading aloud this passage from the prophet Isaiah:

> Like a sheep that is led to the slaughterhouse,
> like a lamb that is dumb in front of its shearers,
> like these he never opens his mouth.
> He has been humiliated and has no one to defend him.
> Who will ever talk about his descendants,
> since his life on earth has been cut short?
> (Acts 8:32–33 [Isa. 53:7–8])

Scholars continue to speculate on the identity of the "suffering servant" in this passage from Isaiah. Some have thought him to have been an individual whose godliness the prophetic writer has recognized and whose mistreatment he has witnessed. Some have thought him to be a prophet himself, whose fate was commemorated by his sympathetic followers. And some have considered the Suffering Servant poems to be allegorical references to the people of Israel. The power of these "servant songs" comes through regardless of which of these interpretations is favored. Christians have tended to understand these texts as referring to an individual, a prophetic forerunner of the Crucified One, and this is presumably the way in which the Ethiopian is reading the passage here quoted. Though he feels an affinity with this despised figure, as a reasonably cosmopolitan inhabitant of the Greco-Roman world, the Ethiopian is as perplexed by the biblical text as are many modern readers of the Bible. Perhaps, like many who read the Bible today, he has turned to this strange anthology for inspiration and spiritual fortification. Instead, he has found a story of mob violence. He cannot make sense of it, and he asks Philip to help him.

Luke tells us only this of Philip's instruction: "Starting, therefore, with this text of Scripture Philip proceeded to explain the Good News of Jesus to him." When has one sentence summarized so much! From the grim story of persecution in Isaiah to the gospel in one sentence. From its effect on the Ethiopian, we are made aware of the shock that Philip's interpretation delivered. As a result of this shock, there on the desert road from Jerusalem to Gaza, the Ethiopian insisted on being formally admitted into the Christian fellowship. To appreciate the larger anthropological implications of this little story is to have the Bible explode in one's hands, much the way Philip's insights caused the text from Isaiah to explode in the Ethiopian's.

What makes the text so haunting and bewildering is that it tells the story of mob violence, and its perspective is to a great extent that of the victim. Not altogether so; it is laced with the perspective of the religiously scrupulous and righteously indignant community that persecuted the victim. In other words, it is a text in transition, one that clearly is moving *away* from myth — the story that flatters the victimizers and sanctions their violence — and toward "gospel" — the story that exposes the violence, strips it of its religious justifications, and reveals to the world a God of powerless love. The Ethiopian has in his hands, therefore, a text of inestimable anthropological value, inasmuch as it is a candid presentation of cultural violence shorn of most of the mythological trappings. It reveals a truth that myths suppress in order to make culture possible. It is a truth that slowly works its way to the surface of the biblical text beginning with the Cain and Abel story in Genesis and culminating with the crucifixion.

The Bible's anthropological distinction lies in the fact that in it an empathy for victims again and again overwhelms the Bible's own attempt to mythologize its violence and venerate it as divinely decreed. Ask ten people what they think of the Hebrew Scriptures — the "Old Testament" — and even if they've never opened it, eight of the ten will tell you that they are put off by its violence. The world over which myth presides with its majestic poise is no less violent. Its violence is simply better veiled and suffused with grandeur. As a gentile, the Ethiopian would have been accustomed to having official tribal violence shrouded in an aura of myth. The passage from Isaiah, however, is haunted by a crude specter of mob violence. Since the Ethiopian is still bound up in mythological thought patterns and the primitive religious cosmology made plausible and morally palatable by myth, he hasn't a clue to the meaning of the text from Isaiah. Philip, on the other hand, has known the passion story. He has been effectively exposed to the story of righteous violence in which an innocent victim died forgiving his murderers, realizing that "they know not what they do." With that story as his interpretive key, the few mythological vestiges that survive in the Isaiah text offer no serious impediment to Philip's revelatory interpretation of it. The mob was wrong and its sense of righteousness was a delusion. It is the victim who is the chosen one of God, the agent of God's self-revelation to the world.

The Suffering Servant Songs combine two insights: first, that the victim was innocent and his persecutors wrong, and, second, that his victimization was socially beneficial and that his punishment brought the community peace. The fact that it combines these two perspectives is what makes it such a trustworthy text. It has suppressed neither the moral offensiveness of the violence nor the social fact that the violence had beneficial cultural effects. In order for these two antithetical facts to be reconciled, of course, it was necessary to subordinate one to the other. If the social harmony it produced was to be enjoyed and extended, the violence would have to be found morally acceptable. All cultures have had to choose between confronting the truth about their mob violence, on the one hand, and enjoying the camaraderie it generated, on the other. What is distinctive about the Bible is that it is the first literature in the history of the world to grapple with the moral dilemma this choice represents.

The author of the Isaiah text has seen both the innocence of the victim and the social revival that his victimization brought about. He tries to reconcile them, and he knows only one way to do so. He assumes that "Yahweh has been pleased to crush him with suffering," that the victim was allowed to be struck down by a God who counted his sufferings as an atonement for the faults of the very mob that inflicted them on him. With one important difference, this is a variation on an ancient and universally prevalent myth. The difference is that the speaker in the Suffering Servant Songs in Second Isaiah sees perfectly clearly how morally upright, how wretchedly abused, how pathetic, and how arbitrarily chosen the mob's victim really was. This knowledge is at war with the conclusion that the text makes, namely, that God was somehow pleased with the results of the violence. In other words, the passage that the Ethiopian found so troubling embodies an unstable balance between culture's dependence on collective righteous violence and the growing empathy for the victims of it, an empathy that develops within and is documented by the biblical literature as a whole. The moral and religious solution the text pronounces is an unstable one because these two forces — the empathy for victims and the need for rituals of victimization — are incompatible. Sooner or later, one of them will have to prevail over the other.

Reading the Signs of the Times

Now let's not forget what has happened in this vignette. The Ethiopian, perplexed by a strange text, underwent a profound change when someone who understood the larger implications of the crucifixion was able to point out to him the text's deeper meaning. Philip's interpretation focused the illuminating power of the Cross on a biblical account of mob violence. Like the Ethiopian, we too are on a journey, and, like him, we are too enmeshed in the myths and scandals of contemporary culture to be able to make sense of what we read about them. Unlike the Ethiopian, however, it's not the Bible we're reading. On *our* homebound journey we read the newspaper. (Or we wait until we get home and have the TV anchor read it to us.) If the interpretive power of the Cross is what it purports to be in this story, then might that interpretive power shed light on the evening newspaper as much as it does on an ancient Hebrew text? Is it possible, in other words, to see in the newspaper what the Ethiopian, with Philip's help, was able to see in Second Isaiah? On opening the newspaper, how long would one have to search to find righteous crowds making common cause by uniting against culprits or adversaries that have been chosen more or less at random?

In John's Gospel, Jesus tells his disciples that they will do greater things than he. One wonders. Nevertheless, I think we *are* called upon to do something even more audacious than what Philip did, for Philip brought the revelation of the Cross to bear on one of the passages in the Hebrew Scriptures that most closely resembles it. It is precisely this resemblance between the crucifixion and the Suffering Servants Songs in Second Isaiah that provided the first Christians with such an important clue for understanding the crucifixion in the first place. In fact, because the early Christians weren't able to eliminate entirely the implications of sacrificial atonement found in these Servant Songs, institutional Christianity perpetuated the idea of placating divine wrath, a notion that is squarely at odds with the God revealed by Jesus' life and death. To say that we are challenged to do something more audacious than Philip, therefore, means two things. First, it means that, as beneficiaries of gospel revelation, we are now better able to distinguish the New Testament revelation from its sacrificial antecedents, and that we have a responsibility to do so. Second, it means that we are challenged to focus the interpretive power of the Cross on texts and on personal and historical experiences that, in contrast to the Suffering Servant Songs in Isaiah, seem to bear no relationship to the New Testament whatsoever.

The modern heir to Philip's task will not encounter a eunuch returning home to Ethiopia and reading with incomprehension a passage in the Hebrew Scriptures. He will more likely encounter a modern commuter returning home reading a newspaper and being confounded by the stories of fierce ethnic violence in foreign lands, or savage and sometimes gratuitous violence in urban America. If Philip's modern counterpart is to offer bewildered moderns what Philip offered the Ethiopian, he will have to bring the specifically Christian revelation to bear on these sources of contemporary bewilderment. He will have to comment as decisively on those newspaper stories that are as much a source of consternation to moderns as the Suffering Servant Songs were to the Ethiopian.

If, for instance, a homeward traveler has before her the March 28, 1991, edition of the *Los Angeles Times,* would a modern Philip be able to explain the Good News of the gospel to her by explicating the story by Janny Scott that appeared on page one? The story, entitled "Violence Born of the Group," tries to analyze the beating of Rodney King by a number of Los Angeles police officers on March 3, 1991. The beating, videotaped by an onlooker unnoticed by the officers involved, gained prominent national attention. This story appeared more than a year before the verdict in the Rodney King beating case touched off riots in Los Angeles and elsewhere. In order to better understand how the senseless act of violence against King could have happened in the first place, the *Times* writer interviewed sociologists and psychologists and reported their conclusions.

Summarizing these conclusions, Scott noted that there is a tendency for "tightly knit groups" to "devalue and dehumanize outsiders and, under certain conditions, to commit terrible violence against them." She highlighted three main points made about cases such as the King beating by social and psychological researchers:

- The larger the group of attackers and the fewer the victims, the more savage the attack.
- The presence of multiple bystanders in an emergency appears to reduce the chance that any one of them will step in.
- A witness is less likely to step in when the victim is black.

"Forming groups is natural, psychologists say, and a strong group identity can build morale," wrote Scott. "But in some groups, members manipulate the sense of 'us versus them' to bolster group spirit and divert attention from internal problems. A sense of identity forms from denigrating outsiders." According to the specialists Scott interviewed, then, denigrating outsiders contributes to a strong group identity and a strong group identity "can build morale."

One of the experts Scott interviewed for the article was Brian Mullen, an associate professor of psychology at Syracuse University. Mullen pointed out that people's behavior "can quickly gravitate to the lowest common denominator." The *Times* article continues:

> According to Mullen, members of a group tend to focus on whatever is unusual or different, just as one's eye is drawn to one part of a pic-

ture and the rest blurs. A group's attention centers on the rare thing, the outsider.

"When a group of people is victimizing one lone victim, they are paying a great deal of attention to that lone victim," said Mullen. "They might notice the sounds that he makes or the dirt and blood on his clothing.

"But they don't recognize that I, John Smith, am a father and husband. I have a job where I am sworn to uphold these rules, and the behavior that I'm engaging in violates that person that I am."

But as early as the next morning, Mullen said, they wake up and say, "How could I have done that? . . ."

"As early as the next morning" the victimizers feel the moral revulsion that the contagious rage of the mob managed to annul for the duration of its violence and for a time thereafter. Speaking anthropologically, one can say that conventional culture lives in the interim between the act of unanimous mob violence and the moment when its social beneficiaries find it morally problematic. It is at least metaphorically true, and arguably even literally so, that what was to become Christianity began when Peter, having been drawn into complicity with the Jesus' tormentors, heard the cock crow — "as early as the next morning."

"History," in the special sense in which I have used that term, takes place in the interstices between the violence and the contrition. The practical effect of the Gospels has been to shorten that interim, to narrow the period during which the human community could say with composure "the rest I did not see, nor do I speak of it." The penchant for resorting to such self-exonerating self-delusion was countered by the words of Jesus from the Cross: "they know not what they do." If the effect of the crucifixion has been to shorten the interim between the violence and the contrition, the purpose of myth has always been to try to extend that interim indefinitely. The surfacing of moral misgivings "as early as the next morning" simply means that we live in a world where violence is being unveiled.

The *Times* reporter interviewed Ervin Staub, a social psychologist, a professor at the University of Massachusetts at Amherst, and a noted authority on the social and psychological preconditions for violence. Staub argues that the crowd persuades itself that the victims deserve to be harmed. Its participants engage in what he calls "moral exclusion," deciding that certain people are "not really human and that moral rules do not apply." Staub also pointed out that those who get caught up in violence tend to regard their behavior as morally justified the more it is joined in by others. Bystanders, he notes, "move along that same continuum." In other words, this newspaper article is a text that ponders something parallel to what the author of the Servant Songs was pondering. Here Janny Scott is helping the reader try to comprehend a strange episode of victimization carried out by those whose task it is to prevent bad violence, and to prevent it, if need be, by the exercise of good violence. Something has obviously gone awry. The distinction between good and bad violence has blurred. The *Times* reporter is trying to shed light on what went wrong. We will never be able to fully appreciate stories such as this one, however, until we see them as symptoms of a very large and very profound cultural, spiritual, psychological, and anthropological upheaval. As we shall see in the later chapters, beatings like the one Rodney King suffered have been going on since the beginning of human social systems. What's new is, if you will, social science. What's new is the conscious attempt to understand the process and to assess its morality. What's new is the concerted attempt to reveal the perversity of the scapegoating mechanism and to dispense with it.

Lessons of Los Angeles

What is rarely enough appreciated is that the historical process that has led to the work of Staub and Mullen has its source in the Hebrew prophets and the Christian Gospels and those cultural imperatives that they spawned. What we must try to recognize is how the events of the sort described in this story fit into the anthropological drama for which the biblical empathy for victims is the central motif and the crucifixion the decisive turning point. For the moment, it will suffice simply to point out the elements in this story that cry out for anthropological and historical understanding. "Now, experts say," wrote Scott, "the shocking video tape of the March 3 incident... offers society an important lesson in *the evil that can emerge from the insidious comfort of groups*." To recognize a link between violence (evil) and social solidarity (the insidious comfort of groups) is to put a spotlight on cultural processes that cannot operate effectively in the spotlight.

The *Los Angeles Times* article, of course, makes no appeal to the gospel or to the story of the crucifixion. The appeal is to the social and psychological sciences. The light these sciences are able to shed on the beating of one man by a group of armed men consists of three basic insights. The broader implications of these insights almost leap out at the reader. I need only reiterate them. The first is that the larger the group of attackers and the fewer the victims, the more savage the attack. There is a kind of algebraic formula at work here whose most irreducible formulation is "unanimity-minus-one," a phrase René Girard uses to describe the cathartic moment of scapegoating violence. When, as Mullen puts it in the article, a group is reduced to "the lowest common denominator," that denominator is one. This lowest common denominator is accompanied by the highest possible numerator. At the crescendo of the violence, the numerator is "everyone." It is all against one.

Staub had remarked that as mobs approach this maximum degree of polarization they cease to experience their victim as "really human." When a modern mob experiences the nonhumanity of its victim, what it sees in the victim's stead is some deranged animal, a source of social pollution, a beast, a pervert. When a primitive mob experienced the nonhumanity of its victim, what it saw in the victim's stead was the demon-god who was the source of violence in life and the source of peace in death. In both cases, the human victim disappears, only to be transfigured into an icon in the sacred system that his victimization generated or regenerated. The victim becomes Dionysus or Tiamat, a god or goddess of mythical proportions whose killing was in accord with the divine plan. As the victim is being thus metaphysically transfigured, his or her corpse remains as a corporeal reminder of a shocking and unmythologized fact, potentially at least an unwelcome reminder of the humanity of the victim. "One psychologist who studied lynchings," wrote Scott in the *Times* piece, "found that large mobs not only shot and hanged their victims but left them 'lacerated, mutilated, burned and flayed.'" This comment suggests that, at the supreme moment of the mob's violence, its narrowed and intensified focus on the body of the victim has a tendency to literally consume the body, removing thereby an important obstacle to its mythological interpretation of what it has done. The fact that the Rodney King beating didn't approach this maximum level of polarization is, of course, not the point. The point is that the beating involved a discernible movement in the direction of that ultimate polarization.

The second insight Scott was able to glean from social science research is that the presence of multiple bystanders appears to reduce the chance that any one of them will attempt to interrupt the violence. The larger the crowd, the more mesmerizing its madness. In other words, a unifying force is at work on the bystanders comparable to the one at work on the perpetrators of the violence, a force that leads to unanimity. What is that force? Where does it originate? What are its paradoxes? That these questions perplex us is no accident. Misconstruing the social phenomena that would have obliged us to face these issues is what myths have always done, and what modern ideologies continue to do, less and less convincingly. Unwittingly, enormous effort has gone into not realizing that these questions are *the* questions.

The key to understanding these and so many other of humanity's social anomalies is a profound human predilection for imitation, for which Girard uses the Greek word *mimesis*. Since modernity is practically defined by its reluctance to recognize the degree to which we humans are imitative, Girard's insistence on the central role of mimesis in human affairs goes against the grain of much of today's popular cultural discourse. Confounding the consternation is the fact that Girard stresses the mimetic nature of precisely what both nineteenth-century romanticism and twentieth-century Freudian anti-romanticism acclaimed as the very essence of individuality and spontaneity, namely, *desire*. Just as Girard's notion of mimesis is something more powerful and less consciously intentional than the merely conscious act of imitation, so his notion of desire is broader and deeper than the highly eroticized and romanticized notion of desire that has reigned and ravaged in our society for much of the modern era. The exaltation of desire in popular culture, enthusiastically embraced by commercial interests, has completely drowned out the words of caution with which our tradition has spoken of desire and warned of its alienating, morally debilitating, and socially ravaging potential. It is not surprising, therefore, that Girard's notion of mimetic desire is one whose significance and larger implications it takes time for us moderns to appreciate. I will explore the issue of mimetic desire and its complexities in later chapters. It is necessary to mention it at this point, however, because the issue before us is that of crowd contagion, and crowd contagion is one of the last and most predictable stages in a social phenomenon the underlying dynamic of which is mimetic desire — the human predilection for falling under the influence of the desires, positive or negative, adulating or accusatory — of *others*. It is that predilection that explains the inverse relationship between the size and agitation of a crowd, on one hand, and the moral independence of its individual members, on the other.

The last of the three observations social science research offers on the subject of collective violence is that a witness is less likely to try to stop the violence when the victim is in some way distinguishable as an outsider or an alien. It is as though, Scott writes, "the desire to conform outweighs the urge to help." In other words, whatever the degree to which an empathy for victims might have been awakened, in the presence of group violence there is aroused a countervailing phenomenon that tends to eclipse this empathy. It is somewhat misleading to refer to what eclipses this empathy as a "desire to conform," inasmuch as it is almost never a conscious desire. It is a mimetic desire. It involves little or no conscious decision-making for exactly the same reason that myth involves little or no act of rational discrimination. Conscious decision-making is mentally and morally antithetical to the social unanimity into which violence tends to sweep both its perpetrators and its spectators.

Beyond the insights into contagion and collective violence to which the *Times* article alluded, it makes several additional observations that are worth noting. One is that the "us verses them" motif can be manipulated to revive a group's *esprit de corps* and to "divert attention from internal problems." That is to say, communal violence is an antidote for internal strife and the "civil" or domestic violence to which it might otherwise lead. Campaigns against outsiders or evildoers revive the camaraderie jeopardized by internal conflict. As the *Times* article puts it, the members of such a community achieve a "sense of identity" by jointly "denigrating outsiders." What is so surprising is that none of this is really surprising. We know all this perfectly well. Not only does mere *knowledge* about the workings of scapegoating violence do little to prevent its recurrence, but it can easily lull us into a naive sense that, knowing what we know, we are free from the mesmerizing power of such violence and immune to its contagion.

In one sense, we *are* liberated from these things. Gone are the days when collective violence could produce *lasting* social and psychological benefits. "As early as the next morning," Mullen is quoted by the *Times* corespondent as saying, those who have joined in group violence "wake up and say, 'How could I have done that?' " Perhaps the best measure of humanity's maturation is the length of time that elapses between the acts of mesmerizing violence and the moment when the moral misgivings that should have accompanied those acts are finally felt.

According to the psychologists consulted by the author of the *Los Angeles Times* story about the beating of Rodney King, the "us verses them" motif can be manipulated in order to "divert attention from internal problems." Successful scapegoating violence results in the social solidarity of the community. Gradually, however, in cultures under gospel influence, acts of violence that once endowed its perpetrators with religious and cultural preeminence gradually begin to rob them of it. As this happens, those who employ violence undermine their moral authority even as they solidify their physical control. Rather than ending the unofficial violence, their official violence becomes a model for the vengeance of those morally offended by it. The fact that vengeful resentment lingers in the aftermath of official violence is a symptom that the culture has lost its ability to distinguish effectively between good and bad violence. It means that the once categorical distinction between official "force," on the one hand, and the "violence" of rebels, criminals, or vigilantes, on the other, is breaking down. In a world where the difference between holy violence and evil violence still existed, violence could still effectively end violence. Increasingly today violence destroys the moral legitimacy that was once its chief by-product.

In other words, societies are slipping deeper into violence, not because violence is now more powerful, but because, however physically powerful it is, violence has been shorn of much of its once shimmering moral and religious prestige. Violence is physically devastating and increasingly difficult to terminate because it has lost its capacity for generating the metaphysical aura that gave it its sovereign power and its moral privilege. Violence is physically more vandalistic because it is morally more dubious. If the modern day Philip can understand the relationship between the crucifixion and the growing moral dubiousness of violence, then he will be able to shed light on what James Clad, a senior associate at the Carnegie Endowment for International Peace, referred to as "the disintegration of any meaningful civic order in many parts of the world still masquerading as sovereign states."[4] He will be better able to understand ethnic passions that are at this moment sweeping so many people around the world into the madness of violence. He will understand the anthropological significance of the fact that today one person's terrorist is another person's freedom fighter.

"Riot" or "Insurrection"

The August 3, 1992, edition of the *Los Angeles Times* carried a front-page story about the dispute among Los Angeles residents about how to refer to the violence that broke out after the 1992 acquittal of the police officers accused of beating Rodney King. According to the story, the two most prevalent terms used to describe the violence that occurred in South Central Los Angeles on April 29 and 30 of 1992 were "uprising" and "riot," terms with two distinctively different connotations. While those on the political left prefer the former, those on the right insist the latter more accurately describes the violence. Responding to those who had used the terms "riot" and "rioters," Sandra Cox, president of the Southern California Association of Black Psychologists, countered: "They never stopped to think that this country was conceived in this manner . . . that America was conceived in violence." According to *Times* reporter Bob Sipchen, Cox prefers the term "insurrection" to the term "riot." "I think what we're seeing here closely resembles the French revolution," said Cox. Sipchen also interviewed Sarah Maza, Northwestern University professor of history. "People on the left are squeamish in describing what crowds do if they're violent and lawless," Maza remarked. "They focus instead on the composition of the crowd and the short- and long-term causes. The right is interested in what the crowd does and not who they are or why."[5]

We may live in a period of extraordinary moral confusion, but the moral revolution being effected by the gospel works in season and out. In today's world, both the political right and the political left, if they are to remain morally coherent, must speak on behalf of victims. The left champions the cause of those who suffer structural violence — the deprivations and indignities to which the poor, the underprivileged, racial minorities, and those habituated and socialized to ghetto life are often subjected. The left justifies or excuses the violence committed by the victims of structural violence. The right champions the victims of criminal violence, violence committed in disproportionate numbers by the underprivileged who have suffered most from social neglect and structural violence. The right justifies the violence necessary to control crime and excuses its occasional excesses as regrettable but unavoidable. Looking abroad, where the right sees "freedom fighters," the left sees the forces of counter-revolutionary oppression. Where the left sees a liberation movement, the right sees terrorists. Domestically, where the left sees an "uprising," the right sees a "riot." It is a mistake to think of this as a merely political disagreement. Seen from a larger perspective, it is a society losing its convictions about the nature of violence. It is a society floundering in its attempt to determine whether violence is destructive or beneficial. It is another symptom that we live in a world no longer able to make a coherent distinction between good and bad violence.

"They never stopped to think that this country was conceived... in violence," said the psychologist Sandra Cox. The larger implication of Cox's comment is that all who enjoy the benefits of cultural life have an inherently ambivalent relationship to violence. Every intact culture looks back on the violence that brought it into being with admiration and gratitude. President Reagan tried to wrap the Nicaraguan "Contras" in the mantle of legitimacy by referring to them as "the moral equivalent of the Founding Fathers," and Cox is doing the same thing with the rioters in Los Angeles, declaring them the moral equivalent of the Founding Fathers of the French Republic. In both cases, the social instinct is a perfectly predictable one. Reagan's right-wing ideology and Cox's more liberal sensibilities function in identical ways, as each tries to salvage the last remnants of the primitive sacred—the aura surrounding culture-founding violence—and bestow its moral halo on selected acts of contemporary violence.

The real issue here, of course, is not a political but an anthropological one. How are we to distinguish violence that creates culture from violence that destroys it? All over the world, the inability to definitively make such a distinction has thrown societies into chaos. Today we awaken routinely to a new Lebanon or a new Bosnia, a fierce and bloody conflict in which factions struggle to perform acts of violence that will create social order out of chaos and succeed only in deepening the chaos. In almost all of these cases, the partisans try to lend moral legitimacy to their violence by claiming it to be the spiritual successor to violence performed at a glimmering moment of cultural origin or revival. Not only Reagan and Cox, but people all over the world are employing intellectual, moral, and rhetorical ingenuity in an effort to endow the violence they favor with culture-founding authority, and all over the world they are failing.

Some of the aphorisms of the ancient Greek philosopher Heraclitus have become focal points for modern philosophy. "Strife," Heraclitus wrote, "is the father and king of all things.... Everything originates in strife.... All things both come to pass and perish through strife."[6] Almost everyone today can see that things perish through strife. Even though we do not understand it, and even though with each passing day it becomes less and less of a real possibility, instinctively we talk and act as though something can still originate in strife. In the period just before and during the U.S.-led war in the Persian Gulf, the world was abuzz with something called "the new world order," and enthusiasm for the war effort was remarkably high. More remarkable still, however, was the speed with which the patriotic spirit, fanned by the war, faded. The "new world order" became a term of mockery. Heraclitus was once right, but not any more. Now he is only half-right. Things can still perish through strife. Violence is losing its culture-founding and culture-rejuvenating power.

"A Crisis of Ungovernability"

Just three days before the *Los Angeles Times* reported on the dispute over how to refer to the Los Angeles riots, The *New York Times* carried a story that bears on the present discussion.[7] The *Times* reported on violence in an impoverished South African township that had been dubbed "Beirut" by its residents and those of nearby townships. According to *Times* reporter Bill Keller, the "Beirut" township in South Africa and others like it are sliding into anarchy. Many factors had contributed to this anarchy, prominent among them, no doubt, the oppression and neglect caused by South Africa's system of apartheid. For the moment, however, it isn't the cause of the anarchy I want to analyze but the nature of it.

According to Keller's report in the *Times*—alarmingly entitled "Bullied by Its Children, a Township Is Festering" — the nature of social chaos underwent a change in South African townships during the decade of the 1980s. What had earlier been the political protests of oppressed people and, later, the violent rivalry between and among the black political factions, became what many believed to be, as Keller put it, "a kind of wild mutiny of a lost generation raised to adolescence without prospects or discipline." At the time of Keller's article, members of teenage gangs, their heads filled with revolutionary slogans, had begun to take control of the township's neighborhoods. The township was being terrorized by its own youth. As the caption under a photograph accompanying the *Times* article put it: "The township is deteriorating into a state of near anarchy where teen-age gangs rule neighborhoods with violence and terrorism."

"There is a serious concern, even if one reached an agreement with the parents, whether the kids will listen to them," the *Times* reporter quotes S. Nigel Mandy as saying. Mandy was an urban planner for Transvaal Provincial Administration, an agency responsible for providing services to black townships. "We're talking today about a crisis of ungovernability," Mandy concluded. According to one of the few doctors still willing to practice in the township, Dr. Josiah Musundwa, "It's almost a free-for-all now. . . . You don't know whether it's political or the thugs or whatever. It almost has created an element of insanity where you find all the basic structures in the community collapsing." When René Girard speaks of a *sacrificial crisis,* he is speaking of precisely this: the collapse of the basic structures of communal life and the simultaneous disintegration of moral and psychological coherence. Musundwa's bewilderment is apparently widespread. Just as there was in Los Angeles after the widespread violence in the spring of 1992, so in the South African township there seemed to be a difference of opinion about whether the violence and those who are committing it were sources of anarchy or order. As Keller put it:

> Leaders of the Sebokeng branch of the African National Congress and its ally, the Communist Party, insist the street barricades and teen-age

> "defense units" represent not anarchy but a precaution against assassins from rival political organizations and the police.
>
> Local residents, however, are not so sure. They refer to their self-appointed defenders as "com-tsotsi" (a wry combination of "comrade," the township badge of militancy, and "tsotsi," the township slang for thug).

"Com-tsotsi" — *comrade-thug*. Here is a neologism, if ever there was one, that deserves to take its place alongside "Lebanonization" and "Balkanization" in the eerie lexicon of cultural dilapidation. "Com-tsotsi" is the necessarily oxymoronic attempt to describe the effect of violence on what remains of a culture that is trying in vain to overcome violence with violence. While the residents of Sebokeng had to invent a new term to describe the ambivalence they felt toward the wild young "defense units" that prowled the streets of the township, they were equally ambivalent about the South African police forces. "The settlement seemed to be of two minds about the security forces," Keller wrote, "the majority who regard them with suspicion, and assume their arrival heralds fresh conflict, and the rest who regard them with secret, guarded relief."

Even in this shrinking world, crises occurring in South Africa may seem to have little bearing on our own cultural situation. In fact, however, the increasing inability to distinguish the violence of "thugs" from the violence of "comrades" is a worldwide phenomenon, one that is heavy with historical implications. The nuclear arms standoff that was the defining reality of the post–World War II international order was (and is) a situation much like that experienced by the residents of Sebokeng. In both cases, those the violence purports to protect tremble to think how much destruction it might unleash in its pathetic attempt to end violence violently.

Comrades and Thugs

In its October 22, 1993, edition, the *New York Times* carried a front-page story by John F. Burns about the breakdown of social structures in the former Yugoslavia. Burns wrote:

> More and more, the residents of Sarajevo are speaking of the city as a "new Beirut," a place once celebrated for its cultured ways that is descending into chaos. As in the Lebanese capital, armed gangs have profited from the disorder of war to turn whole neighborhoods into personal fiefs.

> Touring the city in stolen cars, the gangs spread terror, murdering those who cross them.... The gangs' power is so great that the leaders of the Bosnia Government and army said recently that they dared not challenge them directly for fear of setting off an internal war in Sarajevo that would weaken the city's defenses.

What one sees in this story is that the line separating criminal "violence" and authorized "force," illegitimate and legitimate power, is blurring. Evidence of this same phenomenon crops up almost daily in the press.

"The residents of the Lichtenhagen neighborhood [in Rostock, Germany], who *cheered* and *applauded* on Monday night when rioters firebombed a hostel for foreign refugees, now worry that the explosion of racial hatred has ignited a *chain-reaction of uncontrollable violence*" (emphasis added). Thus wrote Ferdinand Protzman in the August 27, 1992, *New York Times*. Cheers and chain reactions. Comrades and thugs. The story of the rioting in Germany's northern port city was perfectly typical of riots everywhere and at all times. However dissimilar the causes of these outbreaks may appear to be, and as idiosyncratic as their justifications might be, the outbreaks themselves have an unmistakable structural identity. According to the deputy chairman of Germany's Social Democratic Party, quoted in the *Times* article, "It used to be the Jews in Germany. Now it is the weakest and the foreigners."

Is not the world convulsing with the most grotesque resurgence of scapegoating violence? Is this not decisive evidence against the central premise of this book — that an empathy for victims awakened by the biblical tradition is crippling the "surrogate victim" system upon which humanity has depended for social solidarity since culture began? No, for the biblical revelation has not eliminated the human predisposition for resolving social tensions at the expense of scapegoat victims. Overcoming that predisposition is essential to what the New Testament calls conversion, and it is a lifelong process. Meanwhile, however, what the biblical tradition *has* done to those cultures it has significantly influenced is to destroy the mesmerizing power of their myths of righteous violence, myths once compelling enough to make the Caiaphas formula for warding off catastrophe viable; making conversion an option that could be ignored more or less with impunity. Today, to paraphrase Einstein, everything has changed save our social and psychological reflexes. The ancient recipe for whipping human passions into a frenzy and then turning them into piety at their victim's expense no longer works. The medicine has become the poison. Things fall apart; the center cannot hold. A mob unable to glory in its violence will be unable to perpetuate for long the social solidarity that accompanied the violence. It was a robust sacrificial system the ancient Greek Heraclitus was observing when he declared that violence both destroys and creates. For cultures exposed to the biblical revelation, it can no longer create. What makes so many of today's outbreaks of mob violence different, therefore, is the increased likelihood that the cheers of the violent mob will turn into a "chain reaction of uncontrollable violence."

As the *Times* reported, the Rostock rioters were at first supported by many residents of the neighborhood where the riots occurred, but as the rioting continued, fear that it was getting out of hand caused the support to dwindle. (The foreign refugees against whom the violence was directed surely felt that the violence had gotten out of hand at the outset.) The *Times* reporter interviewed one of the teenagers involved in the riots:

> "We had to get rid of the gypsies because of the mess they were making and we did," said a red-haired youth of about 17, with a greased ponytail, mirror sunglasses and four gold studs in his left earlobe.
>
> "But now it's the cops. We have to settle scores with them. They are jerks. They won't talk with us, they just start hitting. Then we go after them. And we'll keep doing it."

As far as the older residents of Lichtenhagen were concerned, whether this young man and his fellow rioters were comrades or thugs was an open question. The inability to distinguish the two is a growing phenomenon and one of the most ominous features of our age. Is the experience of the people of Lichtenhagen an early warning? If we continue to try to solve the problem of violence violently, can we or our children or grandchildren expect to have our cheers turn into anguished cries, as the remedial violence in which we placed our hope for order turns first into random violence and finally into recreational violence?

The dynamic of the present cultural and psychological crisis is so paradoxical that it is difficult to determine whether in any given situation one is witnessing the *disintegration* of a social unit or a clumsy, primitive, and faltering attempt to reconvene one. The reason for this confusion is simple. The two phenomena are indistinguishable. When cultures lose their ability to generate lasting forms of camaraderie at the expense of their victims and enemies, they are soon overtaken by the social tensions and factional rivalries their sacrificial mechanisms can no longer reconcile. Unless one of these factions can convincingly declare its violence to be *metaphysically distinct* from violence that is *physically indistinguishable* from it, no resolution is possible, and the society teeters on the brink of "apocalyptic" violence. Religion, or, if you will, archaic religion, is what bestows the metaphysical and moral privilege on one of the acts of violence — often the most spectacular of them. That is how the primitive sacred managed to make culture possible. The problem is that we now live in a world in which the primitive sacred has lost most of its mystifying power. It cannot save us any more.

Empathy and Pathology

The realization that this is so might also be dawning on one of my imaginary homebound commuters, one reading, for instance, Mike Davis's review of *Do or Die*, Léon Bing's study of urban gangs, which appeared in the August 11, 1991, edition of the *New York Times Book Review.* [8] Would Philip's spiritual heir be able to illuminate this traveler's perplexity over this review? Quoting from Bing's book, Davis wrote:

> "...The more articulate gang members explicitly compare being 'down for the "hood"' with patriotism. Bopete, for example, carefully explains that the Jungle [a ghetto apartment complex] is not just turf, but a 'nation' — an all-encompassing, absolute rationale for sacrifice and destruction. Monster Kody, a famous veteran Crip turned black revolutionary in prison, emphasizes that in any epoch or context he would have belonged to the extreme fringe of nationalism (his examples are the Nazis, the Jewish Defense League and the Black Panthers). Meanwhile his young successors dream about 'a big, humongous meeting' to bring all the warring gang factions together in one all-powerful Crip nation."[9]

In many parts of the world, multiethnic nations groan under the difficult task of subordinating racial, ethnic, and cultural differences to an increasingly elusive sense of overriding national identity. Except under conditions very much like those that ended with the end of the Cold War, modern nation-states seem less and less able to inspire the kind of national loyalty to which their resident subcultures are willing to subordinate themselves. Meanwhile, these subcultures have exactly what most nations do not have — namely: ethnic, religious, or ideological homogeneity, or at least an illusion of such. Not only do many of these subcultures have an unabashed relish for celebrating the social and psychological fruits of that homogeneity, but they often have a knack for reproducing in miniature the cultural and political dynamics that accompanied the heyday of the multiethnic nation-states from whose weakening gravitational field they have begun to break away.

The implication of Bing's book is that, in the Spartan urban gang subculture, ad hoc attempts are being made to reproduce conditions very much like those that ended with the end of the Cold War. By fits and starts, these gangs are experimenting with homemade versions of the "all-encompassing, absolute rationale for sacrifice and destruction" which is the oldest known recipe for generating social solidarity. In subcultural enclaves such as these, social solidarity and psychological identity are still profoundly dependent upon the specter of a common enemy. Like ethnic enclaves in other cultural settings, urban street gangs function in a social niche relatively insulated from the historical processes that have aroused an empathy for victims and undermined the myths of sacred violence in the surrounding culture. Sometimes the only visible sign that the gospel revelation has made any inroads at all into these subcultures and proto-cultures is that the myths with which they try to justify their violence employ the anti-victimage rhetoric without which no violence can any longer hope to justify itself. Unless the adoption of the anti-victimage ethic is accompanied by the recognition of one's own penchant for victimizing, in due course the moral force of the ethic will be giving legitimacy to acts of cruelty virtually indistinguishable from those that its advocates purport to be trying to end once and for all.

Some of the gang members Bing interviewed may have been sociopaths, but they were better anthropologists than those who naively think that today's resurgence of ethnic and gender and class identifications is a harbinger of peaceful times ahead. "Neither Greek nor Jew, neither slave nor free, neither male nor female," declared Paul to the Galatians, dismissing as dangerous and irrelevant the three most conspicuous cultural markers of his world (and ours). Like today's gang members, but with the mythological blinders removed, Paul had experienced first hand how easily these fundamentally accidental distinctions allied themselves with the structures of sacred violence that the crucifixion had decisively revealed and repudiated. The *Times* review of Bing's book recognized this. "Fatalism, bonding by violence, xenophobia — the ingredients of gang culture evoked by Bing's informants — define a kind of pathological *Gemeinschaft* not dissimilar to what most of us admire in the Marines or in police officers," wrote Davis. What an extraordinary thing to say. What an extraordinary thing to *see*. *Gemeinschaft* is the German word for "social bonding," "community," and "camaraderie." The fact that even a subtle similarity between the *Gemeinschaft* of the Marines and police, on one hand, and that of criminal gangs, on the other, is detectable is weighty with historical implications.

Davis may think of fatalism, bonding by violence and xenophobia as a kind of "pathological *Gemeinschaft*," but some of the gang members obviously regard these things as essential for the formation of a "nation." If the *Gemeinschaft* of street gangs is a pathological version of the *Gemeinschaft* of the Marines or the police, questions might arise about the nonpathological claims of these more respectable forms of this *Gemeinschaft.* Freeman Dyson has suggested that all military establishments "have been expressly designed to make it possible for people to do things together which nobody in his right mind would do alone."[10] A *Gemeinschaft* that allows its participants to do what no one "in his right mind" would do alone may not be as easy to distinguish from a "pathological" *Gemeinschaft* as it at first appears.

Except for the accidents of time and space, by his own admission Monster Kody might have been a Nazi or a Jewish Defense League partisan or a Black Panther. Or, Davis adds, a Marine or a police officer, both of whom participate in a "*Gemeinschaft*" that may not be regarded as "pathological," but that nevertheless cannot altogether be distinguished from the one to which Monster Kody and his fellow gang members are loyal. A. C. Jones, a counselor at a Los Angeles correctional facility housing street gang offenders, was interviewed by Bing in her study of gang violence. For his part, Jones recognized a similarity parallel to the one recognized by Monster Kody. "I'll tell you one thing I'm real sure about and that's the commonalities between gangs and cops," Jones, an ex-gang member and Vietnam veteran, told Bing. "Look," he said, "take away the moral imperative and the legal aspect of who has the right to kill and who does not, and what you have left is the very same organization."[11]

Both Bing's book and Davis's review appeared many months before the riots in Los Angeles following the verdict in the Rodney King beating case. The riots seared the nation's imagination, and, as I have noted, extensive discussion of the causes and implications of the riots followed. Dozens of articles that analyzed the riots could be cited for their insight into the collapse of the distinction between "good" and "bad" violence. I will cite only one newspaper article, one of the most explicit in this regard. The June 1, 1992, *San Francisco Chronicle* carried an article by Suzanne Espinosa in which she interviewed a number of Los Angeles police officers. The article brought to light two glaring facts: first, that as an institution the police department was losing its prestige along with its ability to assert an unchallenged monopoly on the use of violence, and second, that even the police officers themselves were seeing the similarity between themselves and the gangs with whom they were almost daily in mortal combat. According to Espinosa, the battle for the streets was not only a struggle for physical control but a contest over "respect."

The most striking feature of the contest for respect was that in many places the police and the criminal gangs began on more or less equal footing. The implications of this one fact are enormous. "In dozens of interviews," Espinosa wrote, "police officers said a badge and uniform no longer win them automatic respect and cooperation. Too many times, they say, officers are driven to using fists, batons, and harsh language to counter hostility and disrespect." As long as the badge and the uniform command respect, those who wear them can counter "bad" violence merely with the moral force that the symbols of "good" violence emanate. Once "good" violence can no longer convincingly radiate that *moral* force, then the violence that might have been exuded as "authority" has to be exerted as physical force. The result is that those whose disrespect made the force necessary will harbor an even greater degree of disrespect, further compromising the institution's moral prestige.

If Espinosa's article is any indication, the police and the criminal gangs are meeting each other on the streets of Los Angeles on more or less equal footing as far as the social prestige of the violence they sponsor is concerned. Increasingly, each side understands itself to be a mirror image of its adversary. Where there is still any respect between the two sides, it is the kind of respect between equals that was once a hallmark of military professionals. "During the riots," Espinosa wrote, "looters approached officers on the street and asked if they wanted to buy stolen goods." The growing sense of moral symmetry between the criminals and the cops corresponds to what Girard speaks of as the doubling effect of violence, the tendency of violence to erase all difference between the adversaries while at the same time enflaming the passions and causing the level of violence between them to escalate.

On condition that she use the pseudonym Eddie instead of his real name, Espinosa interviewed an officer who decided to join the police force so that he could take revenge on gang members who had terrorized his neighborhood, killed one friend, and sexually humiliated another. For him the police force offered an opportunity to retaliate in more or less the same way that gangs retaliate. "Even as a policeman, Eddie still sports the look of a gangster — Levi's, white cotton shirts and slicked-back hair," Espinosa wrote. "Leaning forward, he said in a hoarse whisper: 'We are the biggest gang in L.A.' "

What the Los Angeles police officer, the reviewer Mike Davis, the correctional officer A. C. Jones, and the veteran gang member Monster Kody recognize explicitly is that the necessary asymmetry between "good" and "bad" violence is breaking down. Unless and until the world comes to grips with that fact, the catastrophes of the twentieth century will have taught us nothing, and they will be but the prelude to greater ones in the twenty-first. Monster Kody sees the resemblance between the violence of his street gang and the violence of extreme patriots. Jones and "Eddie," the Los Angeles police officer, see the parallel between "gangs and the cops." Davis sees the underlying similarity between the gang violence and the official violence of the Marines and the police. The pathology of the former may be obvious, but the absolute difference between official violence and criminal violence, and the moral privileges accorded the former, are vanishing.

At this point, let me stress as strongly as I can what I am *not* saying. I am not saying that there is no moral difference between the violence of those trying to restore order and restrain criminal behavior and the violence of criminals, sociopaths, and terrorists. There most certainly is a moral difference, and to disparage it would be morally irresponsible. The point I am trying to make is that this moral distinction is no longer categorical. The distinction between violence used or readied for use by those striving to restore order and the violence it countermands is no longer universally regarded as *absolute*. As a result, we live at an unparalleled moment in human history. While we have so far been too preoccupied with its many symptoms to realize it, what we are witnessing is the passing of a historical epoch during which the sacrificial mechanisms for resolving violence violently still functioned.

"Enmeshed in the Same Evil"

The issue to which I am trying to call attention is vividly exemplified at the end of William Golding's novel *The Lord of the Flies*. The novel is about English schoolboys stranded on an island during World War II with no adult authority on which to rely. With remarkable speed, the boys re-create crude social arrangements and turn to primitive superstition and ritual sacrifices. In the final scene of the novel, Ralph, the boys' former leader, flees the others who are trying to sacrifice him to their primitive deity. Ralph scrambles in the sand in his desperate effort to avoid his attackers when suddenly there before him stands a British naval officer.

> He staggered to his feet, tensed for more terrors, and looked up at a huge peaked cap. It was a white-topped cap, and above the green shade of the peak was a crown, an anchor, gold foliage. He saw white drill, epaulettes, a revolver, a row of gilt buttons down the front of a uniform.

> A naval officer stood on the sand, looking down at Ralph in wary astonishment. On the beach behind him was a cutter, her bows hauled up and held by two ratings. In the stern-sheets another rating held a sub-machine gun.[12]

When the boys chasing Ralph find him standing before the British officer, they abruptly stop, sobered by the unexpected presence of an adult authority. They begin to come to their senses. It has been humanity's recurrent dream that it would eventually be able to do just that, come to its senses. For ten thousand years it has been trying to do so by countering wild and primitive "violence" with stately and authorized "force." This is precisely what works to restore order on the island at the end of Golding's novel. The moral authority of the British naval officer and the institutions he represents enable him to put an end to primitive violence by his mere presence, making him no doubt the envy of the Los Angeles police officers Suzanne Espinosa interviewed for her story. "In dozens of interviews," she wrote, "police officers said a badge and uniform no longer win them automatic respect and cooperation."

Golding was an anthropologically well informed writer, much as W. H. Auden was. When he was later asked to comment on the novel, he spoke of the irony of the final scene:

> The whole book is symbolic in nature except the rescue in the end where adult life appears, dignified and capable, but in reality enmeshed in the same evil as the symbolic life of the children on the island. The officer, having interrupted a man-hunt, prepares to take the children off the island in a cruiser which will presently be hunting its enemy in the same implacable way. And who will rescue the adult and his cruiser?[13]

The real question, the question for our time, is: What happens if the boys chasing Ralph realize the underlying moral similarity between their chase and that of the naval officer? What if they learn the truth made explicit in Golding's epilogue while remaining blissfully ignorant of the warning implicit in Golding's novel? Will they stop as abruptly when they see the naval uniform? Will they as obligingly drop their crude weapons? Will they as meekly obey his instructions? There is still a real moral difference between the *Gemeinschaft* shared by gang members and that of the Marines and police. There may even be a modest moral difference between the criminal violence of urban gangs and that of nationalist extremists. The question we must ask is, in such cases, is that moral difference great enough? Is it shrinking? And what would happen if it vanished all together? The answer is that we would either have to begin living more or less according to the Sermon on the Mount or slide into the abyss of apocalyptic violence. The unlikelihood of the former should not be used as an excuse for dismissing the likelihood of the latter.

What an heir to Philip's ministry must be prepared to explain is what the crucifixion has to do with the disappearance of the distinction between good and bad violence. If he is to continue to speak of the "good news" of the gospel, he must further be able to show that the crisis of culture, however grave and dangerous, is an opportunity to emancipate ourselves from social melodramas that are unworthy of us and that are no longer either morally tolerable or culturally effective.

As the once absolute distinction between righteous and wretched violence blurs, attempts to revive what was once thought to be holy violence will plunge culture ever deeper into crisis. As cultures lose their ability to distinguish good from bad violence, they will lose their ability to terminate the latter with a spectacular display of the former. As the last vestiges of the system of sacred violence dissolve, in the words of Robert Hamerton-Kelly, "the only barrier between us and violent self-destruction is our own restraint."[14] I hasten to add that there is abundant evidence suggesting how inadequate in the face of a full-fledged social contagion even the most resolute forms of moral and social self-restraint are. By itself, moral muscle is no more reliable a defense against such social contagions than is knowledge of the mimetic processes that produce them. Understanding these things is extremely important, and without more robust forms of moral resolve our prospects are no doubt grim. But the present historical crisis is ultimately a religious one, and both the intellectual acuity and moral sinew it demands of us are religious derivatives. It has been said that several drinks of whiskey can produce an effect similar to that of intoxication. Humans in crisis easily succumb to social contagions that end in a violence that is accompanied by a primitive form of religious intoxication. In the final analysis, the only alternative to the simulated transcendence of social contagion and violence is another experience of religious transcendence, one at the center of which is a God who chooses to suffer violence rather than to sponsor it.

Chapter 4

Shaken Witnesses

> If the Judeo-Christian ferment is not dead, it must be engaged in an obscure struggle against deeper and deeper layers of the essential complicity between violence and human culture.[1]
>
> RENÉ GIRARD

> That corpse you planted last year in your garden,
> Has it begun to sprout? Will it bloom this year?
> Or has the sudden frost disturbed its bed?
> Oh keep the Dog far hence, that's friend to men,
> Or with his nails he'll dig it up again!
>
> T. S. ELIOT, *The Waste Land*

In 1777, more than a century and half before William Golding wrote the last scene in *Lord of the Flies,* a similar scene occurred. Like Golding's scene, it involved a confrontation between a British naval officer and a people on a remote island in the midst of a ritual sacrifice. At first, the two encounters hardly seem comparable. One is an episode in twentieth-century literature, the other an event in eighteenth-century history. Structurally, however, there are striking parallels between them. In each, the naval officer casts a cold eye on the sacrificial ritual under way before him. In each, his glance has a debilitating effect on the ritual and an unnerving effect on those participating in it. Whereas the final scene in Golding's novel is extremely brief and his comment on it in his epilogue pithy, the parallel scene that took place in 1777 was recorded in illuminating detail. To this advantage is added the fact that it actually happened. Because of its greater detail, this event, though it historically predates Golding's parallel scene by almost two centuries, can even be read as a sequel to it, which is why I turn to it now.

The British explorer and scientist, Captain James Cook, visited a number of Polynesian islands on his voyages between 1769 and 1774. He was impressed with the charm and seeming nobility of the islanders, naming one archipelago "The Friendly Islands" no doubt because of the cordiality shown to him and his crew by the natives. He visited Tahiti on two occasions, and on the latter visit a young Polynesian joined him as an interpreter and returned with him to England. The young man's name was Omai. Introduced to fashionable society in England and on the continent, Omai impressed his admiring hosts with his poise. Sir Joshua Reynolds painted at least one portrait of him, as did other painters. The young man seemed living proof that Rousseau had been right about the noble savage. In 1777, Omai returned with Captain Cook to the Polynesian Islands, landing at Tahiti in August of that year. Cook and his party were treated warmly. Shortly after their arrival, however, it was learned that the people of a neighboring island were preparing for war. The next day, a subordinate chief ordered a man to be killed so that he could be offered as a sacrifice to the god Eatooa, whose assistance in the coming war would thereby be assured. Cook was allowed to witness the ritual that ensued, and he recorded it in some detail.[2]

As Cook soon learned, the Tahitians believed that their god, pleased to have a fresh corpse (or its spirit) to devour, would be favorably disposed toward whatever request the corpse might have brought from the land of living. The god would grant boons to those who offered the sacrifice. The task is neither to assess Polynesian mythology aesthetically (as romantics do), nor to mine it for psychological symbolisms (as popular therapies do), nor to dismiss it as nonsense. Our task is to recognize the anthropological phenomena that such myths camouflage and that the accompanying rituals re-present in stylized form. For the Tahitians, what is important about the ritual human sacrifice is that it promises to enhance their upcoming military campaign against a neighboring tribe. The belief that ritual sacrifices have such effects is an anthropological commonplace. We must ask how could so many cultures in so many different historical settings have thought that human sacrifice was socially or even militarily efficacious?

There is only one explanation: in the actual experience of these cultures such ritual sacrifices actually had such effects. The next question is: how could that have been their experience? The simplest answer is that successful ritual sacrifices climax in an intense experience of social solidarity, a solidarity that is crucial to the success of any military venture. In fact, the situation is somewhat more complex. The prewar sacrifices that serve to galvanize a tribe are *preliminary* rituals. The war itself is the ritual main event.

It is almost impossible for someone to recognize, much less critically analyze, the system of sacred violence upon which one's own culture relies. Once one has inhaled the sacrificial fumes, one tends to justify the sacrificial fires that produced the fumes. Should one witness the sacrificial violence of others, however, one will sooner or later understand—and if one has been significantly exposed to the Bible, one will *instantly* understand—that what one is seeing is scapegoating violence. We have Captain Cook's extraordinary and invaluable record of the sacrificial rituals on Tahiti because Cook could see those rituals through eyes made wary of such things by a European culture under the considerable influence of the gospel.

Rites and Wrongs

From the point of view of the Tahitians, it was a terrible mistake to allow their sacrificial rituals to be observed by one so immune to the accompanying myth of sacred violence. Cook did what cultures infected with the gospel virus have been doing for hundreds of years. He started asking questions. He tried to learn from the Tahitians how they could possibly believe what was to him such utter nonsense.

> They said, that it was an old custom, and was agreeable to their god, who delighted in, or, in other words, came and fed upon the sacrifices; in consequence of that, he complied with their petitions. Upon its being objected, that he could not feed on these, as he was neither seen to do it, nor were the bodies of the animals quickly consumed, and that as to the human victim, they prevented his feeding on him, by burying him...they answered that he came in the night, but invisibly; and fed only on the soul, or immaterial part, which, according to their doctrine, remains about the place of sacrifice, until the body of the victim be entirely wasted by putrefaction.

One doesn't quite know which is the more naive, the simple faith of the Polynesians in their myth and ritual or Cook's apparent belief that such myths could be swept away by common sense. Nevertheless, as the priests groped for ritual justifications that would satisfy Cook's inquiries, Cook showed himself an astute observer of social reality. He noticed certain social facts which he was perceptive enough to regard as significant. He observed divisions within the community. He noticed a difference of opinion concerning the essential matter of the upcoming war with the nearby tribe. Moreover, these divisions existed *after* the ritual sacrifice had taken place. On the basis of this last observation, Cook astutely concluded not only that the rite had failed, but that, having failed, its practical consequences would be the opposite of the intended ones. He told the Tahitian chief that in his opinion the ritual would result in a curse rather than a blessing. In his journal, Cook wrote:

> This was venturing pretty far upon conjecture; but still, I thought, that there was little danger of being mistaken. For I found, that there were three parties in the island, with regard to this war; one extremely violent for it; another perfectly indifferent about the matter; and the third openly declaring themselves friends to Maheine [the enemy chief] and his cause. Under these circumstances, of disunion distracting their councils, it was not likely that such a plan of military operations would be settled, as could insure even a probability of success.

Brilliantly Cook intuited that the ritual's efficacy had to do with social solidarity, and he observed that no such solidarity had been achieved. The question for us is, What had gone wrong? Why was the ritual unable to produce the necessary catharsis and the social unanimity it fosters?

Ironically, and I suppose paradoxically, one of the reasons Cook gives for the fact that he was so morally offended by the Tahitian sacrificial rite was that its liturgical performance was so slipshod and unconvincing. He writes:

> The custom, though no consideration can make it cease to be abominable, might be thought less detrimental, in some respects, if it served to impress any awe for the divinity, or reverence for religion, upon the minds of the multitude. But this is so far from being the case, that though a great number of people had assembled at the morai, on this occasion, they did not seem to shew any proper reverence for what was doing, or saying, during the celebration of the rites.

The lack of genuine religious fervor at the Tahitian ritual may well have been due in part to the fact that the victim had already been killed by the time the formal sacrificial ritual began. On examining the victim's body and by inquiring among those who knew something of the preliminaries, Captain Cook was able to find out that the victim "had been privately knocked on the head with a stone." The Tahitians chose to perform in secret the ritual's *coup de grâce,* the act that would ordinarily have served as the ritual's dramatic and cathartic crescendo. As a result, their ritual no doubt lost both its religious solemnity and its social utility. By comparison with the innumerable cults of human sacrifice known to have thrived in antiquity, those participating in this eighteenth-century Polynesian one seem to have become ambivalent about it. They carried out its most potentially cathartic event surreptitiously. Not only was the victim no longer actually killed during the ritual itself, but the process by which the victim was selected seems to have degenerated. Cook was able to report:

> Those who are devoted to suffer, in order to perform this bloody act of worship, are never appraised of their fate, till the blow is given that puts an end to their existence. Whenever any one of the great Chiefs thinks a human sacrifice is necessary, on any particular emergency, he pitches upon the victim. Some of his trusty servants are then sent, who fall upon him suddenly, and put him to death with a club or by stoning him.

There can be little doubt that this ritual derives from one in which the killing occurred at the center of the ritual arena and served as the ritual's dramatic dénouement. Covert activity of the sort Cook reports is almost surely a sign that the Tahitian rituals and myths are being haunted by misgivings.[3] After the rites were concluded, the Tahitian chief asked Cook whether they had met his expectations, what he thought of their efficacy, and whether such rituals were performed in Cook's native land. "I did not conceal my detestation," Cook writes.

The myths and rituals of an intact culture do not answer questions; they extinguish the will to ask them. Once a mythological system fails to eliminate such questions, it can never make up for that failure by being logically persuasive. In fact, as I earlier pointed out, those who use persuasion to try to rehabilitate myths actually undercut the myths all the more. Persuasion involves a detectable mental or moral effort, and mythological conviction demands a mental tranquility that even rudimentary acts of reasoning disrupt. A culture attempting to rationally defend its sacrificial myth is a culture in an irreversible crisis. When a myth fails to extinguish the will to question, the more brilliant the reasoning offered by its defenders, the more the sophisticated reasoning destroys mythological consciousness. Perhaps open skepticism had yet to surface in the Tahitian society Cook was observing, but clearly the culture's ritual and mythological system had ceased to be compelling. In such a culturally precarious situation, a critical question asked aloud can go off like a grenade.

The "Spirit" and the "Wrath"

In communicating his disgust with the rituals and his opinion that they were doomed to failure, Cook asked Omai, the young Polynesian who had been in the company of the Europeans for three years, to interpret. As Omai translated Cook's critique of the ritual to one of the tribe's chieftains, the young man became visibly moved by the strength of Cook's argument. Cook writes:

> In conveying our sentiments to Towha, on the subject of the late sacrifice, Omai was made our interpreter; and he entered into our arguments with so much spirit, that the Chief seemed to be in a great wrath; especially when he was told, that if he had put a man to death in England, as he had done here, his rank would not have prevented him from being hanged for it. Upon this, he exclaimed, maeno! maeno! [vile! vile!] and would not hear another *word.* (emphasis added)

The "word" to which the chief objects is the same word Agamemnon tried to silence at the sacrifice of Iphigenia. It is synonymous with the scream the German diplomat heard on that fateful night in Moscow. It is the word whose effects Nietzsche so despised. It is the word made flesh in the life of the Crucified One. Neither Cook nor Omai could ever have uttered it had it not first been thus made flesh.

Though Cook seemed only dimly aware of the cultural and religious influences upon which his objections were based, the words he spoke to the Tahitian chief were an extension of the revelation of the Cross, and they carried with them some of the explosive power of biblical revelation. As I said, however, it is considerably easier to recognize the mythological delusions of others or of other cultures than it is to renounce the delusions on which we ourselves have grown culturally and psychologically dependent. The *logos* with which Cook challenged the *mythos* of Tahitian sacrificial thinking may have gone off like dynamite, but its explosive effects were occurring more gradually in Cook's own Europe. European culture had managed a rapprochement of sorts between gospel sensibilities and cultural conventions antithetical to them. As a result, Europe had been able — precariously to be sure — to manage a kind of time-released explosion of the *dynamite* of the gospel. In Europe at the end of the eighteenth century, a number of sacrificial structures were still standing. This is why Cook was able to scold the Tahitian chief and, without a hint of irony, tell him that if he were to perform in England such sacrificial rites as he performed in Tahiti, he would be hanged for it!

Cook could not see that he was proposing his culture's sacrificial system as the solution for the outrages of the Tahitian sacrificial system. An increasing number of people today *can* see this, but not because they are wiser than their predecessors. On the contrary, it is because since Cook's time Western culture's sacrificial institutions and sacrificial reflexes have continued to be exposed to moral scrutiny by the gospel revelation. We moderns have begun to notice the similarity between the wretched violence from which the world must be saved and the righteous violence by which it has heretofore tried to save itself. It may be that the gradual recognition of this similarity is what finally defines what we call "the modern world." What we moderns have yet to understand — and what Girard's important work now makes it possible to see — is what Nietzsche saw: namely, that it is the gospel that is responsible for what is happening to us.

Cultural leaders can sometimes be the last to realize how dangerously fragile is the system on the summit of which they teeter. This seems to have been the case for Chief Otoo. He solicited Captain Cook's opinion on the just concluded sacrificial ritual. Little did he realize the danger of exposing elements of the primitive sacred to the scrutiny of those not under the spell of its justifying myth, and especially those in whom an empathy for victims had been awakened. By inviting Cook to express an opinion, therefore, and by allowing his Polynesian translator to broadcast this opinion to all those within earshot, he was letting the victim's voice be heard.

We are left to speculate what might have been the effect had Cook's comments been translated in a perfunctory way. They were not, and this is part of the wonder of Cook's account. Omai, the young Polynesian man, translated Cook's remarks, and, as Cook put it, he "entered into our arguments with so much spirit, that the Chief seemed to be in a great wrath." Here we have not only the confrontation between the forces of revelation and the forces of mystification, but, more strikingly, we have each of these forces in their most compelling and persuasive manifestation: the *spirit* by which Omai has been suddenly moved to "speak on the victim's behalf" and the *wrath* of the sacrificial spokesman who refused to hear another *word*. This is nothing less than a parable of the cultural crisis of our time. It is a showdown between the forces of cultural concealment and the forces of gospel revelation. Omai's ardor in rebuking the sacrificial *myth,* and the chief's furious refusal to hear another *word,* represent the two forces struggling today for the soul of the human race.

In the midst of translating Cook's objections, Omai was suddenly seized by a "spirit," and Cook's words became his own. Ardor in defense of victims is hardly the sum and substance of the Christian revelation, but it involves a significant break with the cultural mystifications that have veiled the truth of that revelation since the dawn of human culture. There is nothing whatsoever fanciful, therefore, about suggesting that the spirit by which Omai is suddenly seized is the *Paraclete* of which the Jesus of John's Gospel speaks. In fact, no other explanation can adequately account for it. Jesus of John's Gospel declares that the crucifixion will have the effect of turning the *Paraclete* (the Spirit) loose on the world, and that this Spirit will show the world how wrong it was about righteousness and condemnation (John 16). Just as the word "Satan" implies the "accuser," the word "Paraclete" implies the "defender of the accused." The Johannine Jesus declared that unless and until he was crucified, the *Paraclete* could not come into the world. Whatever perplexity might have surrounded this statement for us in the past, the anthropological meaning of these words is now perfectly clear. Neither Cook nor Omai was aware that it was the *Paraclete,* the spirit of the gospel, that was speaking through him, but we can become aware of that, and in doing so we can begin to understand the anthropological meaning of what they did and said.

The Hebrew prophets were the first to speak in condemnation of the sacrificial system and in defense of its victims. They were largely ignored, but their words took on a life of their own, eventually becoming the moral ballast of the Hebrew Scriptures and the essential link in the Judeo-Christian revelation. The Gospels carry forward what the Hebrew prophets began, announcing from the supreme perspective of the Cross that those united by their common victim "know not what they do." By the time Cook spoke his rebuke to sacrificial thinking in Tahiti in 1777, Europe had been haunted by these anti-sacrificial voices for centuries. What happened to Omai has happened to countless numbers of people who have been exposed to the biblical aversion for sacred violence.

In the Meantime

In general, a functioning sacrificial system is less violent than a malfunctioning one. The people that have sensed this have sometimes striven to restore the sacrificial system, content with the wisdom of Caiaphas: it is better that one (or a limited few) die than that the whole culture disintegrate. The moral shortcomings of that position aside, the only machine capable of restoring a conventional cultural system is the machine whose linchpin is a lynching, and the effect of the crucifixion has been to remove the linchpin. Even if a force as benevolent as the gospel is responsible for the resulting cultural disarray, unless and until we learn to live without resorting to these now dilapidated sacrificial mechanisms, we will be courting disaster. Encouraging the human race to live without them, and instructing us about how to do so, is what the gospel and the Christian movement exist to do. In the meantime, one can be morally offended by the sacrificial system, indeed, one *ought* to be offended, but we continue to rely on vestiges of it. For as long as it remains a plausible distinction, most will be grateful to be able to dial 911 when threatened by "bad" violence and to have the forces of "good" violence intervene posthaste. The effectiveness of such intervention is to a large extent dependent upon the degree of residual sacrality the institutions charged with the task of intervening (and their agents) continue to enjoy. What is obvious is not only that the sacral status of these institutions is declining, but that the sacrificial mechanisms for replenishing their waning prestige are themselves in gradual decline.

In the *meantime,* inept sacrificial systems tend to resort to greater violence in an effort to achieve the results they could once achieve with minimal violence. Cook noticed, for instance, that as the Tahitian sacrificial system lost its religious awe and those in attendance ceased to find the rite religiously transfixing, the sacrificial killing *increased.* Cook writes:

> Though we should suppose, that never more than one person is sacrificed, on any single occasion, at Otaheite, it is more than probable, that these occasions happen so frequently, as to make a shocking waste of the human race; for I counted no less than forty-nine skulls, of former victims, lying before the morai, where we saw one more added to the number. And as none of those skulls had, as yet, suffered any considerable change from the weather, it may hence be inferred, that no great length of time had elapsed, since, at least, this considerable number of unhappy wretches had been offered upon this altar of blood.

A sacrificial system reeling from the revelation of its murderousness grows more murderous. Desperately trying to achieve a catharsis and fumbling with ever more spectacular acts of violence, it drifts inexorably toward regicide or genocide. To the extent that an empathy for victims has been awakened, however, more brazen violence against cultural leaders or violence on a more prodigious scale will have to justify itself as a campaign not only against violence but against *victimization.* In other words, the sacrificial system will have to try to defeat the empathy for victims by turning that empathy into its rallying cry. The culture in question will have to try to revive its *esprit de corps* by selecting only certified victimizers and other perpetrators of violence as victims of its righteous zeal.

Remarkably, Cook's account contains the prefiguration of this development as well. It occurs just after Cook has written of the chief's displeasure at hearing Omai criticize the ritual sacrifice. This is symbolically important for our inquiry, for what we are concerned with at the moment is how the sacrificial myths and sacrificial logic survive in a social environment made wary of them by the presence of rudimentary gospel sensibilities. In Cook's report, such sensibilities have just been expressed by Omai. A gospel-aroused empathy for victims has encroached on the myths that justify Tahitian sacred violence. How will those whose social and psychological lives depend on the sacrificial system respond? Cook makes the following wry comment:

> During this debate, many of the natives were present, chiefly the attendants and servants of Towha himself; and when Omai began to explain the punishment that would be inflicted in England, upon the greatest man, if he killed the meanest servant, they seemed to listen with great attention; and were, probably, of a different opinion from that of their master, on this subject.

The logic behind the theoretical London hanging alluded to by Cook and Omai is simply the Tahitian sacrificial logic operating with a different triggering mechanism. In the imaginations of the lesser Tahitian priests, a sacrificial scenario more likely to earn the approval of their impressive European visitors is forming. In it, the victim is not a hapless vagabond but the high priest of a sacrificial cult whose justifying myth has been revealed to be a sham, and who has therefore lost his moral exemption. This is not only a harbinger of the chief priest's precarious social fortunes, it is a throwback to one of the sacrificial system's most primitive forms, the sacrifice of the tribal leader. Given what Cook reports, and seen against the backdrop of modern history, there is little doubt that were the Tahitian priest to become the victim of the lesser priests, the rationale for his "execution" would be "justice," though it might take more exposure to European customs for Tahitians to formulate the rationale in explicitly juridical terms. The cry of the crowd for precisely this sort of "justice" has given the modern world a rational banner under which a reformed and weakened version of the sacrificial system has been able to survive. Riding on successive waves of anti-victimage rhetoric, the sacrificial system has been able to reestablish the sacrificial logic by vehemently denouncing earlier forms of that logic as repulsive and scapegoating its former exponents. The sacrificial mechanisms given new legitimacy by this development combine a conscious feeling of moral rectitude with sublimated moral misgivings — a recipe for brutality. Compared to Chief Otoo's clumsy sacrificial efforts, the incessant clacking of Robespierre's guillotine hardly seems the moral leap forward those who operated it thought it to be.

Were such abominable Polynesian rituals performed in England, Cook says with unflappable conviction and sincerity, the perpetrator would be taken to a carefully constructed scaffold and, after scrupulously performing the social rituals designed to imbue the event with the full aura of legitimacy, that methodical murderer would be solemnly and methodically murdered. Neither Cook nor Omai seems to have noticed that it was not an unbridgeable moral chasm that separated eighteenth-century Tahiti and London. Neither, however, is the distance between them to be dismissed as insignificant.

Cook, as I've said, was unable to recognize the similarities but he *was* able to pronounce a judgment on Tahitian sacred violence. And not one letter of his judgment would need to be altered in order for it to rebound on both his own society and ours. He wrote:

> It is much to be regretted, that a practice so horrid in its own nature, and so destructive of that inviolable right of self-preservation, which every one is born with, should be found still existing; and (such is the power of superstition to counteract the first principles of humanity!) existing amongst a people, in many other respects, emerged from the brutal manners of savage life.

Two hundred years after Cook condemned the Tahitian sacrificial cult, his condemnation reverberates in our own world with greater power than when it was first uttered. Whatever progress we who are Cook's cultural heirs can claim to have made since 1777, the best measure of that progress is our capacity for recognizing, as Cook himself could not, that the sentence applies to us as much as to the eighteenth-century Tahitians.

Though the differences are obvious, there remains a similarity between the scene at the end of Golding's *Lord of the Flies* and the scene in Tahiti in 1777 described in Captain Cook's journals. In each, a British naval officer glares at those participating in a primitive ritual of human sacrifice, blissfully unaware of the underlying resemblance between the more respectable versions of the rite upon which his culture depends and the cruder versions which have aroused his moral contempt. A little more than two hundred years after Cook suggested hanging as a cure for sacrificing, a street gang member can see the similarity between his gang and nation-states; a correctional facility counselor is able to see the similarity between "the gangs and the cops"; and a journalist is able to see that gangs "define a kind of pathological *Gemeinschaft* not dissimilar to what most of us admire in the Marines or the police officers."

What kept the Tahitian priests from feeling the moral revulsion that Captain Cook felt was the same thing that kept Captain Cook from seeing the structural similarity between the violence he loathed and the violence he advocated as a cure for it. It was the lingering aura of holy or righteous violence. The ritual violence the Tahitian priests supervised without moral compunction was "holy" violence, a killing required by religious scruple. The violence Cook proposed as a cure for this "abominable" custom was "righteous" violence, a killing required by principles of retributive justice. It would be silly to deny that the judicial version represents a moral improvement over the explicitly sacrificial one, but it would be disingenuous to argue that the judicial version serves no sacrificial purposes or that it has no sacrificial effects.

"Thousands of Upturned Faces"

In August of 1777, Captain Cook warned Chief Otoo that he would be hanged in England for what he was doing with religious impunity in Tahiti. At daybreak on November 13, 1849, Charles Dickens was taking an early morning walk in London when he came upon a raucous and jubilant crowd. Pausing to investigate, he found that the crowd had gathered for a public hanging. A woman, one Mrs. Manning, was shortly to be hanged. The jeering crowd was in the process of making the woman the butt of its gibes and jokes. Later that day, Dickens wrote an open letter to the *Times of London,* saying he had seen an "inconceivably awful" sight, "the wickedness and levity of the immense crowd" that gathered to watch a public hanging. Dickens went on to say that as the sun rose it lit "thousands and thousands of upturned faces, so inexpressibly odious in their brutal mirth or callousness that a man had cause to feel ashamed of the shape he wore."[4]

With this scene before us and with the memory of the rather clumsy and embarrassed Tahitian version of it still in our minds, how are we to judge the two societies, the Christian one and the heathen one? Lest a variation on Captain Cook's moral sanctimoniousness be aroused, let us admit that we are the heirs of both Dickens and the jeering mob whose behavior he found so repulsive. Were we thrown back to 1849, would we have spent the morning writing a letter to the *Times* or rejoicing over the society's latest victory over evil? Did not President Bush receive a 91 percent approval rating for crushing the Iraqi military on live TV? Who during that brief war did not find almost daily evidence of what Dickens called "brutal mirth and callousness"? As for more recent forms of what so shocked Dickens, Janny Scott, the same *Los Angeles Times* reporter who wrote the story analyzing the phenomenon of mob violence in the Rodney King beating, wrote a subsequent article that could be a postscript to Dickens's letter of 1849. In it, she said:

> The scene outside Florida State Prison at the 1989 execution of serial killer Theodore Bundy was one of the wildest. Parents brought children, men brought wives. Hundreds of reporters camped out in a pasture. It was like a tailgate party, someone said. Or Mardi Gras.[5]

Scott then asks precisely the right question. "Why are people fascinated?" she wonders. Answers to this question abound, but none seem to finally account for the fascination. Scott gets close to the underlying dynamic when she concludes a litany of possible explanations with a perceptive observation. The execution, she says, "is a brutal act," but it is one carried out "in the name of civilization." It would be difficult to think of a more succinct summation of the underlying anthropological dynamic at work: *a brutal act done in the name of civilization,* an expulsion or execution that results in social harmony. Clearly, after the shaky justifications based on deterrence or retribution have fallen away, this is the stubborn fact that remains: a brutal act is done in the name of civilization. If we humans become too morally troubled by the brutality to revel in the glories of the civilization made possible by it, we will simply have to reinvent culture. This is what Nietzsche saw through a glass darkly. This is what Paul sensed when he declared the old order to be a dying one (1 Cor. 7:31). This is the central anthropological issue of our age.

Fascination

Janny Scott's brief article comes especially close to the essential point when she quotes Louis West, a UCLA professor of psychiatry. "Society uses its occasional legal victim of the gas, the rope or the electric chair as a lightning rod to focus divine wrath upon a single offender," says West, "while at the same time magically insinuating the survivors into the good graces of the gods by the blood sacrifice." Curiously, and tellingly, the ancient language of blood sacrifice goes more directly to the heart of the issue than does the more conventional language of modern social science. If West has found such language relevant, and if he achieves greater clarity using such explicit sacrificial language, it may well be due to the fact that, like Captain Cook and Charles Dickens, he has had first-hand experience. Here is what Scott writes in her article:

> West of UCLA became curious about the phenomenon in the summer of 1952 when he agreed to assist a fellow physician at a hanging in Iowa. His role was to help certify the moment of death. It came, West said, 12½ minutes after the man was hanged.

> "So as I stood there taking turns with my colleague listening to the man's heart, I had time to look at the spectators," he recalled. The sight stunned him.
>
> "There was a kind of glitter in their eye that I found strange, some of them, as though this was a fascinating kind of entertainment," West said.

The fact that the 1989 Florida execution bore a marked resemblance to the "brutal mirth or callousness" that so disturbed Charles Dickens in 1849 should serve as a sober reminder that whatever the social and psychological dynamics of such crowds are, they cannot be dismissed as a thing of the past. "Why are people fascinated?" Janny Scott asked. West was puzzled by the strange glitter of "fascination" in the eyes of the "spectators" witnessing the *spectacle* of holy violence. If we are to understand the driving force behind the violence that has played so dominant a role in human history, we will have to understand this "fascination" far better than we have in the past.

Etymology is often a good place to begin. The original meaning of certain words, like the originating events of a culture, tends to recede as the word adjusts to a conventional and respectable place in a culture's vernacular. This is especially true of those words that have the most potential for shedding light on culture-founding events. "Fascination" is just such a word. The root of "fascination" is the Latin verb *fascinare,* which means to bind or hold spell-bound. It is related to the Latin *fascis,* which means a bundle bound together. The symbol of authority in ancient Rome was a *fasces,* a bundle of rods bound together around an ax with the ax blade projecting from it. From these roots, the modern term "fascist" is derived.[6] What are we to make of this? It suggests that when the journalist Janny Scott and the UCLA psychiatrist she interviewed puzzle over why humans find public executions fascinating, they are touching on an anthropological issue of the first order. The complex etymological background of the word "fascination" suggests an underlying link between fascination, the *esprit de corps* of a violent mob, and the structures of cultural authority that institutionalize the *esprit de corps* and extend its social benefits over time. Were we to fully understand the complex phenomenon of fascination, we would know more than we generally care to know about the origin and nature of conventional culture.

For a culture to choose only the certifiably guilty as victims of its sacrificial spectacles is undoubtedly a moral improvement, but it is an innovation that will only temporarily be able to override the empathy for victims aroused by the gospel. Even when proven evil doers are publicly scorned or punished by persons or institutions representing the righteous indignation of the whole community, not even their glaring moral failures and criminal behavior will be enough to entirely cancel out the empathy for victims that the gospel inspires. Punishing wrongdoers or protecting society from them is an inevitable fact of social life. The system for doing so may be clumsy and cruel, or it may be scrupulous and attentive to the humanity of even the most heinous criminals. (In all cultures that have fallen under the gospel influence, the tendency toward the latter is unmistakable.) And yet, vestiges of ritual sacrifice survive in even the most ideal criminal justice systems. How morally problematic future generations will find these vestiges and how they might seek to eliminate them remains to be seen. Reversals in any historical development can be expected, but, in the long-term, I haven't the slightest doubt that the exposure and renunciation of sacrificial violence will continue. In which case, to the extent that societies under gospel influence exploit their criminal proceedings for the purpose of venting their resentments, indulging their lust for vengeance, and basking in the glow of unearned moral rectitude, they will sooner or later have the devil to pay.

"Behind the Glass Wall"

When a culture or subculture turns the system for protecting law-abiding citizens into a social ritual for generating its camaraderie, it sets up a social pattern structurally similar to the crucifixion. Eventually, in such situations, the objective wickedness of the culprit will not be enough to offset the moral misgivings aroused by that similarity. For obvious reasons, this is especially so in the case of "public executions." This is no doubt why of the very few Western societies that still impose the death penalty, in none of them are the executions carried out "in public." In California this matter was debated not long ago when the San Francisco public television station KQED sued to be given the right to televise executions at California's San Quentin prison. On the Op-Ed page of the May 16, 1991, edition of the *New York Times,* an Anna Quindlen column appeared in which she discussed the lawsuit. The column begins as follows:

> Before he was executed by the state of California in 1960, Caryl Chessman arranged with a reporter to communicate from behind the glass wall of the gas chamber. As the cyanide pellets mingled with the sulfuric acid, the convicted murderer brought his head up and down violently in a last

> nod. Yes, he was saying, it hurts. The reporter wrote: "Whatever medicine says, the eyes said Chessman did not die quickly, not even gracefully, after his twitching reflexes took over from a dead brain. It is probably for the best that only 60 shaken witnesses have to know exactly how it happened."

Clearly the anguish felt by the sixty shaken witnesses was in large measure a moral phenomenon. Probably none of them believed in the condemned man's moral innocence, and most probably had no philosophical objections to capital punishment. To what, then, are we to attribute their discomfort? Was there something about his death that made it especially disturbing, even though the criminal was guilty and the punishment legal? Yes. It is summed up in a comment Girard makes in *Things Hidden since the Foundation of the World:*

> Since the truth about violence will not abide in the community, but must inevitably be driven out, its only chance of being heard is when it is in the process of being driven out, in the brief moment that precedes its destruction as the victim. The victim has therefore to reach out at the very moment when his mouth is being shut by violence.... But this must not take place in the dark, hallucinatory atmosphere.... There must be witnesses who are clear-sighted enough to recount the event as it really happened.[7]

The irony here is that in this passage Girard is talking of the death of Christ. At one level, of course, there is literally a world of difference between the state execution of a convicted murderer and the public execution of the innocent Palestinian Jew Christians call their "Lord." Is it not absurd, therefore, to apply Girard's words to the execution of a depraved and convicted killer? At another level, however, what these two executions have in common can hardly be dismissed on the basis of that moral distinction alone. "It was not because the *innocence* of the sacrificial victim had been discovered that it was associated with Christ, but the other way round," wrote Cesáreo Bandera, in another context, but speaking precisely to the issue before us.[8] The structural similarity between the Chessman execution and the crucifixion endows the convicted criminal with a kind of "innocence" that has nothing to do with moral flawlessness, an "innocence" based not on moral or legal criteria but on the degree of one's social isolation. The innocence of Christ to which the Gospels attest should not be reduced to strictly behavioral or ethical terms. No doubt Jesus was innocent in these terms, but the innocence on which the gospel revelation throws light is the structural "innocence" of the isolated victim.

The experience of being morally shaken by a public execution is the beginning of an anthropological and spiritual revolution for which the term "Christianity" was coined decades after the public execution of Jesus. Jesus' moral rectitude surely contributed to the shock felt by his followers. And yet the recognition of the victim's moral rectitude alone could not have set in motion the anthropological revolution from which the world is now reeling. This revolution was set in motion by the revelation of Christ's structural innocence, by which I mean that his "innocence" was deducible from the fact that all accused him and no one rebutted the accusation. He was *perfectly* innocent, not just because he was ethically beyond reproach, but because he stood *perfectly* alone before a *perfectly* unanimous mob. What Christ has in common with all those against whom a unanimous mob has risen up will eventually outweigh the moral differences, however vast, that separate them. Societies under biblical influence will little longer be able to nullify the empathy for scapegoats aroused by the Cross by reserving its righteous and socially galvanizing contempt for certified moral failures.

At roughly the same time Dickens's indignant letter was being published in the *Times,* Coventry Patmore was writing a poem entitled "A London Fête."[9] Like the last scene and epilogue of William Golding's novel, Patmore's poem represents a marvelously insightful reflection on the demise of the sacrificial system in the Western world. It deals with a public hanging in London, around which a great crowd gathers. It anticipates the disintegration of Western culture's most explicitly sacrificial institution, but it does so in marvelously subtle and insightful ways. With a keen eye for the true purpose of the execution, Patmore's poem explores the ritual's diminishing capacity for restoring social order and harmony. At first, however, there are indications that such a harmonious outcome might still be possible.

> ...They brought the man out to be hanged.
> Then came from all the people there
> A single cry, that shook the air;
> Mothers held up their babies to see,
> Who spread their hands, and crowed for glee;
> Here a girl from her vesture tore
> A rag to wave with, and joined the roar...

That *single cry* is precisely what such rituals are all about. It is the verbal equivalent of the stones rained on the victim by a maddened mob. This single cry, achieved without anyone consciously acting to produce it, seems almost miraculous and is essential to the mob's *conviction,* its sense of having found the real *convict.* In terms of its primitive origins, it is probably not coincidental that this cry occurs at the moment when the victim would most likely be screaming protestations. Drowning out the victim's protests—effectively silencing the victim's voice—would be another function of the unanimous cry.

Removing criminals from society and deterring would-be felons from emulating them is a necessary task for any society that wishes to remain civil. As Patmore's poem underscores, however, these legitimate concerns can sometimes serve as a rational justification for an essentially irrational sacrificial ritual. This is especially so, of course, in the case of public execution or "capital punishment." Patmore makes it clear that the issue of guilt is extraneous to the social ritual he is examining in his poem.

> ...There's a man, with yelling tired,
> Stopped, and the culprit's crime inquired...

By the time of the ritual expulsion or elimination, the victim's culpability — or at any rate the rightness of the punishment — must be so completely clear that "it goes without saying." In myth, of course, what always "goes without saying" is the righteousness of the mob. When the condemned one's culpability "goes without saying," it suggests that what is happening is a social or religious ritual more than a criminal proceeding. When, for instance, Captain Cook attempted to ascertain the grounds on which the Tahitian chieftain had chosen the man who had been bludgeoned, he found only that the man had been a member of a Tahitian underclass called towtow. He inquired further:

> But, after all my inquiries, I could not learn, that he had been pitched upon, on account of any particular crime, committed by him, meriting death. It is certain, however, that they generally made choice of such guilty persons for their sacrifices; or else of common, low fellows, who stroll about, from place to place, and from island to island, without having any fixed abode, or any visible way of getting an honest livelihood.

Cook, standing outside the prevailing mythology, was able to perceive how socially circumstantial and morally insignificant was the victim's guilt—if, in fact, he had been guilty at all. These are two separate issues; they must not be confused. The first issue is the guilt or innocence of the accused, their responsibility for wrongdoing, and the question of what is to be done to protect society. The second issue is the use to which such persons are put in a social ritual in which their guilt is incidental, except that it helps allay moral misgivings in those obliged to witness their torment.

The Medicine Becomes the Poison

That the whole spectacle Patmore is presenting is taking place against a backdrop of heightened social tensions is indicated at several places in the poem, but from the point of view of an eventual resolution of these hostilities, a disconcerting note is sounded. Among the crowd were many who "blasphemed and fought for places" from which they could get a better view of the hanging.

As casually as the poet may have used it, we must not overlook the reference to blasphemy. The most common blasphemy is the most revealing: "God damn!"—with any number of prefixes and suffixes. It is the invocation of divine retribution. A more successful sacrificial ritual would have succeeded in channeling all such curses toward the despised culprit. Here, that has not happened. Two of the witnesses, who might have been expected to have joined in the "single cry," are God-damning one another instead.

As the ritual at the scaffold approaches its solemn climax, therefore, the poet focuses the reader's attention carefully on the essential *ritual* issue—not the issue of the victim's fate, but the issue of the community's solidarity. This is the ultimate moment when a religious awe might be expected to settle over the crowd, a crowd that had been in such a state of frenzy just the moment before.

> ...At last, the show's black crisis pended;
> Struggles for better standings ended;
> The rabble's lips no longer cursed,
> But stood agape with horrid thirst...

The crowd's suddenly altered mood is a keen reminder that, as Andrew McKenna put it, the legal system of retribution "remains party to a more primitive liturgical imperative."[10] In the beginning was the hush. This might be a new beginning. Patmore, having awakened such an expectation, now disappoints it.

> ...The rope flew tight; and then the roar
> Burst forth afresh; less loud, but more
> Confused and affrighting than before...

As Girard says of the murder of Caesar in Shakespeare's *Julius Caesar,* the sacrificial violence must "cure the body politic either instantly or not at all."[11] Here, it did not. The center did not hold. The spectacle of violence proved not to be religiously enthralling after all.

It is hardly an idle question to ask: What happens when a culture continues to attempt the periodic restoration of its social harmonies by relying on myths and rituals of sacred violence that have lost their religious authority and moral immunity? The Patmore poem is ready with an answer, and it is as clear an answer to that question as we have a right to expect. In the poem, the hush at the climactic moment is shattered by a roar, a roar "less loud" but nevertheless one that is *more confused and affrighting than before.* The last lines of the poem proceed then to present a sweeping and haunting image of a sacrificial scapegoating ritual that has failed to achieve its social purpose. Its violence begins very slowly to rebound on the society that sponsored it.

> The dangling corpse hung straight and still.
> The show complete, the pleasure past,
> The solid masses loosened fast:
> The thief slunk off, with ample spoil,
> To ply elsewhere his daily toil;
> A baby strung its doll to a stick;
> Two children caught and hanged a cat;
> Two friends walked on, in lively chat;
> And two, who had disputed places,
> Went forth to fight, with murderous faces.

What makes Patmore's poem so helpful is that he shows us what happens when a society continues to resort to such rituals after they have begun to malfunction, and *that* is the real issue before us. In ancient Greece, the victim of sacrificial, scapegoat violence was called the *pharmakos.* The Greek word *pharmakon,* from which we get "pharmacy" and its cognates, means both "medicine" and "poison."[12] Sacrificial rituals that cure the social realm of its tensions under certain circumstances, can poison it under other circumstances. More to the point, if a sacrificial event fails to function as a cure, it will inevitably function as a poison, which is what is happening in our day.

As we will see in subsequent chapters, it is humanity's inordinate capacity for imitation or *mimesis* that primarily determines our social arrangements. When scapegoating rituals *work,* the ritual violence achieves sacred status. The primary function of the sacred is so to privilege one form of violence, and to confer upon it such transcendent prestige, that a profane imitation of it becomes unthinkable. In the modern age, however, the process has begun to break down. Spectacles of holy violence that once put an end to episodes of vulgar violence, and resolved the social tensions underlying it, now function as prototypes for the violence of those who gawk at the spectacles and whose sacrificial appetites the spectacles arouse but fail to satisfy.

> ...A baby strung its doll to a stick;
> Two children caught and hanged a cat...

Whether it is a public hanging, a war, or a televised glorification of violence, a culture's righteous violence will fascinate its onlookers. It will be a spectacle. Regardless of the rhetoric and details of its justification, if a society can heighten that fascination and bring it to a cathartic sacrificial conclusion, then the sacrificial violence will be a pharmacological cure for the society's internal animosities. (Those not caught up in it might find it morally repugnant, but those swept into its ritual vortex will be uplifted and socially harmonized.) When, however, the violence loses its religious aura, the fascination that the spectacle of violence arouses will not lead to a reverence for the sacred institution that unleashed it. Rather, the spectacle of violence will become a model for similar violence, and those who were its most entranced spectators will replicate it — beginning with the youngest and most mimetic in society. "A baby strung its doll to a stick."

Patmore's poem is fiction; what can we learn from fiction? If we read the right fiction, we can learn a great deal indeed. An eerie echo of Patmore's reference to the baby stringing its doll to a stick and the children catching and hanging a cat was reported in the press a few weeks after the verdict in the Rodney King beating case set off the Los Angeles riots in 1992. Sixth graders at a southern California school, who had obviously seen some of the many replays of the videotaped beating, apparently found the example of the beating more powerful than the moral condemnations that accompanied it. One day following the riots, as the children were standing around during lunch talking about what they wanted to be for Halloween, Gerald, a black student, said he wanted to be Rodney King. "Then," according to the Associated Press report, "one of the boys tripped Gerald and when he fell, they started talking about King's videotaped beating. Then the kicking started." Asked about the episode, Gerald told the reporter: "They were all standing around kicking me and singing, and everybody came and watched." He recalled that while kicking him, the boys — who were white, Hispanic and Filipino — chanted to the tune of the "London Bridge" nursery rhyme: "Rodney King is falling down, falling down... My fair black man."[13]

Contagious Violence

When a culture's sacrificial rituals "work," they transfer the existing rivalrous antagonisms onto one figure against whom all can unite, an act that miraculously dissolves existing tensions and replaces them with a social bond. Conversely, when a culture's sacrificial routines fail to generate this combination of camaraderie and moral rectitude, the existing rivalries fester and the social fabric begins to fray. In the Coventry Patmore poem, the violence of the ritual fascinated its spectators but failed to end in catharsis. As a result, the superficial consensus that occurred at the ritual's climax vanished almost instantly, leaving the social frictions more vexed than before. No sooner had "the solid masses loosened fast" than the rivalries returned with a vengeance.

> ...And two, who had disputed places,
> Went forth to fight, with murderous faces.

Brilliantly, Patmore uses these two contentious characters as a symbol of the hanging's sacrificial efficacy. In the immediate aftermath of the ritual killing, at the height of its potential for dissolving social tensions, these two go off to fight. Whereas before they had only "blasphemed and fought for places," now they glower at one another with "murderous faces." This gives vivid specificity to Patmore's comment that at the moment of the hanging a murmur was heard, "less loud, but more / Confused and affrighting than before." The poetic hints Patmore has left us make it clear that, far from reconciling social antagonists at the expense of a figure all could jointly despise, the ritual has had the effect of aggravating social tensions. This rivalry has intensified, as a matter of fact, to the point that what was once the *object* of the rivalry—choice views of the scaffold—can now disappear without in the least diminishing the passion of the rivalry. In point of fact, the rivalry becomes "murderous" at exactly the moment when it ceases to be *about* anything, except eliminating the rival. I will have more to say on this very important matter later. For the moment, however, I want to explore a point that is raised by the three most glaring images in the last lines of Patmore's poem: the baby who strings its doll to a stick, the children who catch and hang a cat, and the two who go off to fight with murderous faces. The issue underlying each of these grim images is the *contagiousness of violence.*

A few years before Dickens took his early morning walk and found himself being so disgusted by the brutal callousness of the crowd gathered for a public hanging in London, Søren Kierkegaard came upon a morally troubling sight of his own while taking a walk in Copenhagen. Dickens had seen an organized and officially sponsored episode of righteous violence. What Kierkegaard encountered was a more spontaneous episode of violence, a mêlée in the street. He writes:

> I was once the witness of a street fight in which three men most shamefully set upon a fourth. The crowd stood and watched them with indignation; expressions of disgust began to enliven the scene; then several of the onlookers set on one of the three assailants and knocked him down and beat him. The avengers had, in fact, applied precisely the same rules as the offenders. . . . I went up to one of the avengers and tried by argument to explain to him how illogical his behavior was; but it seemed quite impossible for him to discuss the question: he could only repeat that such a rascal richly deserved to have three people against him.[14]

Just as the Tahitian chieftain had remained deaf to the moral objection raised by Captain Cook, so the assailants to whom Kierkegaard expressed his objection were impervious to his reproach. If Cook did not have to be a moral genius to see through the sacrificial logic of the Tahitian ritual, Kierkegaard need hardly have been one to see the moral absurdity of the act of vengeance he witnessed. What is striking, and what struck Kierkegaard himself, is that those whose moral indignation had compelled them to take vengeance were oblivious to the absurdity. Even after Kierkegaard explicitly pointed out to the assailants that they had only replicated the act that they found offensive, they seemed not to be able to see the parallel. They were unable to see the unmistakable identity between the violence they loathed and the violence with which they proposed to counter it. The morally outraged ones were as blind to the injustice of their own violence as they were incensed by the identical injustice that provoked their outrage in the first place. The gospel's insistence on forgiveness is both profound and pragmatic, but we cannot fully appreciate either until we realize how routinely moral indignation leads to the replication of the behavior that aroused the indignation. Moral outrage is morally ambiguous. The more outraged it is, the less likely it is to contribute to real moral improvements. Righteous indignation is often the first symptom of the metastasis of the cancer of violence. It tends to provide the indignant ones with a license to commit or condone acts structurally indistinguishable from those that aroused the indignation. When moral contempt for a form of violence inspires so explicit a replication of it, there is only one conclusion to be drawn: *The moral revulsion the initial violence awakened proved weaker than the mimetic fascination it inspired.*

Nor is this ability of morally repugnant violence to inspire imitation limited to spontaneous street fights between and among the coarser elements in society. When the Japanese bombed Shanghai in 1937, moral revulsion in the U.S. was strong. When the fascists bombed Barcelona in 1938, Cordell Hull, the U.S. Secretary of State, declared: "No theory of war can justify such conduct." In June of 1938, the U.S. Senate passed a resolution condemning the "inhuman bombing of civilian populations." Following the outbreak of war, one of Franklin Roosevelt's first pronouncements was an appeal to the belligerents to refrain from bombing civilian populations. By 1944, however, the bombing of German cities had the backing of military strategists, and in August of 1945 atomic bombs were dropped on Hiroshima and Nagasaki.[15] The nuclear-era doctrine of Mutual Assured Destruction (MAD) was nothing less than the supreme manifestation of this deadly reciprocity: two death machines, each on a hair trigger, ready to replicate and reciprocate the morally reprehensible acts of the other and, if necessary, destroy the whole world.

Violence is immensely compelling. Those who witness spectacles of violence can be seduced by its logic even when — perhaps especially when — they are morally scandalized by it. Violence is *labyrinthine.* It turns back on itself in serpentine ways. The paths that seem to exit from its madness so often lead deeper into its maze. Violence is literally a-mazing. That is why it gave rise to primitive religions. We may no longer be able and willing to turn violence into religion, but neither are we able to turn the other cheek, and the conventional way of resisting evil causes the contagion of evil to spread, perpetrated by those who are most determined to eradicate it. How to resist evil in ways that prevent its spread is now history's most fundamental dilemma. When exposed to violence, the most likely response is to replicate it. An eye for an eye, a tooth for a tooth. What is astonishing, then, is not that the kind of violence Kierkegaard witnessed inspires imitation, but that *some* violence does not.

Catharsis or Mimesis

Sacred violence ends in catharsis, and it satisfies the appetite for violence that its preliminary rituals awaken. In those who witness violence that fails to achieve catharsis, on the other hand, an unquenched appetite for violence lingers, and it tends to model itself on the violence that has just failed to quench it. Whether those who replicate the violence that has aroused an appetite for violence do so out of admiration for the perpetrators of the prior violence or out of a moral revulsion for it, the effect is very often the same. Cultural violence that does not climax in *catharsis* will result in *mimesis*.

There is a growing tendency for spectacles of "good" or "righteous" violence — whether historical ones like wars or fictional ones like those that occur so frequently in popular entertainment — to be followed by an *increase* in violence. The growing incidence of "copy-cat" acts of violence is a case in point, but such conscious acts of imitation are only the most conspicuous and predictable versions of violent mimicry. A vastly greater degree of social violence is mimetic, but since its perpetrators do not consciously set out to mimic prior violence, the mimetic linkage is less clear. Public displays of official violence that may have once provided a cathartic resolution for various and sundry social tensions now provide only fascinating models upon which the spectators can base their own ad hoc attempts to achieve a cathartic resolution. We have crossed a fateful threshold, and once that threshold is crossed, violence has effects opposite to those that it had before the threshold was crossed. Until we come to grips with the fact that we have crossed this threshold, we will deepen and hasten the cultural catastrophe on the edge of which we now stand.

Even those who support the institutional versions of sacred violence with the heartiest gusto will be morally and politically distraught by its unofficial replicas, but they may be less able or willing to recognize the mimetic relationship between them. They will be reluctant to realize that we are now living in a world in which flagrant displays of righteous violence will increasingly fail to achieve ritual effects — even when they achieve their penal or military purposes — and that as a result, the society once made more peaceful by these policies will now be made more violent by them. As a result, each time we resort again to violence, the cogs and gears of the sacrificial system — which can operate effectively only when shrouded in myth and mystification — are more glaringly exposed to view. Moral misgivings are inevitable, their mimetic results are predictable, and the process is irreversible.

Chapter 5

A Land of Mirrors

> Once violence has reached a certain threshold, social and cultural institutions themselves are of no avail to limit its diffusion. Every attempt to diffuse the conflict is seen as a further provocation and usual mechanisms of arbitration lose their transcendence. They are seen by all as a party in the quarrel rather than as a judge....Just as violence reduces the individual opponents to mirror-images of each other, so it destroys the differences that normally distinguish justice from revenge, arbitrator from opponent, and finally friend from foe.[1]
>
> PAUL DUMOUCHEL

The Patmore poem and the incident observed by Kierkegaard exemplify our present situation perfectly. The end result of the London hanging described in the Patmore poem and the street fight described by Kierkegaard is the same: the violence that was witnessed was imitated. Both Patmore and Kierkegaard have presented this issue in memorable ways. What Kierkegaard's account does not explain, however, is why a loathing for violence can so easily become the license for similar violence. What Patmore's poem does not tell us is what it is that caused the public execution to go awry. Both are tremendously helpful in showing how the violence that fascinates but fails to achieve catharsis leads to imitation. They are of less help to us in understanding why this is so.

In Patmore's poem, there is no indication that moral qualms played any role whatsoever in the failure of the ritual to achieve catharsis. In the street fight Kierkegaard observed, the moral indignation of those who witnessed the original act of violence was clearly driven more by a fascination for the violence than by an empathy for the victim of it. (For all the implied concern for the original victim, Kierkegaard records no effort on the part of the second group of attackers to actually minister to the wounds of the first victim.) Injustice has merely been exploited for whatever degree of sacrificial legitimacy it could momentarily bestow on its avengers.

Superficially, the second group of assailants appear to be motivated by moral principle. A phrase in Kierkegaard's report, however, suggests something much more complex and troubling. As the original attack arouses indignation in those witnessing it, Kierkegaard says that "expressions of disgust began to *enliven the scene.*" We have a word for the kind of disgust that enlivens the scene. We call it revenge, and revenge is violence imitating violence.

The violent imitation of violence takes two forms. The first is simple imitation, and it occurs when one becomes so fascinated by the violence and so riveted by the daring of its perpetrator that one follows the example shown in a straightforward way. In his famous quatrain, Alexander Pope captured the chilling essence of this form of imitation:

> Vice is a monster of so frightful mien,
> As to be hated, needs but to be seen;
> Yet seen too oft, familiar with her face,
> We first endure, then pity, then embrace.

The second form that the violent imitation of violence takes is what Kierkegaard saw. It involves the same fascination with violence. The moral valence of the fascination has reversed, but that has little or no effect on its mimetic power. As a matter of fact, the imitation involved in revenge tends toward *more* violence, for it tends to repay the violence it avenges "with interest." It tends to escalate the violence. The ancient injunction, "an eye for an eye, a tooth for a tooth," was an attempt to keep revenge from spinning out of control. Revenge, then, is violence succumbing to the deadly and unstable cycle of reciprocity that cultural structures exist to prevent. As self-righteous as it always is and as prone to invoke the principle of justice, the spirit of revenge qualifies as a moral response only in the most rudimentary sense. What Kierkegaard saw — faces enlivened by the imminent prospect of justified vengeance — is comparable in every way to what West noticed at the Iowa hanging in 1952 — the "glitter" in the eyes of the spectators. Together, they provide a suitable backdrop for Nietzsche's remark, quoted earlier, that pity prevents us from experiencing the "tonic emotions which heighten our vitality." As chilling as it is to allow the deeper implication of these things to sink in, they refer to that sense of satisfaction we have all felt when a spectacle of righteous violence — whether actual or theatrical — brings down those we know to be evil-doers. The trace of moral acuity we might possess at such moments does little more than give legitimacy to the spirit of revenge it unleashes.

It would be naive, therefore, to make too much of the fact that the street fight Kierkegaard described initially aroused moral misgivings whereas the hanging Patmore's poem depicts did not. The distinction between them is not great, and on the most important point, the issue of imitation, the two are essentially identical. The fact that they are indistinguishable in this crucial way, even though one was a contemptible and cowardly act of ruffians and the other an act solemnly sanctioned by the culture's most prestigious institutions, must not be overlooked. As I have earlier stressed, the collapse of the distinction between "official" and "unofficial" violence is the salient fact of modern cultural life.

A Star Is Born

The historical phenomenon that I am trying to approach using Patmore's poem and Kierkegaard's reminiscence is marvelously summarized by W. H. Auden in his poem "Diaspora." In this poem, Auden deals with the bitter ironies involved in historical Christianity's complicity in anti-Semitism. The poem treats Christ as Jew and the Jewish victims of Christian anti-Semitism as Christ.[2] In a larger, more anthropological sense, however, Auden has seen both the central role of the victim in human culture and the effect that the revelation of the victim's plight was having. He speaks of how the scapegoat provided ages past with their social center of gravity and how a gradually developing empathy for victims was finally robbing the scapegoating system of its effectiveness. Auden shows us a victim who slowly becomes a source of immense perplexity to the society formerly united in its contempt for him.

> How he survived them they could never understand...
> No worlds they drove him from were ever big enough...
> And he fulfilled the role for which he was designed:
> On heat with fear, he drew their terrors to him,
> And was a godsend to the lowest of mankind,
> Till there was no place left where they could still pursue him
> Except that exile which he called his race.
> But, envying him even that, they plunged right through him
> Into a land of mirrors without time or space,
> And all they had to strike now was the human face.[3]

This sums up precisely the effect that the passion story in the Gospels is having on human history. Once the persecutors could no longer avoid the face of their victim, Auden writes:

> ...they plunged right through him
> Into a land of mirrors without time or space.

As many of Auden's poems suggest, for him this land of mirrors consisted of precisely the kaleidoscopic world of social imitation for which Girard has used the term "mimetic desire."

Violence is so inherently fascinating that it distracts us from the more fundamental mechanisms that underlie it. To understand the human predicament, we must not fall for the seductions of violence as easily as did the children in Patmore's poem (who mindlessly replicate it) or the ruffians in Kierkegaard's recollection (who replicate it out of revulsion for it). From time immemorial, the well-intentioned have tried to find a way out of the violent labyrinth by following the trail of violence, and it has always led them back into the labyrinth. The trail that can lead us out of the "land of mirrors" is the path that led into it. So the trail we must follow is not the trail of violence but the trail of *mimesis,* of social contagion. I have used the Patmore poem and the Kierkegaard story because they dramatically illustrate the point I am trying to make about the contagiousness of violence in our world. Yet the underlying issue in both the Kierkegaard story and the Patmore poem is *mimesis* and not violence. Ultimately, violence is just the fiercest and most enthralling form of mimesis. We cannot understand violence, and we cannot begin to understand the role it has played religiously and anthropologically, until we understand the mimetic mechanism that produces violence and gives it such mystifying power. And so, beginning with the scapegoating violence to which it leads, I want to follow the trail back to mimetic desire and its role in social and psychological life.

Patmore has used his poetic license to collapse into one vivid scene a process that in actual social life is usually much more complex and convoluted. It is a process that leads from the waning of sacrificial rituals, to an increase in social imitation, and then to more and more violence, but it usually does so more gradually than it did in the Patmore poem. Sacred violence usually loses its cathartic power and its moral authority, not with a bang, but a whimper. To better understand that process, I want to return one last time to Captain Cook's report to George III and to compare it first to a recent event and then to a very ancient one.

What was clear from Cook's account was that the Polynesian tribe was performing solemn rituals that had lost their solemnity. Those *physically* engaged *in* them were not being *psychologically* engaged *by* them. Not only did the climactic violence fail to achieve cathartic effects (it took place in secret), but the ritual was no longer even fascinating, much less religiously compelling. Again, Cook's eye for the significant detail is a keen one. The lack of fervor on the part of those performing the Tahitian rites is coincident with the keen interest the Tahitians have begun to take in their European guests. Cook notes:

> Indeed, the priests themselves, except the one who chiefly repeated the prayers, either from their being familiarized to such objects, or from want of confidence in the efficacy of their institutions, observed very little of that solemnity, which is necessary to give to religious performances their due weight. Their dress was only an ordinary one; they conversed together, without scruple; and the only attempt made by them to preserve any appearance of decency, was by exerting their authority, to prevent the people from coming upon the very spot where the ceremonies were performed; and to suffer us, as strangers, to advance a little forward.

The priests seem eager to please their foreign guests, more eager in fact to do that than to perform their assigned ritual with the reverence and care that might have partially redeemed it in their guests' eyes. The Tahitian priests, forsaking their ritual duties, use what remnant of authority they have left for holding the other tribal members at a distance from the sacrificial scene and for clearing a path to it so that the Europeans might have a better view. What a telling gesture that is! Moreover, at precisely the moment Cook is noting how lackadaisically the ritual is being observed, how "they did not shew any proper reverence" for the ritual they were observing, he perceives the effect the arrival of Omai, Cook's Tahitian interpreter, has on those assembled for the ritual:

> And Omai, happening to arrive, after they had begun, many of the spectators flocked round him, and were engaged, the remainder of the time, in making him relate some of his adventures, which they listened to with great attention, regardless of the solemn offices performed by their priests.

Without knowing it, Cook has here given us a parable, one symbolizing the extremely elusive moment when a traditional society begins to become a modern one. Here, in a nutshell, is the modern spiritual situation. There is a direct line from this scene to *People* magazine, the TV talk shows, and all the modern cults of personality and celebrity. Collective fascinations, no longer enthralled by the religious cult and its rituals, begin to bestow the prestige once reserved for the religious cult and its priestly representatives on those in the social order on whom the fickle finger of social fascination happens to fall. The gods are dying, and a "star" is being born. *This* is where the fascination has gone. The fascination the Tahitians have for the Europeans has grown in inverse ratio to their fascination for their gods and the sacrificial rites required to keep these gods appeased. In other words, the Tahitian culture seems to have been abandoning the traditional (sacrificial) mechanisms for resolving social passions in favor of the kind of social melodrama that engenders and enflames these passions. The Tahitian world was plunging right through its victim into a "land of mirrors."

The West Invades Itself

A little more than two hundred years after Omai brought his anti-sacrificial message right into the heart of the Tahitian sacrificial arena, Bob Dylan gave a concert at West Point. An article reporting on the concert appeared in the October 15, 1990, edition of the *New York Times.* Here, in part, is what the *Times* article said.

> It could have been just another Bob Dylan concert, complete with sneering, pointed lyrics, jamming electric guitars and a few reflective ballads. But this time the hall was packed with future Army commanders.
>
> Mr. Dylan, who galvanized the 1960's anti-war movement, played to a standing ovation Saturday night at the Dwight D. Eisenhower Hall theater at the United States Military Academy. Among the crowd of 4,020 were hundreds who were clearly in bliss from the music.
>
> The clean-cut future officers, in their dress-gray uniforms, with military medals and patent leather shoes, danced in the aisles, shimmied their shoulders and pumped their arms in the air. Some accompanied the songs with riffs on imaginary guitars, still others pogoed up and down, and a few just smiled as they mingled with civilian "groupies" in tie-dyed T-shirts.

Now imagine Captain Cook and his entourage arriving at Chief Otoo's social setting. It all seemed innocent enough. The Tahitians actually welcomed the Europeans, blissfully unaware that by doing so they were placing their culture's sacrificial system in peril. They actually gave the Europeans a place of prominence. When Cook and Omai began to say things that were troubling to the tribe's leaders, the tribe's less prominent members gathered around, eager to hear. They stood fascinated by these strangers and what they were saying. In an intriguingly similar way, the Bob Dylan concert at West Point caused the Army's most promising future leaders to *mingle* "with civilian 'groupies' in tie-dyed T-shirts." Listening to the Dylan concert, the cadets seem mesmerized by the prestigious stranger from beyond their world.

The *Times* article quotes Lucian K. Truscott IV, a West Point graduate and author of a critical portrait of the institution entitled *Dress Gray*, as saying the Dylan concert was "extraordinary" for the academy. He went on to say:

> "What the place exists for—what it's done since 1802—is to allow older officers to pass on the knowledge of how to exercise power," Mr. Trus-

> cott said. "They socialize you so that when you're 45 or 50, you can be the national security adviser in the White House. The idea that they'd introduce Bob Dylan into that is amazing."

If there is a chief priestly role in the modern nation state, it is the national security advisor. Like the priests of old, it is his task to advise on the proper use of sanctioned violence. Efforts must be made, and they are made in places like West Point, to preserve these future national security advisors from influences that would do to their zeal what the Europeans did to the zeal of the eighteenth-century Polynesians. Efforts must be made to keep these future officers from *mingling* with those with moral misgivings about the operations for which they are being trained. A version of what happened at Tahiti in 1777 happened at West Point in 1990. A voice speaking on behalf of victims rang out where the priesthood and its novices were gathered. Just as the Tahitians were fascinated by Omai and animated by the contagious zeal with which he spoke, many of those who listened to Dylan were mesmerized by his message, his music, and his mannerisms.

> When Mr. Dylan played his most famous anti-war song, "Blowin' in the Wind," at the end of the concert, many of the cadets stood, closed their eyes and quietly sang along.

As Cook noted, those who found Omai more fascinating did so even though he rebuked their culture's most hallowed institution. In exactly the same way, the West Point cadets became fascinated with Bob Dylan. At Tahiti, Western culture, infected with a gospel-inspired empathy for victims, invaded a sacrificial cult ill prepared to repel the Western ethos. At West Point, the empathy for victims at the heart of Western culture was overtaking one of the more formidable of its own cultural institutions. In each case, a stranger with a new message, one speaking on behalf of victims, was found to be more fascinating than the official sacrificial system whose physical premises he was invading and whose sacrificial premises he was undermining. What is implied in Cook's account is made explicit in the account of Dylan's concert: the result of this fascination was mimesis. While we are told only that the Tahitians lost interest in the rite in favor of Omai's tales of adventure, it takes no special insight to realize that many of them would soon be modeling themselves on the one they found so fascinating. In the case of the West Point cadets, this is explicit. Not only did they sing along with Dylan, but during the concert many "accompanied the songs with riffs on imaginary guitars."

Here is my working definition of a *reactionary.* A reactionary is someone who isn't aware of what Patmore's poem reveals: namely, that we live in a world where even the most sanctioned forms of violence are losing their ability to restore order, while the mimetic power of violence is still as potent as it was ten thousand years ago. Here is my working definition of a *revolutionary.* A revolutionary is someone who isn't aware of what Kierkegaard's report reveals: namely, that converting moral outrage into complicity with the kind of behavior that provoked the outrage is not likely to lead anywhere. Here is my working definition of a *romantic.* A romantic is someone who sees the Tahitians flocking around Omai or the West Point cadets dancing in the aisles at the Dylan concert and feels that the world is finally coming to its senses. The three Rs. Beware of them.

The Fascinating One

With Cook's visit to Tahiti and Dylan's visit to West Point still fresh in our minds, let us turn, then, to a parallel story, this time, a mythological one. Unlike the Cook and Dylan visits, it is one that allows us to see the entire process whereby an intact religious cult is thrown into crisis, collapses into social chaos and violence, and then is sacrificially restored. The fact that we moderns can no longer achieve such sacrificial restorations makes the story *more,* not *less,* relevant, for diseases for which cures do not exist are the ones it is most urgent to understand and avoid. To that end, we must try to appreciate the paradoxes involved in what Girard calls "mimetic desire" — the centerpiece of his anthropological theory and the key to its universal applicability. Perhaps the best way to appreciate the paradoxes of mimetic desire is to see how it operated in archaic society, and for that I would like to reflect briefly on a widely known myth.

A major figure in the mythology of the Aztec culture of central Mexico was the great god-king Quetzalcoatl, the feathered serpent. For many years his worshipers enjoyed a thriving culture. Available accounts suggest that during the Toltec golden age, when Quetzalcoatl was the incarnate deity, the cult devoted to him offered few, if any, human sacrifices. The sacrificial system was able to sustain itself by sacrificing snakes, birds, and butterflies. Had Captain Cook been able to observe the Toltec culture in its heyday, he would have seen something quite different from what he saw at Tahiti. And yet Toltec and Aztec mythology suggests that this period of religious fervor and cultural stability was suddenly interrupted by the arrival of a stranger who introduced a new kind of music and who wantonly flouted the culture's taboos. Like the Greek Dionysus, the flamboyant behavior of this strange and fascinating man plunged the society into social chaos. Eventually he was slain by the very crowd that had found him so intriguing, a slaying that coincided with such a sudden restoration of religious awe and social harmony that it was obvious to everyone that the one they had slain must have been a god. A cult dedicated to him arose, and on its altars regular human sacrifices were offered.

In order to fully appreciate the relevance of this mythology, we must be willing to read it as a distorted misrecognition of real events. As I have already pointed out, myth, from the root *mu,* always involves a *mu*tation or *mu*tilation of the memory of an actual event. To go to the myth in search of anthropological insight, one must try to reconstrue the event that the myth misconstrues. I will read the myth in this light.

Quetzalcoatl's reign had been glorious, but finally he grew old and weary. One day the people were struck by the arrival of a strikingly handsome and powerful stranger. Like Captain Cook at Tahiti, he was a foreigner. Like Omai, he was young and physically attractive. Like Bob Dylan, he was gifted, and he sang a new song. All, especially the young, found him completely mesmerizing. Increasing numbers of people began to follow him and mimic his ways. The old revered Quetzalcoatl and the cult rituals his worshipers performed grew less and less spellbinding as the strange and intensely vigorous figure grew more and more so. Of course no one at the time knew that this strange man was the god Tezcatlipoca. As is typically the case, his divinity was only brought home to them after he had been killed by his worshipers.

Tezcatlipoca, whose name means "Smoking Mirror," carried with him a mirror wrapped in rabbit skin, or so the legend has it. With this mirror, he went to the palace of old Quetzalcoatl and demanded of the servants that he be given an audience with the great Lord himself. As bold as Cook and Omai at Tahiti or Dylan at West Point, he entered Quetzalcoatl's realm with little deference for its idols and prestigious figures. Quetzalcoatl graciously received the stranger, as graciously as did Chief Otoo or the West Point program committee. Suddenly, Tezcatlipoca uncovered the mirror he was carrying with him and held it up so that Quetzalcoatl could see his own reflection. "Look now upon your own flesh," said Tezcatlipoca. "See yourself as you are seen!"

In the presence of this robust and virile young man, the old god-king Quetzalcoatl saw himself with distressing clarity. The mirror and the handsome stranger that carried it arrived at the same moment and were, in fact, the same thing. Quetzalcoatl, with the vigorous and dazzling Tezcatlipoca standing before him, saw that he had grown old and wrinkled and weak. After gazing upon his own withered image, Quetzalcoatl sank back on his throne, his greatness sabotaged, evidence of his waning power and virility no longer to be denied. Meanwhile, just as the Tahitians found the object of their fascination shifting from the familiar cult deities and rituals to the Europeans, and just as the West Point cadets found themselves spellbound by the fascinating musician to whose lyrics they began to sway, so the followers of Quetzalcoatl began to find the stranger more fascinating than the old god-king.

With Quetzalcoatl still shaken from the revelation of his mortality, Tezcatlipoca produced a potion concocted by the goddess Mayahuel, the arouser of passions, and he offered it to the old king. The myth says that Quetzalcoatl at first declined to drink the potion. He was encouraged by Tezcatlipoca to wet at least one finger in the brew and touch the finger to his mouth. This he did. The potion was, of course, intoxicating. Quetzalcoatl took the drinking vessel from Tezcatlipoca and drank lustily and grew drunk. Then he sent servants for his sister, Quetzalpetlatl, and had her drink the potion as well. In a fit of drunken lust, the two of them fell to the floor in incestuous embraces. At dawn, Quetzalcoatl recognized that, drunk on the tonic of rejuvenation, he had violated the incest taboo, the very taboo whose supposed violation triggers so many regicides and sacrifices in primitive society. He said: "I have sinned. I am not fit to rule." Various accounts of Quetzalcoatl's subsequent fate exist. Each clearly involves either a sacrificial immolation or an expulsion or both.

As I have said, Quetzalcoatl had been the supreme object of fascination for his culture. As long as his worshipers found his radiance and power enthralling, the merest of sacrificial gestures served to maintain social coherence. As we readers of his myth watch Quetzalcoatl's radiance begin to wane, the same question arises that arose about the waning of the social prestige of Chief Otoo and his sacrificial priests. What will become the next object of that fascination? Given the circumstances surrounding the withering of Quetzalcoatl's image, the question need hardly be asked. The dazzling young man on whose polished surface Quetzalcoatl had seen his decrepitude had become "the observed of all observers" even before Quetzalcoatl was dispatched. The young women of the court were especially intrigued by him. He managed with little difficulty to seduce a number of them, and he provoked a general breakdown of the customs and standards of decorum to which all had previously adhered. Added to his physical splendor, his brazen disregard for the codes by which all Aztec non-gods were trained to live would have made the intriguing stranger even more fascinating and lent credibility to the later myth of his divinity.

At one point, during an important religious ceremony, it was the impressive and princely stranger from elsewhere and not the familiar rites on whom the eyes of the community were riveted. This is an exact replica of the scene Captain Cook described at Tahiti when Omai caused such a flurry of excitement and interest and parallel to the one at West Point when Bob Dylan so captivated the cadets. As the official ritual continued, all eyes were on the intriguing stranger, who completely disrupted the proceedings by dancing and singing in tune with a song all his own. No doubt to the dismay of the ritual priests, all began to *mimic* this man's dance and song. It was an ancient version of Bob Dylan's appearance at West Point, where "clean-cut future officers... danced in the aisles, shimmied their shoulders and pumped their arms in the air... accompanied the songs with riffs on imaginary guitars [and]... pogoed up and down." Aztec society was becoming a "land of mirrors." Had the Aztecs not had a viable sacrificial system to fall back on, they might have enjoyed about one breathless week of modernity before collapsing into savagery. Instead, they resorted to the discrete and surgical form of savagery that is at the heart of primitive religion.

The Making of a God

The ritual over which Quetzalcoatl had presided was forsaken in favor of the new dance and song of the mesmerizing Tezcatlipoca. He danced and sang, like a frenzied Dionysus, and the people followed him wherever he went. As those fascinated by him grew in number, the fascination grew in intensity. Like a bacchanalian pied piper littering the cultural landscape with the discarded taboos and customs once so scrupulously observed, Tezcatlipoca led his revelers out to the river. So great was the throng, the myth tells us, that the bridge over the river collapsed under the weight and many people fell and were turned into stone.

Except in myths, people don't turn to stone. When bridges fall under the weight of too many people, people drown or are crushed, but they are not turned to stone. In many primitive societies, however, the most typical form of spontaneous violence involves the throwing of stones. Stones fly and people fall dead. When the mythological mind recollects the frenzy of a full-blown violent crisis, it *muses*. Evidence of mob violence doesn't always disappear, for if the myth is to serve as the "sound-track" for future sacrificial reenactments, these hints of violence cannot be altogether erased.

24 To mine the myths for anthropological insight, one must look for signs of where the narrative seems to be glossing over violence. In this myth, one such sign is the reference to people dying and turning to stone. So, clearly, what the myth is recollecting is not the merely physical accident of a bridge collapsing under too much weight. Rather it is re-membering a moment when the social order collapsed under the pressure of too much mimetic stimulation, something that still happens at rock concerts and soccer matches. In another hint of the same sort of spontaneous violence, the myth tells of a later occasion when Tezcatlipoca again appeared to the community. He held out his hand, and a puppet magically danced on it. A crowd quickly gathered and, in its eagerness to see the astonishing magic, the crowding became so intense that, the myth says, many suffocated and died. In both instances where the myth makes oblique allusions to violence, the violence it alludes to has no perpetrators. If we are attentive, however, we can see that the myth describes a society in a violent crisis.

Unless a society that has descended into such a crisis can find a way to restore order, it will disintegrate. It will be able to restore order only if another god as fascinating and terrifying as Quetzalcoatl takes the old god's place. Astonishingly, just such a god arrives just in the nick of time. Lo and behold, the very man who flouted the taboos and threw the society into such a frenzy is discovered to have been a god in disguise. The social chaos that began when he broke the taboos is resolved when his godliness manifests itself and he becomes the divine destroyer of those who break taboos. The society thrown into violent chaos by the handsome stranger who was merely *profanely* fascinating is restored to order again when he becomes *profoundly*—that is, religiously—fascinating. How, we ask, does such an extraordinary transformation take place? How does a society cross the magical threshold from profane to profound fascination, from imitation to worship? The myth tells us.

After many of those fascinated by Tezcatlipoca had been turned to stone at the river and many more had suffocated and died, those once merely fascinated by this strange Dionysian figure become both fascinated and terrified by him. As fascination reaches religious levels, it produces frenzy, dread, and holy apprehension. To fascination (*fascinans*) is now added terror (*tremendum*). These, according to Rudolf Otto's classic study of religious emotion, are the key features of primordial religious experience. A society seized simultaneously by the kind of fascination and holy dread of which Otto speaks is a society whose cultural crisis is beginning to generate its own resolution, a resolution that will be accompanied by violence and followed by the kind of precarious peace that archaic religions preserved as best they could with their myths, rituals, and prohibitions. Otto aptly describes the mental meltdown involved, but he does so with no reference whatsoever to the social contagion that is its true source:

> The daemonic-divine object may appear to the mind an object of horror and dread, but at the same time it is no less something that allures with a potent charm, and the creature, who trembles before it, utterly cowed and cast down, has always at the same time the impulse to turn to it, nay even to make it somehow his own. The "mystery" is for him not merely something to be wondered at but something that entrances him; and beside that in it which bewilders and confounds, he feels a something that captivates and transports him with a strange ravishment, rising often enough to the pitch of dizzying intoxication; it is the Dionysiac-element in the numen.[4]

Here Otto captures something of the extreme psychological ambiguity of the social frenzy that turns first into violence and then into archaic religion. While the community is in this heightened state, events begin to unfold that will later be remembered mythologically. In the case of the Tezcatlipoca legends, the myth tells us that Tezcatlipoca spoke to the community, now little more than a frantic mob, and told them that in order to avoid future catastrophes — such as occurred at the river when people turned to stone and at his displays of magic when people suffocated — they should stone him to death. It was his presence, he explained, that had caused such death and confusion.

Except in myth, people don't ask to be stoned to death. *In retrospect,* the stoning of Tezcatlipoca would have been understood as having the god's own warrant, for it is only in retrospect that the sudden peace that accompanied his murder had to be accounted for, and Tezcatlipoca's divinity was the way in which it was accounted for, and gods don't die at the hands of mortals unless they want to. The stoning and the discovery of divinity are synonymous, and that is the answer to our question: how does a society convert profane fascinations into religious ones? But that isn't the end of our investigation. The question remains: how does a culture institutionalize the primitive *esprit de corps* upon which it spontaneously stumbles in its fit of mob madness? Again, let's turn to the myth and ferret out those hints that the myth hasn't fully erased.

Institutionalizing the Whirlwind

So awed were those who stoned Tezcatlipoca that they were unable and unwilling to touch the body afterward. The corpse was initially abandoned. This strongly suggests a spontaneous stoning. Clearly, there are no priests presiding at this sacrifice, for leaving a corpse untended is a liturgical indiscretion that not even the most inexperienced and inept priesthood would commit. The myth as much as confirms this when it says that the stench from the decomposition of Tezcatlipoca's corpse caused many people to die. Here is where romantics trying to exonerate their myths suddenly become medical epidemiologists. People must have died because of diseases associated with a decaying corpse. Please, no. This myth is about violence. If people start dying again in the middle of it, it's not for hygienic reasons. The fact that people are still dying means that the crisis has yet to be decisively concluded. One thing is keeping the community's suspicion that their victim was a god from becoming a religiously unassailable truth, namely, the sight and the stench of his decomposing body, a haunting reminder of human mortality. This stench of decomposition is the palpable metaphor for the dim recognition of what the mob has actually done. The honeyed head of Orpheus is one thing, the stinking corpse of Tezcatlipoca is quite another. Somehow or another, the shattering fact represented by the corpse and the stench of death must be neutralized. The myth goes on to say that, overcoming great fear, the crowd was finally able to drag Tezcatlipoca's body out of town. Once the disturbing sight of the corpse was removed, those who had stoned the "god" were suddenly better able to understand the profundity of what had happened and the sacredness of what they had done. They realized that the stranger had been a god, a god of fascination, frenzy, and violence—an Aztec Dionysus. The god had invited his worshipers to stone him, and when they did, he blessed their obedience with the social unanimity that the stoning of him brought about.

Once he had taken his place at or near the center of their religious cult, the Aztecs remained in awe of Tezcatlipoca, their fascination now completely mingled with dread. They were enthralled. Rituals designed to placate the god became extremely important. The culture's sacrificial crisis had run its course, and social harmony had been restored, but an important key to that harmony was the fear that it might be swept away again — that the god might again unleash his violence — should his worshipers fail to take the necessary precautions. As is true everywhere in archaic societies, these precautions took the form of ritual reenactments of the god's last mesmerizing and terrifying visit, including most essentially the reenactment of his death. The violent death of Tezcatlipoca was clearly the recipe for harmony, and reenactments of it were necessary for extending that harmony over time.

So frightened were the Aztecs that the god might come to sow violence again that they offered him copious blood sacrifices. Lest it decimate the resident population, the cult's need for sacrificial victims required that war parties regularly raid neighboring tribes for captives who could serve as sacrificial offerings. Here, as so often in the most ancient and/or primitive settings, the institution of war was ancillary to the institution of cult sacrifice. In such settings, wars were not primarily driven by political differences or by competition for land or resources, but by the need to supply the sacrificial system with the prodigious number of victims deemed necessary to placate the gods. The almost inevitable circularity of the process can readily be imagined, for the intervention of the gods whose favor required sacrificial victims would have been sorely needed in the raids or wars whose purpose was to obtain sacrificial victims. Whether in crude and primitive ways or in brilliant and sophisticated ones, the system generates its own logic, a logic that vigorously reasserted itself in the aftermath of Tezcatlipoca's death and deification. The new god demanded fresh blood.

Now let me try to shed light on how ancient societies extricated themselves from the "land of mirrors" into which they occasionally fell. The Aztec sacrificial scrupulosity took many forms, but it centered around an elaborate ritual reenactment of Tezcatlipoca's memorable visit to the realm of the mortals. This all-important ritual was the culmination of a year-long preparation that began when the most handsome and fascinating of the foreign prisoners of war was chosen to personify Tezcatlipoca throughout the coming year. The god's impersonator was taught to dance and sing and play the flute. He was carefully instructed in how to look attractive, how to carry himself in such a way that those who saw him would unavoidably find his mannerisms fascinating. He learned how to smoke and sit and walk in the most elegant fashion. He wore the finest garments and he was festooned with flowers. He, like the now divine model he was being asked to impersonate, became the supreme object of social fascination. Eight valets were assigned to attend him constantly, taking care that his appearance and demeanor were always the most appealing. Throughout the year, he received honors and gifts. Twenty days before the solemn feast of Tezcatlipoca, he was given four of the society's most beautiful young women as wives. On that day, the period of feasting and dancing began that would last until the day of the solemn rite itself. When that holiest of days arrived, the god who had lived in their midst for the last year, on whom all had looked with fascination, and whom no one was now capable of recognizing as a hapless warrior from a neighboring tribe, was escorted with unstinted extravagance and with a festive spirit to the terrace of the temple. As the assembled worshipers watched in mounting awe, the great god Tezcatlipoca himself climbed the stairs of the temple, breaking as he took each step a flute that he had played during his earthly visit to his supplicants. At the height of the temple stairs, the god of unparalleled beauty, the god of disorder and peace, of dancing and death, of prestige and violence, was laid across the altar. With one flashing, forceful, and expert blow of the chief priest's obsidian knife, the god's breast was torn open and his still palpitating heart ripped out and held aloft as an offering to the sun.

The rite accomplished what all ancient blood rituals exist to accomplish. It reenacted in a controlled and liturgically choreographed context the spontaneous sacrificial crisis that had actually taken place in the past. In this case, the crisis had begun when a bold and fascinating stranger, mocking the taboos and piping his intoxicating music, threw the social order into pandemonium, was killed by a frenzied mob, and then recognized as a god by those who experienced a cathartic *esprit de corps* at his death. The catharsis and the religious meaning it was given by the myth and ritual reinforced in the most viscerally powerful way the distinction between the *sacred* and the *profane,* upon which all other cultural distinctions depend. By explicitly and methodically directing all mimetic fascination toward the "god," the ritual channeled outside the social order the dangerous passions to which such fascination can lead if directed toward mere humans, namely, envy, jealousy, rivalry, and resentment. These are the passions that would otherwise be the dry tinder for a future social conflagration. The cathartic death of the one on whom all the fascination had been focused had the effect of "transcendentalizing" desire.

To fully appreciate the cultural function of this rite, one need only follow the eyes of its spectators, eyes that for a full year had looked with rapt fascination as the god's impersonator acted like a magnet drawing to himself the desires of his venerators. It was his preliminary task to intensify these desires, and his ultimate task to transfigure them entirely and turn them into worship. For the year during which this radiant being had walked among them, the Aztecs had in their midst one who had been carefully groomed to be more fascinating than all others in the social milieu. On the appointed day, the necks of all his admirers craned gradually *upward* as the god climbed the temple stairs with ritual solemnity. The higher he climbed, the more heavenward did the faces of his admirers turn, and the wider and more glazed did their eyes become. The more the twin radiance of sun and ritual grandeur blinded the worshipers, the more cathartic potential the ritual achieved. At the climax of the rite, blinded with sun and solemnity, the fascination of the Aztecs was turned into primitive religious awe by a murder, and the murder was turned into cult religion by myth and ritual.

Rethinking Our Desires

Since the dawn of human culture, it has been by virtue of just this kind of sacrificial system that we humans have been able to focus mimetic passions on selected victims and restore social solidarity by "scapegoating" them. We now know better. Not only can we no longer believe, with the Aztecs, that our victims are gods, but the belief that our victims are incarnate devils is one we can sustain only for as long as the social contagions that so designate them last. "As early as the next morning" we begin the process of coming to our senses. We have no sacrificial mechanisms that can convert all our mimetic passion into social unanimity, psychological stability, and a renewed sense of moral rectitude. We can no longer save ourselves from our own mimetic passions — adulation, envy, resentment, rivalry — by joining in occasional acts of unanimous violence, but we have hardly begun to calculate the implications of this. We live in a world inundated by these mimetic passions. What we call "modernity" is a world of feverishly mimetic desires and fascinations. With powers of telecommunication of which the Aztecs could not have dreamed, we are given models to emulate incessantly. We are inspired to envy, desire, compete, resent, aspire, and be ambitious. We live in what Auden called a "land of mirrors," but we no longer have a "Smoking Mirror" on whom all our mimetic passions might be focused and who could then be driven out — like a scapegoat — or religiously transfigured — like a god. When, in the aftermath of a public hanging, some go off to fight with murderous faces, a baby strings its doll to a stick, and children catch and hang a cat, then it is *we,* and not just our victims, who are at the end of our rope.

The Aztecs and those who lived under the dispensation of primitive religion were once able to believe that their victims were gods. The witch hunters and their ideological heirs were once able to believe that their victims were demons. But all that we have to strike now is the human face. It is the biblical texts and traditions that have stripped away the mantle of the sacred — the veil of sacrificial mystification — and forced us to see the victim's face and hear the victim's voice. We have every reason to be grateful for being thus freed from the grip of the sacrificial system, but if we are to avoid in the future the kind of cultural catastrophe that has so characterized the twentieth century, we will have to face the problem of mimetic desire, realizing that we no longer have rituals for exorcising its terrible consequences. Even as the sacrificial structures collapse, therefore, the biblical tradition that contributed so to the collapse warns about the ravages of rivalry, imitative desire, covetousness, and resentment. The sacrificial system is collapsing, and good riddance, but, if it collapses while the mimetic passions it existed to tame continue their explosive growth, it will collapse into the kind of pandemic crisis that sacrificial religion existed to prevent.

There is perhaps no better commentary on the situation in which we now find ourselves than that made rather offhandedly but nevertheless pointedly by the *New York Times* columnist Anna Quindlen at the conclusion of the column I quoted in chapter 4. The reader may recall that in that column Quindlen commented on a law suit by San Francisco public television station KQED contesting the refusal of California authorities to allow live television transmission of public executions. In the portion of the column I quoted, Quindlen recalled how a reporter covering the 1960 execution of Caryl Chessman arranged for Chessman to signal if the cyanide was painful. Quindlen ended her column with the following:

> The shocking thing has nothing to do with cameras or microphones. The shocking thing is there whether we reporters are there or not. "It's barbaric," a reporter named Mary Crawford wrote after witnessing the Chessman execution. Having it on television makes it no worse. It simply makes the reality inescapable, and our role undeniable. If we want it, we should be able to look at it. If we can't bear to look at it, maybe it's time to rethink our desires.[5]

As casually as Quindlen may have made that last comment, with it she has nevertheless deftly summed up the situation that I have so far been trying to describe anecdotally. She says that our aversion for our culture's official episodes of sacrificial violence means that "it's time to rethink our desires." This is certainly so. The reason why the demise of these sacrificial routines demands that we rethink our desires is that it is precisely these "desires" that produce the social aggravations for which scapegoating violence has been the perennial remedy. If the human race is now obliged to live without "sacrificial protections," then it is certainly time to rethink the "desires" that for thousands of years made ritual violence the only alternative to "endless conflagration" (Matt. 18:8) and cultural extinction.

I have touched on three stories, each involving the breakdown of an existing system of sacred violence and the corresponding increase in mimetic fascinations. The Tahitians began to find Omai more fascinating than the sacrificial system he had challenged. The West Point cadets mimicked Bob Dylan as he sang lyrics that challenged their most cherished beliefs. The Aztecs abandoned Quetzalcoatl in favor of the dazzling Tezcatlipoca. In each case, an existing sacrificial system gave way under the pressure of what Girard calls mimetic desire. Not only do we no longer have a sacrificial system for saving us from the social and psychological frenzy to which envy, covetousness, rivalry and resentment lead, but we increasingly live in a world consumed by these passions precisely because of the collapse of the sacrificial system. As Girard put it: "Desire is what happens to human relationships when there is no longer any resolution through the victim, and consequently no form of polarization that is genuinely unanimous and can trigger such a resolution."[6]

This "desire," which I will analyze in more detail in the next chapter, is what ravages human relationships and undermines psychological stability. Wherever and whenever the biblical tradition morally incapacitates a culture's sacrificial system, the aggravating effects of mimetic desire flourish precisely because there is no reliable way to focus them on one flamboyant object of lust or loathing and eliminate them at his or her expense.

Casual though her remark may have been, therefore, Quindlen put her finger on precisely the essential issue. To rethink our desires would mean not only jamming the cogs and gears of our present social and economic machinery, but it would mean reckoning with the most deeply embedded of our social and psychological reflexes. If, however, we are to avoid the catastrophes that loom on the horizon, rethinking our desires is exactly what we must do. As Augustine so eloquently insisted so many centuries ago, only when we have begun to rethink our desires can we be said to be thinking at all. And there are a number of things about which we urgently need to start thinking, one of the first being the nature of *desire* itself.

Chapter 6

"To Know the Place for the First Time"

> The tree of liberty must be refreshed from time to time with the blood of patriots and tyrants. It is its natural nurture.[1]
>
> THOMAS JEFFERSON

> All over the world, when sacrificers are asked why they perform sacrifices, their justification is . . . [that] they must do again what their ancestors did when the community was founded; they must repeat some foundational violence with substitute victims.[2]
>
> RENÉ GIRARD

> We shall not cease from exploration
> And the end of all our exploring
> Will be to arrive where we started
> And know the place for the first time.[3]
>
> T. S. ELIOT, "LITTLE GIDDING"

As Girard formulates it, the passions that lead to violence are the product of *mimetic desire,* the term he uses to speak of how predisposed to "suggestion" we humans are and how easily desire is aroused by the tangible evidence of another's desire. Virtually every use of the term "desire" today is suffused with Freud's understanding of desire as autonomous and spontaneous, and in popular culture, desire has become almost a synonym for life itself. Girard's use of the term has its roots in Plato, St. Paul, and Augustine, and it finds its literary reverberation in Shakespeare, Cervantes, and Dostoevsky among others. The desire that interests Girard is the desire that forms and destroys cultures, that shapes and shatters personal identities. So muddled are we about the true nature of desire that one is tempted to drop the term and use another in its place, but that would leave in place one of modernity's most formidable misconceptions and banish to the margins of discourse a discussion that ought to be at its center.

In what follows, therefore, when I speak of desire, or mimetic desire, or the passions born of mimetic desire, please know that for me, as for Girard, the word "desire" means *the influence of others*. I use the term mimetic "passions" or mimetic "aggravations" to refer to the social and psychological effects of such influence. As I have tried to suggest, the mimetic passions include jealousy, envy, covetousness, resentment, rivalry, contempt, and hatred. The same powerful mimetic penchant that gives rise to these passions is responsible for humanity's most laudable traits and most promising potentials. We humans are capable of learning, capable and sometimes even eager to follow positive role models, and willing to emulate virtuous deeds, for example, all because of our mimetic propensities. We are imitative creatures. We may try to hide our imitative behavior — even from ourselves — but we will never be able to dispense with it. The issues are: Whom do we imitate? Does our imitation lead us toward or away from our authentic uniqueness? And, do we eventually turn our models into rivals?

The enormous value of positive mimesis comes into play only in nonrivalrous settings or where rivalry is carefully codified and limited in scope. The intrusion of jealousy, envy, resentment, and all the other mimetic passions into such settings immediately undermines the benefits of healthy mimesis. If the passions born of rivalistic desire are not eliminated or kept severely restricted, few of the blessings of positive mimesis will be able to survive in the social hot-house that results. What protects humanity from the ravages of these passions — and screens us from the apocalyptic violence toward which they would otherwise drift — is culture. As I have shown, in overriding these passions cultures have invoked the sacrificial resources of the primitive sacred or one of its weaker modern vestiges. As the gospel influence began to render the sacred system morally and culturally problematic, the mimetic passions it was once able to tame grew, eventually becoming the social, psychological, and spiritual crisis of our time.

Where We Started

It was in his study of European novels that Girard first found recurring evidence of the social and psychological power of mimetic desire.[4] In analyzing the novel, Girard discovered that the plots of the greatest novelists were driven by mediated or mimetic desire. In fact, the novel appeals to its readers in part because it allows them to experience the ecstasies and agonies of mimetic desire—and all its stirring emotions—vicariously. To some extent, the popularity of the novel was one of the symptoms of the upsurge in mimetic desire that the novel as a literary form was documenting. It was, after all, fictional characters in romances and novels that served as mimetic models for figures like Don Quixote, Madame Bovary, and Dostoevsky's Underground Man.

For Girard, novels provided the first clue that led to his observation that throughout the modern era an epidemic of mimetic desire had been gradually overwhelming the various social structures traditional cultures had always used to prevent such things from happening. Until recently at least, Western societies have been able to exploit the economic—and, to some degree, the political—potential that this explosion of mimetic desire presented. But just as there is eventually a price to pay for exploiting, say, the economic potential of drug addiction or the political potential of racism, the West's attempt to exploit desire rather than to expose its hollowness and renounce its chimeras is one fraught with dangers. Even as the economic miracle made possible by mimetic desire is winning converts around the world, the social and psychological ravages of desire are destroying the social arrangements, the family among them, that make the enjoyment of economic plenty possible.

The fateful question was: under the right economic and political circumstances, could envy, covetousness, ambition, and resentment — the products of mimetic desire — be made into social virtues, or were the Christian warnings about the destructiveness of desire—warnings that the world-after-Freud found so amusing — valid at a level Freud had been afraid to plumb? We would eventually find out, because even as the West turned its economic dynamos with mediated desire, it grew daily less nimble at using the scapegoating apparatus to convert the mimetic aggravations that resulted into healthy camaraderie. In the West, the epidemic of mimetic desire was spreading even as the sacrificial system for preventing its worst consequences was becoming morally problematic and culturally ineffective. Girard's master stroke was simply to see the relationship between these two developments. "Desire is what happens to human relationships," he wrote, "when there is no longer any resolution through the victim."[5] Something that was unique and distinctive to Western culture was apparently throwing that culture into a crisis by *somehow* preventing its scapegoating mechanisms from operating with their full mesmerizing and galvanizing power. What was it?

What was to become modern astrophysics began when researchers discovered that the universe was flying apart. Similarly, Girard's mimetic theory began with his realization that European novelists were chronicling an explosion of mimetic desire in Western culture. In searching for the meaning of that explosion, Girard went next to anthropological records to investigate the role of mimesis in a larger frame of reference. It was this exploration that led him, in *Violence and the Sacred,* to suggest the violent foundation of all culture.[6] An even more audacious proposal came several years later in his *Things Hidden since the Foundation of the World.* In this seminal work he argued that the defining theme of biblical literature was a gradually developing aversion for sacred violence and the religious blood sacrifices that extended its purview, and a corresponding tendency to see historical phenomena from the perspective of its victims. These themes, he then realized, achieved their decisive historical revelation at the crucifixion and their literary summation in the New Testament. Anthropologically, this was decisive: the crucifixion and the New Testament's disclosure of its universal meaning. The historical convulsions of our age are an elaborate footnote to these things. Attempts to comprehend these convulsions that fail to take into account the destabilizing effect of the Bible's aversion for sacrifice and its concern for victims will never get to the heart of the present cultural predicament.

The world plagued by violence, over which no one and no institution has enough prestige to exercise control, is the world that existed prior to the formation of human culture. It is also the world to which we return as the myths that distinguish good from bad violence disintegrate under the disclosing power of biblical revelation. Without that distinction, civilization-made-*possible*-by-violence ("history") becomes civilization-made-*impossible*-by-violence (apocalypse). We face a situation, as Andrew McKenna put it, in which "the prospect of humanity's violent end repeats the dynamics of its violent beginnings."[7] In other words, the human experiment has arrived at where it started. All that is left for us to do — and the one thing, in fact, that we must do if we are to avoid catastrophe — is to know the place for the first time.

The word "religion" comes from the Latin *religare,* meaning to "bind back." Primitive religion is the binding up of the community by binding it back to the moment of its origins, the moment when it gathered together around its first victim. Anthropologically, religion, *religare,* centers on the ritual re-presentations of the community's founding violence. It is a repeated return to "where we started." But it is *not* a return in which the community really knows the place for the first time. It knows, instead, only a mythologized re-membering of the dis-memberment that occurred *in illo tempore,* when the "world" began. Whether we have taken the path of spontaneous collective violence or the path of ritual, we humans have returned to "where we started" ever and again. If ever we come to "know the place," however, it will necessarily be "for the first time," for once we know it, we can never again return to it in the same way. The misrecognition of what happened at the place "where we started" is the *sine qua non* of cult religion and the myths and cultural complexes into which it elaborates itself.

Once we know the place "where we started," when we return there, what we find is not the stirring memories of valorous deeds and the inspiration to perform comparable deeds in our day. Rather, we find the evidence of mob violence and religious mystification that reminds us of the fallen state of our world and of our complicity in its sinfulness. To know the place where we started for the *first* time is to have enjoyed its rejuvenating effects for the *last* time.

To arrive at where we started and to see it without either the mythological veil or the historical screen that vindicates its violence is to stand stupefied before the spectacle of scapegoating violence. To return to where we started and to know the place for the first time is to stand before a scene structurally indistinguishable from the crucifixion. To know the place for the first time is to stand at the foot of the Cross. If one can do so without entangling oneself in what Girard calls the "Lilliputian threads of piety and antipiety,"[8] then one can see "things hidden since the foundation of the world" (Matt. 13:35). To catch a glimpse of such things is to realize both how dependent we are on culture for our sanity and civility, and how suffused culture is with delusion, myth, and religious superstition.

Like the "founding" violence which physicists calculate to have occurred at the beginning of the universe, but for which they have only circumstantial evidence, the "founding" violence that accompanied hominization can only be deduced by an examination of its residual traces. Like the physicists, we too must content ourselves with secondary effects, with the second- and third-generation rituals, and with the founding event's subsequent religious and mythological representations. Lest our explorations cease, therefore, they must follow the trail of these mythological traces and try to reconstruct the events that produced them.

No reconstruction will be satisfactory unless it convincingly accounts for the seemingly inscrutable transition from prehuman life to human life as we know it, that is, the transition from precultural to cultural existence. The idea that violence is the key to this transition may be less of a stumbling block to our understanding than the idea that the source of that violence is *mimesis*. And so, before we return to the "place where we started" in the anthropological sense, I want to try to describe the place where we started in a more psychological sense. We can know the culture-founding events for the first time only if we better understand the social and psychological reflexes that structure these events. Before we try to understand the violence that first produced culture, therefore, let us look more carefully at social and psychological dynamics that first produced the *need* for culture.

The Nursery

Imagine a scene. A small child is sitting alone in a nursery that has a couple of dozen toys scattered about it. He sits there rather dreamily, exhibiting only a casual interest in the toy that just happens to be nearby. Another child comes into the nursery and surveys the room. He sees the first child and a great number of toys. There will come a moment when the second child will choose a toy. Which of the toys will he most likely find interesting? The first parent you meet will be able to tell you. It will likely be the toy with which the first child seems to be interested, although the first child's interest is as yet only a casual one. The second child will no doubt be more interested in the first child than in any of the toys, but this interest will almost instantly be translated into a concern for the toy for which the child has shown some interest. All parents have seen this sort of thing happen hundreds of times. Dealing with the resulting squabbles is an almost constant aspect of child-rearing. We joke about it. We shrug our shoulders. We even try to exploit it in order to elicit the behavior we want. But we almost never ask what this familiar phenomenon tells us about *desire,* and about the little bundle of it that we like to call the *self.*

Imagine, now, what most parents would predict. The second child becomes interested in the toy for which the first child has shown an interest. The second child reaches for the toy. What happens? The first child's nonchalance vanishes in an instant. Suddenly, he clings to the toy for dear life. Extremely vexed, the first child says, "I had that!" His intense reaction arouses in the second child a desire for the toy vastly more powerful than the rather mild one with which he had first reached for it. The two children simply feed each other's desire for the toy by demonstrating to each other how desirable it is. Each further intensifies the desire of his rival by threatening to foreclose the possibility of possession. As the emotions rise, the opportunity for parental compromise declines rapidly. Each child treats the suggestion that he take turns playing with the toy as a betrayal by the adult who makes it. If a perfect facsimile of the toy is produced so that both children can have identical toys, the dispute may well sputter out, but each child's interest in the no longer disputed toy will in all likelihood begin to cool at the same time.[9] As long as the conflict remains unresolved, the suggestion that both children bear some responsibility for the squabble will be resolutely rejected. Each child will be certain that the other is the sole cause of the conflict.

Already in the children's nursery, therefore, we have the basic dynamics of scapegoating fully manifested. In word, gesture, or deed, each child is saying to the other: "What is wrong here is *your* fault!" The dynamics operating in the innocuous little squabble in the children's nursery are the same dynamics — writ large — that operate in religious or ethnic or nationalistic conflicts. The kind of scapegoating that has significant social consequences usually involves a crowd scapegoating a single person or subculture, but social scapegoating is merely the transference onto one person or subgroup of all the private sacrificial predilections with which a society is rife just prior to its paroxysm of unanimous scapegoating.

In children old enough to be verbal, something of the following dialogue can be safely predicted:

> FIRST CHILD: I had it first!
> SECOND CHILD: You weren't playing with it. I wanted it first!
> FIRST CHILD: No you didn't. I wanted it first!
> SECOND CHILD: No, I wanted it first!

Now, let us ask: who's right? Who wanted it first? The astonishing thing is, we cannot completely answer that question. Should either of the children be told that his desire for the toy was aroused by the desire of the child who is now his rival for it, he would vehemently deny it. In a way, he would be right, inasmuch as there has probably been no conscious attempt to copy. That is why the term "imitation" is not entirely satisfactory. It implies a degree of conscious intention that the term "mimesis" does not necessarily imply.

The most glaringly obvious fact about the squabble in the children's nursery, the one that is so familiar we hardly notice it, is the very one that the two children will most vehemently deny and whose implications we adults seem predisposed to ignore, namely, mimetic desire. Clearly, each child's desire for the toy evoked and reinforced the desire of his rival. Neither of their desires was entirely spontaneous. Desire is the product of *influence,* and in turn it has influence on others. The desired object is always located at the *con-fluence* of more than one desire.[10] Should it be pointed out to either child that he wants the toy just because the other child wants it, he would passionately insist that *his* desire was original and that the desire of his rival was secondary and derivative. Older children and adults have had repeated experiences of this sort. In responding to them, they have gradually developed much more subtle reflexes for manipulating mimetic contests to the best advantage. Desire, that most cherished essence of both the romantic and the Freudian self, is not the infallible gyroscope the modern age has acclaimed it to be. It is the most fickle and capricious compass imaginable, whose needle always quivers in the presence of someone else's desire.

Had either of the children recognized the dynamic at the heart of their rivalry — that exhibitions of desire arouse desires in others, making them rivals for the desired object — they would have behaved more like adults. That is to say, they would have manipulated (and been unwittingly manipulated by) desire, envy, rivalry, and ambition in much more subtle ways.

The Sale Table

Imagine, therefore, another scene. This time, imagine yourself rather casually passing by a sale table in a department store. On the table there is an assortment of items that have been marked down for sale. There is really nothing on the table that is of much interest. You have a few minutes before your commuter bus stops in front of the store, so you pause. Presently, someone else pauses. Among the items on the table, there are a few shiny gismos. You have no need for another shiny gismo. As the other person picks one of them up, however, you remember that you don't have a shiny gismo in the den and that the one in the breakfast nook cost three times what these gismos are going for. There are a few other shiny gismos on the table. Maybe you should get one before they're all gone. For some reason, you're embarrassed to pick up a shiny gismo so soon after the other person has picked one up. (Why? Someone might see you and think you don't know how to think for yourself? God forbid.) But there is another reason. You "realize" — without pausing to really become fully aware of it — that were you to pick up one of the shiny gismos, the other shopper might notice, whereupon *he* would "realize" — in exactly the same semi-conscious way — what a bargain the shiny gismos really are, and he would hang on to the one he has in his hands. You don't want to encourage him to do that because you now "realize" that the one he is holding is the only green one on the sale table, and green would look nice on the end table in the den. (You have, you "realize," *always* liked green.)

You try to appear as casual as you can, being careful not to seem too eager about anything lest the other shopper's desire might catch some of the heat of your own, in which case you would have to kiss the green one good-bye. So you pick up a pack of peach-colored queen size pillow cases and try to look interested. The other person has put the green one down and is now looking at a navy blue one. ("Classic color, navy blue," is a thought that doesn't quite have time to reach consciousness.) The green one is now free, but it is still right in front of the other shopper. To reach for it so soon after he put it down would be a little embarrassing, and maybe even brazen, though you're not sure why. You look at your watch. The commuter bus will be leaving the stop in front of the store in three minutes. You feel irritation, even anger. A few minutes later, you are standing on the crowded bus you just managed to catch. Along with your briefcase and your overcoat, you are clutching this foolish looking green gismo. You can just imagine what that smug young man in the horn-rimmed glasses sitting next to the window is thinking. You say to yourself, "Who cares what he thinks."

If this little parable seems even sillier than the one about the children in the nursery, and I would be the first to admit its silliness, then one need only replace the shiny gismos with lovers, wealth, power, spouses, career opportunities, and social prestige to appreciate its relevance. As I hope this little story and the one preceding it show, mimetic desire is *meta*-physical, not physical; it tends to become obsessional faster and more fiercely than merely physical desires—for which it would be more appropriate to use the term "appetite," rather than desire. The desires that churn out the melodramas that are the hallmark of human history have their roots in mimesis and not in physical appetite. Mimetic desires have one exasperating quality: they can never be satisfied. This makes them more, rather than less, powerful. As the old saying goes: you never get enough of what you really don't want. "The world I am trying to understand," writes the economist A. O. Hirschman, "is one in which men think they want one thing and then upon getting it, find out to their dismay that they don't want it nearly as much as they thought or don't want it at all and that something else, of which they were hardly aware, is what they really want."[11]

To make sense of ourselves and our world, we have to ask questions like the one this economist asks, but we must pose the question anthropologically and not merely economically or psychologically. Hirschman has referred to something that is peculiarly human—a desire that is always a desire for something else, something someone else desires. Is it possible, by focusing on this distinctively human characteristic, to locate human origins? Can we imagine the process by which the *anthropoid* became the *anthropos?*

The Birth of Religion

The distinguishing feature of the higher primates is their mimetic capacity. We commonly use the term "ape," for instance, to refer to mimicry. Among the higher apes, however, conflicts can still be settled instinctively. The dominance-submission mechanism interrupts the mimetic rivalry before its most passionate and violent stage is reached. As Aristotle observed, however, "Man differs from other animals in his greater aptitude for imitation (*mimesis*)."[12] Our hominid ancestors were so mimetically excitable that contact between and among them aroused fierce mimetic passions that the dominance-submission mechanism was simply no longer able to suppress. As my two parables suggest, because of this mimetic predilection, sooner or later an acquisitive gesture will arouse in another a desire for the object toward which the gesture has drawn attention. Like the children squabbling over a toy, each claiming his desire for it to be prior to and independent of the desire of the other, the human mimetic predilection generates conflict. Like the second child in the nursery, the one whose desire has been aroused by the first desire will mimic the acquisitive gesture. The two will be in conflict, and, with each other as rivals, the passion with which they desire will grow, causing their acquisitive gestures to become more emphatic. These emphatic gestures will be highly evocative, and they will be mimicked by those looking on. Eventually, bystanders will be drawn into the mêlée.

Once the dominance-submission mechanism has been overridden, the strife increases in social scope, in emotional passion, and in physical ferocity. Again, like children in the nursery, as the rivalry grows more heated, the rivals grow more preoccupied with one another, and in short order this preoccupation with each other surpasses in emotional intensity each rival's interest in whatever the object of desire they each claim. The rivals become for one another the *raison d'être,* and the object over which their contest began remains of interest only as the token by general reference to which the rivals maintain the elusion that their rivalry is about something other than the elimination of the other rival. The rivalry is now a metaphysical one, that is to say, it is driven by passions that the rhetoric and rationale espoused by the rivals serves only to obfuscate. Each one desires the elimination of his rival more than the possession of the desired object over which the rivalry began. As the mimetic passions run their predictable course from desire to rivalry and finally to violence, the acquisitive gestures with which the process began are replaced by accusing and violent gestures. Unless this process had been interrupted, humanity's powerful penchant for emulation — the source of both its violence and its virtue — would have ended in savagery thousands of years ago.

What interrupts this process in ordinary human life is culture. It is cultural structures that take the place of instinctive restraints — such as the dominance-submission mechanism. Obviously, however, we cannot posit a cultural control until we account for the formation of culture, a formation that must have taken place without such a control. How then did culture come to be in the first place? Girard argues, correctly in my view, that there is only one reliable constant in the proto-cultural scene, namely, mimesis and its one predictable result: social strife. Is it possible, then, that some form of the mimesis that is throwing our culture apart in its centrifuge could have brought the first culture together like a mighty magnet? Yes.

To understand how this occurs, it is important to notice that by its very nature mimetic desire is extremely fickle. It moves from one object to another as model-rivals designate these objects as desirable. Mimetic desires are contagious, and as they contaminate the social order, they lead to rivalry and violence. At each stage of this deepening crisis, the mimetic passions grow more volatile, more violent, and more responsive to suggestion. At the height of this madness, fickleness, and volatility, the stunning transformation that gives rise to culture takes place. It occurs at a moment when there is nothing operating except the pure reciprocity of violence. Each does to his immediate rival what his rival has just done to him. When this process achieves its maximum effect, all distinctions vanish. Each person behaves in exactly the same way: reciprocating violence he has been dealt or duplicating violence he has seen. In other words, the violence of the precultural mob is apocalyptic violence.

All of this begins with an *acquisitive gesture* toward an object that awakens other desires for that object. A number of acquisitive gestures made toward the same desired object set the conflict in motion. At the supreme moment of violent dis-integration, another gesture is mimetically replicated with even more speed and ferocity than the numerous acquisitive gestures with which the crisis got under way. At the moment when the social frenzy is at its height, someone designates a rival with a startling *accusatory gesture* that has, under the circumstances, an extremely intense mimetic effect. The mêlée becomes a lynch mob. The chaos that was set in motion when an *acquisitive gesture* had its mimetic effects is resolved when an *accusatory* gesture — made at the height of the crisis — has its even more powerful mimetic effects. To imitate the grasping gesture or the desiring glance is to find oneself in conflict with the one whose gesture inspired the imitation. On the contrary, to imitate the accusatory gesture is to join in a surge of social solidarity. This is the turning point, one that can be accounted for purely in terms of the mimetic forces that are most likely to have been in play in proto-cultural situations.

At the crescendo of an all-against-one crisis, therefore, all it takes to turn the social free-for-all into a *communal exorcism* is for one of those caught up in the furor to heap abuse or accusation on his immediate rival with such hysterical vehemence that the accusation exerts a contagious influence on others. Sooner or later, this is bound to happen. With literally blinding speed, a supremely violent and terrifying and utterly undifferentiated social chaos is replaced, first, by unanimous shouts and, then, by the hush of awe. Primitive religion is born at this moment, the moment when, as Girard puts it, "the atmosphere of terror and hallucination that accompanies the primordial religious experience" reaches its climax, and "the détente that follows only heightens the mystery of the whole process."[13] *In the beginning was the hush.*

Human culture as such begins with the community of victimizers looking at the corpse of its victim in solemn astonishment at the miracle of camaraderie that has just taken place. Whereas but a moment before strife had prevailed, now there is a unanimous religious awe focused on the corpse of the victim. The intensity of that attention, and the fact that it is accompanied by the first experience of social solidarity, justifies the designation of the moment in which it occurs as the moment of hominization. It is the moment when the rupture with the prehuman primate realm can be pronounced complete. The murder, the peace, the *esprit de corps,* and the religious awe all occur at the same moment, the moment commemorated in innumerable myths as the beginning of the world. The profound religious fascination the members of the mob experience at the critical moment is a more or less perfect balance between "desire" for the object — whether it is a desire to acquire as one's own, or to strike yet one more blow, or to dismember or consume the corpse — and a fear that any attempt to act on that desire will renew the violence. Rudolf Otto may have misunderstood the real nature of the primitive sacred, but he understood how powerfully it combined attraction and repulsion. "The daemonic-divine object may appear to the mind an object of horror and dread," wrote Otto in the passage I quoted in the last chapter, "but at the same time it is no less something that allures with a potent charm, and the creature, who trembles before it, utterly cowed and cast down, has always at the same time the impulse to turn to it, nay, even to make it somehow his own."[14]

What checks this impulse to make the sacred object one's own is the existence of this same impulse in all those who participated in the mob murder. To act on this impulse, to actually reach out for the sacred object toward which all have turned their attention, would be an *acquisitive gesture* of such provocative power, occurring at such an intense moment, that the violent mêlée would instantly resume, and the one whose gesture provoked it would almost surely become the next victim. Killing the victim produced the peace. Touching the corpse of the victim destroys that peace. The primitive mind makes the obvious conclusion: the god who gave the community peace when he died will let violence loose on the community again if the sacrality emanating from the corpse or the sacred space surrounding it is trespassed. This is the birth of the sacred. The corpse is the first sacred object. Or as Andrew McKenna puts it: "What first takes place is the victim.... What takes its place is the sacred."[15] In fact, a number of hands reaching out toward the victim's corpse, but arrested at a certain point by the fear of violent repercussions, may well have constituted the first discernible act of religious homage. "Desire" frozen by the terror of the sacred into a gesture of reverence may have been primitive religion's first act of terrified supplication. The mob violence culminates in a culturally "unforgettable" moment in which *hush* and *hesitation* lay the groundwork for the religious system that will thereafter remember this event (myth) and re-present its cathartic power (ritual).

The Victim with an Extended Sentence

As I said, if one especially caught up in the madness should fail to draw back in time and touch the corpse, he would very likely be killed in the ensuing frenzy his grasping gesture provoked. In retrospect, his impious gesture would be understood as a sacrilegious act, a terrible transgression, a violation of the sacred that provoked the god's renewed wrath. He would be seen as the violator of the distinction between the sacred and the profane, the world's first transgressor of taboo. "Violence" and "violation" have the same Latin root, and apprehension about the violent consequences of taboo violation is a driving force in primitive religion.

If, on the other hand, an encroachment on the sacred domain were to be made with sufficient boldness or reverence or authority, the community might be too stunned and fascinated by the brazen audacity of the transgression to converge on the transgressor immediately. In that moment between the "violation" — the touching of the corpse or the entering of the sacred precinct — and the new outbreak of violence, the mob regards the violator with the same combination of horror and deference with which it regards the sacred corpse or sacred space he has dared to approach. For the moment between the transgression and the violence, the sacred aura enjoyed by the transgressor endows him with an immense social prestige. By deftly exploiting this prestige, the transgressor might be able to postpone indefinitely the violent repercussions of his transgression, and perhaps even to transfer the violence to a "surrogate victim" if and when it occurs. In any case, the transgression will not be forgotten, and the social uniqueness the transgressor earned by committing it will insure that the community's attitude toward this figure will thereafter be commingled with dread and fascination. This figure, who has demonstrated an ability to approach the sacred with impunity, will very likely come to serve as both the mediator and interpreter of the mysteries of the sacred, on the one hand, and the community's designated victim, on the other. The community's relationship to this figure will involve the same paradox of attraction and repulsion that characterizes its relationship to the sacred for which he becomes the channel and spokesman. It is in this way that the rudimentary forms of kingship and priesthood emerge. "The king reigns only by virtue of his future death," writes Girard. "He is no more and no less than a victim awaiting sacrifice, a condemned man about to be executed."[16]

The anthropological evidence for Girard's claim that originally the king was a victim with an extended sentence is abundant and persuasive. To illustrate, let me refer briefly to some of this evidence. In his *Crowds and Power,* Elias Canetti quotes a wide array of first-hand anthropological reports, and a surprising number of them indicate an unmistakable relationship between kingship and sacrifice. Two of them are especially interesting in the present context. Canetti quotes from an eye-witness report by Du Chaillu, published in 1861, describing the selection of a new king in Gaboon and the installation ritual that followed. First, the new king was selected in secret by the tribal elders. And then, Canetti quotes Du Chaillu:

> As he was walking on the shore on the morning of the seventh day [of the elders' deliberations] he was suddenly set upon by the entire populace, who proceeded to a ceremony which is preliminary to the crowning, and which must deter any but the most ambitious men from aspiring to the crown. They surround him in a dense crowd, and then began to heap upon him every manner of abuse that the worst of mobs could imagine. Some spat in his face; some beat him with their fists; some kicked him; others threw disgusting objects at him; while those unlucky ones who stood on the outside, and could reach the poor fellow only with their voices, assiduously cursed him.... Then all became silent; and the elders of the people rose and said, solemnly (the people repeating after them), "Now we choose you for our king; we engage to listen to you and obey you...." He was then dressed in a red gown, and received the greatest marks of respect from all who had just now abused him.[17]

As all rituals are, this is a ritual reenactment. The question is: What is it reenacting? Can there be any doubt that it is reenacting a mob murder? I think not. "The insults and blows he is subjected to before entering on his office are an intimation of what awaits him in the end," concludes Canetti. "As he submits to them, he will submit to his ultimate fate."[18] A later study of an installation ritual among the Bambara tribe confirms this view. Canetti summarizes the data, comments, and then quotes from the researcher, Monteil:

> Sometimes the length of [the new king's] reign is fixed from the start: the kings of Jukun...originally ruled for seven years. Among the Bambara the newly elected king traditionally determined the length of his own reign. "A strip of cotton was put round his neck and two men pulled the ends in opposite directions whilst he himself took out of a calabash as many pebbles as he could grasp in his hand. These indicated the number of years he would reign, on the expiration of which he would be strangled."[19]

In the late 1980s, Simon Simonse found comparable rituals still taking place in the traditional societies of Southeastern Sudan. His data is as vivid and persuasive as the reports of nineteenth-century field workers. Summing up the similarity between the ritual installation of a new king and mob violence, Simonse says: "The installation and funeral ceremonies are enactments of the same scenario. They mark the beginning and the end of the victimary career of the King."[20] In other words, the king's reign is nothing more than the extended *intermission* in a violent sacrificial ritual. Like the impersonator of Tezcatlipoca in the Aztec ritual, the fascinating figure of the primitive king might be hailed for some time as the god's representative, a manifestation to the worshiping community of the god's uncanny power, and then sacrificed at a moment determined either by ritual or by social circumstance. If, during this period when he serves as the god's mediator, this figure acquires enough sacred prestige, then at the moment when his sacrifice is demanded, he may be able to remain sufficiently in control of the ritual to offer a substitute victim in his own place, and therefore to retain his role as the culture's reigning personification of religious fascination. This substitution is an important turning point in the transition from cathartic mob violence to durable cultural institutions.

Those who become the god-kings, the shamans, and the priests of a newly forming cult are those who have proven themselves capable of moving across the threshold separating the sacred from the profane without suffering the god's wrath, or at least without suffering it immediately. These cult figures mediate and disseminate the sacred for the community. Ultimately, their role is not to protect the sacred realm from contamination by the profane, but the other way around, to protect the worshipers from the violence for which the sacred shrine is a shimmering reminder. They do this in part by serving as the community's first line of defense against an unwelcome incursion of the scourge of sacred violence. For the religious prestige these figures enjoy and the wary obeisance they are accorded by their community is the prestige of the marked victim. Lest we think that all the fawning over such figures is a sign of social popularity, let me offer one last comment from Canetti's study. Canetti writes:

> The king rarely appeared in public. His naked foot must never touch the ground, for, if it did, the crops would be blasted; he was also forbidden to pick up anything from the ground. If he fell off his horse he was, in earlier times, promptly put to death. It might never be said that he was ill; if he did contract any serious illness he was quietly strangled.... He was believed to be in control of the rain and the winds. A succession of droughts and bad harvests indicated the waning of his strength and he was secretly strangled by night.[21]

Obviously, as cultures manage to further institutionalize themselves, vestiges and vivid reminders of their founding violence tend to recede. They are never altogether eliminated, however, and no matter how recessive the structures of mystified violence become, the fact that culture begins with such violence has enormous implications for our species, implications that we can no longer ignore.

The Mythic Pattern

Behaving in ways for which Girard's mimetic hypothesis fully accounts, mob violence produces the rudiments of the primitive religious cult—the *esprit de corps,* the power of the sacred, and the prestigious figures capable of acting in its name and speaking on its behalf, as well as the myths, rituals, and prohibitions that will henceforth structure social existence. The culture's myths, rituals, and prohibitions are the essential tools for extending the social benefits of the *esprit de corps* that accompanied the founding murder. *Myths,* as I have already indicated, exist to misrepresent the founding violence as divine violence by which the "world" was created. *Prohibitions* censure the kind of behavior that might result in the spontaneous eruption of another violent crisis. In the first instance, the prohibitions strictly demarcate the boundary between the sacred and the profane and severely punish those who disregard the distinction between them. Subsequent prohibitions condemn those behaviors that might easily provoke another social crisis—such things as overt violence, theft, cursing, casting of spells, taking another's sexual partner, and so on. *Rituals* do the opposite of prohibitions. The opening gambit of a ritual reenactment is often the dramatic violation of taboos. Rituals reenact in a strictly controlled setting precisely the violent crisis that the prohibitions exist to prevent or forestall. Whereas in the original violence a transfer of all hostility toward one victim had developed spontaneously (mimetically) at the moment of greatest mimetic frenzy, rituals involve a meticulously controlled transfer of violence onto a ritual victim. The most universal ritual in human anthropology is the blood sacrifice, whose purpose is to periodically revive the religious fervor and the social *esprit de corps* born of the tribe's founding violence and to remind the tribe of the terms under which its relative social peace is being permitted to endure.

We moderns can hardly imagine what an immense relief it must have been for ancient peoples to discover that a powerful god was now in control of the violence that, as they knew so well, might otherwise rage out of control at any moment. We think of religion as a pious and respectable affair; we are horrified to find that it began in delusion and murder. But we must realize that both its delusions and its murders were vast improvements over the recurring waves of homicidal delirium by which the proto-human world must have been deluged once violence could no longer be controlled instinctively and before collective episodes of it produced the first religions.

Its abominations notwithstanding, the primitive sacred made the ancient world a more peaceful place. Calculated and ritualized violence has a special horror, which is the source of its cathartic power, but it often warded off violence on a far greater scale. The ancients may have been deluded by the process in which they were so caught up, but, faced as they were with the ever present danger of savagery, their eagerness to live in a world under the control of the sacred was neither irrational nor cruel. The sacred was their protection. It was the screen by which they protected themselves from the workings of the apocalypse. We have no right, therefore, to be contemptuous of, or condescending toward, our ancestors, but surely the worst form of contempt and condescension is the misty-eyed romanticism that repeats words and gesture of the chorus in Aeschylus's *Agamemnon.*

> The rest I did not see,
> Nor do I speak of it...

Demythologizing Myths

Joseph Campbell admired the mystery cults of the Near East, regarding them as a kind of mythogenic "fertile crescent" from which the greater mythological tradition emanated. Repeating for the thousandth time the cliché that has robbed comparative religion of its one critical tool, Campbell saw in Christianity a religiously mediocre variant of the basic Dionysus-Orpheus-Bacchus myth. For Campbell, Christianity was "a popular, non-esoteric, politically manageable, state-supported variant, wherein symbols that in others were read in a mystic, anagogical way, proper to symbols, were *reduced* to a literal sense and referred to supposed or actual historical events."[22] "For," says Campbell, "the myth of the dead and resurrected god whose being is the life-pulse of the universe had been known to the pagans millenniums before the crucifixion of Christ."[23] But what if underneath "the myth of the dead and resurrected god" that is "the life-pulse of the universe" there are innumerable victims of mob violence whose blood has been the life-pulse of conventional culture? What if the preference for anagogical metaphors over actual historical events amounts to stuffing cotton in one's hears at the crowing of the cock?

Campbell scorned Christianity for depriving the story of mob murder of the metaphorical treasures that the mythological renditions of the story so marvelously preserve. By abandoning the *anagogic metaphor* and insisting on "actual historical events," Christianity, according to this view of things, demonstrated its crudity. What can one say? Should we regard the stories of medieval witch-burning as *anagogic metaphors?* Campbell laments Christianity's humdrum interest in historical events—"supposed or actual"—as if the difference between imaginative events and real ones was insignificant. Campbell had all the pertinent information at his fingertips, but he was too much under the spell of Nietzsche, Schopenhauer, and Jung to recognize it for what it was. He dismissed the *objective realism* of the Judeo-Christian tradition in favor of a vague and mythic form of *subjectivism* whose spiritual dubiousness might have been deduced from the solemnity with which it was declared to be paramount. There is a huge irony here, one that it will take another book to explore in sufficient detail. Briefly, it is that the further away one moves from the heart of the Christian revelation, the greater the antipathy between objectivity and subjectivity, the less reliable the former, and the less substantial the latter. Whereas at the heart of the Christian revelation, where the Cross and the God-centered One who died on it converge, the objective and the subjective are reconciled at a level that only the great mystics have fully appreciated.

Campbell and others were right, of course, when they saw the resemblance between the crucifixion of Christ and the manifold myths of dismemberment and divine revelation. But that similarity doesn't destroy Christianity's claim to universal relevance; it substantiates it. No one denies that the crucifixion *actually happened,* that a Jew named Jesus of Nazareth was publicly executed by decree of Roman overlords of Palestine and at the behest of the condemned man's co-religionists. What gave rise to the "Dionysus-Orpheus-Bacchus" myths was no doubt also a mob murder, an *actual historical event,* but, of course, the mythic rendition of it tranquilizes the curiosity about what it might have been. Be assured, however, that the ancients were not in the habit of concocting *anagogic metaphors* for the purpose of after-dinner discussions about their psychic implications. They were concerned rather with warding off the violence that constantly threatened their fragile societies.

What those who repeat the cliché about the similarity between the crucifixion and the "Dionysus-Orpheus-Bacchus" myths fail to see is that the Gospels tell the story of the crucifixion *from the point of view of the victim.* The Gospels make it perfectly clear that the righteous mob, and the political and religious functionaries that kowtowed to it, were both morally wrong and mentally mesmerized into believing otherwise. "Forgive them, for they know not what they do." Was the scholarly erudition required to recognize the similarity between the passion story and the archaic myths so exhausting that the recognition of the perfectly obvious dissimilarity between them had to be forsworn? To refuse to see this difference is to renounce any hope of moral clarity and to turn comparative religion into a parody of what its name implies. Refusing to interpret stories of mob murder as *anagogic metaphors* and concerning oneself instead with "actual historical events" is the victory of gospel over myth. Swooning over the missed psychological or literary opportunities cannot eliminate the fact that it is that victory that is removing the cultural linchpin, throwing the world into its maturation crisis, and, in the process, saving us from sin and death.

When one catches a glimpse of the violence myths formerly veiled, the myths that once served to allay moral suspicions serve instead to awaken them. And that is precisely how we must now use myths. We must learn from myths. But we have much more to learn from them than those who wax poetic about them realize. Instead of being marvelously imaginative maps of "the unconscious," myths are the narrative remnants of the source of human unconsciousness, namely, the *fascinans* and *tremendum* of the primitive sacred.

The spirit born of the sacrificial murder inspires the community of its perpetrators to remember the murder as holy and creative. The Spirit of the Gospels, on the other hand, remembers the false accusations, sordid plots, the sham trials, and the weak faith of those who fled. Those inspired by the Paraclete awaken from illusion and experience dis-illusionment, contrition, and cultural alienation, as did Peter and Paul. The truth to which the Paraclete will lead humanity is not a truth that can be acquired by a simple intellectual transaction, the way, for instance, knowledge can be acquired in a classroom or in a book. The truth (*aletheia*) that the Paraclete reveals is a cure for the kind of forgetfulness that myth makes possible. It is a revelation that occurs as those to whom it is revealed stop forgetting the price they have paid for their social and psychological poise and for their religious righteousness. That is why, again according to John's Gospel, the Paraclete draws those it inspires to the Cross, for the Cross is the counter-mythological, meta-religious revelatory image par excellence, the pivot around which a worldwide anthropology revolution is now turning.

Joseph Campbell had a working familiarity with an impressive range of myths and mythological traditions, and he had a gift for mining this material for insights into *the* "unconscious" as mapped by Carl Jung and his disciples. When he treats "actual historical events" as contemptible, however, he abandons the element of realism that has been crucial to the West's intellectual curiosity, and he repudiates the very tradition that makes a lucid understanding of myth possible. The word *historia* means "inquiry." As I suggested in the first chapter, conventional historical inquiry, that is, inquiry not under the influence of the gospel revelation, exempts from its scrutiny that which, if scrutinized, would destroy the meaningfulness of its conclusions. The foray into "actual historical events" launched by "history" is no doubt too deferential, not robust enough to demythologize with the requisite moral and religious determination. If it is to be superseded, however, it should be replaced only by a less deferential inquiry. Campbell spoke for the romantic remnant that would dismiss the inquiry precisely in order to squeeze the last few psychological drops out of myths whose sacrificial underpinnings the gospel had already begun to expose and whose spellbinding and culture-sustaining power it had thoroughly compromised. The modest and psychologically dubious results of this undertaking are achieved at the expense of the enormous anthropological insights to be gained from a serious investigation of the "actual historical events" that lay behind the mythological constructs.

Perhaps sensing what might come from an unchaperoned historical inquiry, the Greeks took the precaution of assigning to history its own special Muse, Clio, whose name (from the Greek, *kleiein*) means "to praise." With the laurel wreath as her celebrated symbol, Clio saw to it that remembering the past would awaken only the zeal to reenact its great deeds and emulate those who performed them.

Even a determined effort to discover the truth and eschew mythic fabrications will fail, therefore, if it has no tool at its disposal for deciphering the scapegoating and sacrificial nexus at the heart of mythic reality. It was the biblical empathy for victims that aroused a truly historical interest in "actual historical events," and it is this interest that helped define the world's first counter-cultural culture — what we call "Western culture." The poet Howard Nemerov renounced the mythic fabrication of the Muse in words that go straight to the crucial issue.

> ...tell us no more
> Enchantments, Clio. History has given
> And taken away; murders become memories,
> And memories become the beautiful obligations:
> As with a dream interpreted by one still sleeping,
> The interpretation is only the next room of the dream.[24]

At the *crux* of the West's historical realism is the *Cross,* but the full impact of the revelation of the Cross demands that we understand it in the context of the extraordinary religious and anthropological journey that led to it: the history of biblical Israel. Under the influence of Clio, murders have become memories and memories the solemn duties. Interpreting these things while still under her soothing influence does nothing more than seduce us into the next room of the dream. When the next room of that dream begins to look like Auschwitz, Hiroshima, or Bosnia, it is time to dispense with the soothing interpretations. For a more troubling one, but one that has real revelatory power, let us turn to the biblical texts.

Chapter 7

A Text in Travail

> The Bible has given us the privileged tool of demystification, but we either do not know how to use it, or do not want to use it. Perhaps we are secretly afraid it will wreak too much havoc.[1]
>
> René Girard

> The man of today . . . must read the Scriptures as though they were something entirely unfamiliar, as though they had not been set before him ready-made, . . . as though he has not been confronted all his life with sham concepts and sham statements which cited the Bible as their authority.[2]
>
> Martin Buber

The Bible I have before me has 1679 pages. On page 8 the first violence occurs. It results in the first death. Since shortly before this murder occurs, death is declared to be the punishment for sin, the fact that the death that follows the first sin is a murder hardly deserves to be considered merely incidental. As one would expect, the biblical tradition responds to the central and profound fact of human mortality in rich and complex ways. If the New Testament is to be trusted, however, the most profound of these understandings concerning our mortality occurs at, or shortly after, the moment when we have been freed from our unconscious complicity in the structures of sacred violence. (It must not be forgotten that it was those whose sacrificial delusions were the most thoroughly shattered by the Cross who found themselves suddenly living in the light of the resurrection. One must not ignore the subtle but essential link between, for instance, the moral shock Paul felt upon realizing his complicity in sacred violence and his subsequent attitude toward death. "Death, where is your sting?")

So it is hardly coincidental that death is conspicuously declared to be the punishment for the sin of Adam and Eve and that the first death to occur in the aftermath of that sin is a murder. In the Bible, the fact that murder is prior to natural death and that the one murdered is *innocent* is one of the clearest and earliest indications of the anthropological character of biblical literature. As soon as Abel's blood touches the ground it cries out. The biblical God hears the blood crying out from the ground and demands a reckoning in terms that force the murderer to confront the truth. "What have you done?" asks Yahweh.

Not only is the Bible's first death a murder, but the Bible's first murderer is also the founder of the Bible's first culture. But the Bible doesn't sing the praises of this founding figure and celebrate the gloriousness of his violence; it remembers him as a murderer. Unfortunately, the Old Testament's moral lucidity — its tactless preference for truth — does not always carry the day as conclusively as it does in the Cain and Abel story. Neither, however, is it ever fully subdued, and it grows more irrepressible with each successive attempt to repress it. In the biblical literature, the forces of myth and revelation contend with each other in the boldest and most explicit ways. Though the struggle between them is occasionally both morally unedifying and theologically misleading, the literature in which it occurs is the most important one we have for understanding the journey from religion to faith, from myth to gospel.[3]

There is plenty of violence in biblical literature. These are obviously troubled texts, but what troubles them is the truth. Myths exist to spare us the trouble. The greatness of the Hebrew Scriptures lies in the candor with which they document a struggle between Israel's dependence on a system of sacralized power and violence and its moral and theological ambivalence about the workings of such a system. This tension fairly defines the religious life of biblical Israel. Eric Gans has perceptively described the Hebrew Bible as a "discovery procedure" whose larger relevance is that the discovery it undertakes is "a global moral revelation."[4] Moral revelations, by their very nature, are rarely morally uplifting. Discovery procedures as serious and as sustained as the one that takes place in the Bible exist only because something in these texts has managed to survive both the mythologizing tendencies of the authors of the texts and the pious expectations of their readers. If any literary artifacts might be deemed "divinely inspired," perhaps it is those texts that reveal what neither their authors nor their readers wish to have revealed.

The story that the Hebrew Bible tells is both grand and garish; it is both utterly unique and perfectly typical. It is both fictional and factual, and a fair amount of it is the kind of amalgamation of hoary fact and lionizing fancy that characterizes legendary literature. As with myths and the literary vestiges of myth, however, even those biblical passages whose strict historicity is most doubtful were not, as Martin Buber put it, "born at the writing desk." Whatever historical figure or figures lie behind, say, the biblical Moses or Joshua, and however the accounts of their trials and exploits may have been embroidered in the retelling, that historical kernels lie behind these accounts should not be doubted. To get at these kernels, we will sometimes have to handle the texts in which they occur a little more roughly than conventional piety is accustomed to handling them. Compared to mythological materials, however, the biblical literature fairly cries out, inviting the reader to strip away whatever weak and clumsy myth might obscure a view of its historical rudiments.

As an account of a people's origins and destiny, the Bible is the world's most striking example of a non-myth, not because those who produced these texts renounced the impulse to mythologize their violence, but because something operating in the consciousness of this people made them very clumsy myth-makers. The true biblical spirit works like a lie detector. It magnifies subtle signals of nervous anxiety that always accompany the Bible's attempt to speak mythologically, and it turns these signals into a proof against the textual obfuscations that accompanied them. In many ways, the Hebrew Bible is one long account of how a people averse to myth and disenchanted with primitive religion strove with only intermittent success to find an amalgam of myth and religion with which they could sustain their cultural enterprise. The intentions of the original authors and editors of these texts no doubt varied, but if it was religious devotion they strove to awaken, what they wrought was something much more complex and contradictory. To try to make a morally reassuring manual of religious piety out of these texts requires either a mighty editing effort or a mighty interpretive one. Both have been tried. Some have tried, either by discrete omission or by scissors and paste, to make the Bible into a nicer book. Some, for laudable reasons, have chosen to read the most troubling texts allegorically. The ultimate fruit of such labors is a tame and agreeable text capable of flattering, but not flabbergasting, the modern mind. It's been flattered enough.

The complaint that the revelation of an infinitely loving, merciful, and nonviolent God is too often obscured by the biblical representations of a god who is hardly more than a synonym for delusion and mob violence misses the point. It is a complaint based on the misunderstanding of the true anthropological and spiritual significance of the biblical literature. One can sympathize with the efforts to keep some of these texts from having the dubious effects they have occasionally had in a world where a nostalgia of sacred violence is still strong. If history has shown that an overly pious reading of these texts can awaken that nostalgia, it has more recently shown that we will never be cured of that nostalgia by abandoning these troubling texts in favor of more superficially edifying ones. There is a struggle within the biblical texts between the mesmerizing power of sacred violence and the realization that Israel's God was the champion of the weak, the outcast, and the victims. This struggle is not one of the Bible's ironic peculiarities; it is *the* essence of the Bible. The crisis into which our world is now sliding is nothing less than the latest stage of that struggle. Speaking of the Judeo-Christian Scriptures, Andrew McKenna has said: "We do not read them, they read us, and our task in attempting to understand these texts is to understand ourselves as well as they do."[5]

As I have said, Buber was right to insist that the Bible's spiritual discoveries were not born at the writing desk. Often they are discoveries made in the midst, not only of historical defeat, but in the midst of moral and spiritual failures as well. Girard, in a memorable phrase, has described the Old Testament as a "text in travail." Though a developing theme can be detected in this body of literature, it is not, to quote Girard again, "a chronologically progressive process, but a struggle that advances and retreats."[6]

I am constrained by the scope of this book to limit my discussion of biblical literature to a distressingly few texts. The passages upon which I have chosen to comment are ones that I feel uniquely illuminate the role of the Bible as the original chronicle of humanity's struggle to extricate itself from primitive religion and blood sacrifice and to renounce its dependence on the structures of sacred violence. Contrary to the tendency of most who insist on the value of the biblical literature, in many instances I will go straight to the most troubling texts. I will have ample occasion to point out how this literature tries to sacralize violence and perpetuate the myths that justify it. The mysterious genius of this literature, however, is precisely that an interpreter needs no additional genius in order to see through these efforts to the disturbing violence that they repeatedly fail to camouflage. The texts often provoke a moral shudder in the reader for the same reason that the history of institutional Christianity often provokes a moral shudder in Christians. In each case, the text's justifying mythology is inept and its moral self-disclosures are vivid.

According to the biblical tradition, the essential thing about the human race is that it has fallen. It lives cursed by its own waywardness, insolence, pride, and absurdity. This idea of a fallen humanity has not been a popular one in the modern world, but that is not because the evidence for it has become any less compelling. What we must realize is that the biblical idea of a fall is inextricably linked with the biblical idea of the goodness of creation and the goodness of God. When the Bible says we are fallen creatures, it is saying that the question of what's wrong with the world is really the question about what's wrong with *us*.

The Garden and the Fall

The story of the fall in Genesis is the story of contagious desire, not desire in the romantic or the Freudian sense, but precisely the kind of desire that is awakened by displays of another's desire. The serpent's alluring gesture inspires Eve to see the fruit of the forbidden tree as desirable, as "pleasing to the eye." Behind this desire is the desire to be *God-like,* for the serpent tells Eve that the fruit will make her *like God.* The fall, then, involves two things: mimetic desire for the fruit and mimetic rivalry and resentment toward the divine. The forbidden tree is simply the author's device for making mimetic desire and resentment intelligible in narrative form.[7] Here, then, is the fall: mimetic desire and resentment in a situation in which there is no unsatisfied appetite and only One Transcendent Being against whom resentment might be aroused. It is, one might say, a perfect test case. The "test" that the tree represents is whether or not humans can tolerate even the most innocuous form of self-restraint and even the most beneficent form of transcendence without becoming resentful and rivalrous. If, under these circumstances, we humans chafe and connive for godlikeness and dissemble in our efforts to match or surpass our model/rival, how much more certain is it that we will find whatever social prestige our fellow creatures enjoy a perpetual stumbling block to our happiness and peace of mind. As the book of Wisdom has it:

> ...it was the devil's envy that brought death into the world, as those who are his partners will discover. (Wisd. 2:24)

Even in a situation that is as unconducive to envy, covetousness, and resentment as the Garden of Eden, the serpent's gaudy desire is all that it takes to unhinge the human race and shove it on its grasping and violent "career."

We are creatures "made in God's image." Consciously or otherwise, we shape our lives according to our experience of God or whatever functions as a god for us. It is a truth we may deny, but we will never be able to keep from behaving in ways that validate it. As the prophet Jeremiah put it, once we humans fall into the caldron of mimetic desire, we behave like frantic camels in heat, running in all directions — a frenzied "career" that ends, as Jeremiah points outs, at the sacrificial altar where human victims die (Jer. 2:23–24).

In verse 6 of the third chapter of Genesis, Adam and Eve eat the forbidden fruit. In verse 12, Adam scapegoats Eve: "It was the woman you put with me; *she* gave me some fruit from the tree." In verse 13, Eve scapegoats the serpent: "The *snake* tempted me and I ate." The fallen condition is summed up with breathtaking economy. The story is about how we humans fall into an alien and duplicitous relationship with God and one another because of an inability to be in the presence of the "other" — whether a human other or the divine Other — without succumbing to envy, resentment, guile, and dissembling. Adam and Eve cover their nakedness, now sensing that sexuality is fraught with uncertain dangers, as of course it tends to be in a world saturated with mimetic desire. Whatever the social dangers that sexual appetite might occasion, they are insignificant compared to those created when that appetite is contaminated with mimetic desire. After the fall, physical appetite becomes the slave of metaphysical desire. The fig leaf is by no means incidental. It is both a symptom of the dissembling that accompanies the fall and a symbol for the dangers that sexual attraction entails in a world where the mimetic passions — covetousness, envy, and jealousy — bedevil humanity's sexual relations.

As I said, the Bible's first act of violence is the killing of Abel by his brother Cain. Because siblings offer each other the most readily available models for mimetic desire, they very frequently become mimetic rivals. Myths, legends, and scriptures are filled with stories having to do with siblings in rivalry. Resentment, the product of those passions, is the stuff violence is made of, and in the Cain and Abel story it comes to violence. The Bible's first violence is as clearly the result of *mimetic rivalry* as humanity's fall is the fall into *mimetic desire.* The murder of Abel by Cain happens in chapter 4 of Genesis. Chapter 5 is taken up with a catalogue of patriarchs. In chapter 6 we learn that the earth is now "filled with violence" (6:11). It doesn't take the Bible long to lay before us the human problem.

Sacrificial Substitution: Cain and Abel

In the Cain and Abel story, the conflict reaches its crisis as sacrifices are being made to Yahweh. We're told that Yahweh found Abel's animal sacrifice more pleasing than the first fruits of the harvest that Cain offered. This seems unfair and even historically regressive if we think of an agricultural civilization as an advance over a nomadic one. The crucial issue here, however, is not the author's preference for shepherding over farming. The real issue — of which the ancients were necessarily more aware than we — is that blood sacrifices "worked" whereas those that involved no ritual slaughter often did not. In the Cain and Abel story, a *bloodless* sacrifice failed to resolve the rivalry between the two brothers in the same way that the London hanging in Patmore's poem failed to resolve the rivalry between the two spectators who had "disputed places" and left the hanging "with murderous faces." In both cases, and in others, the way to find out what the purpose of the sacrifice was is to notice what happened when it failed. *The purpose of sacrifice is to prevent what happens when it fails.* The one thing that can be said with utter certainty is that Cain's bloodless offering failed to extinguish his resentment. Like all sacrifices that fail, it exacerbated the tensions it was incapable of dissolving. In the end, the Cain and Abel story provides a parable of the sacrificial dilemma with which the Israelites would wrestle for centuries and with which we are still confronted. Under the cumulative pressure of the biblical revelation, the sacrificial system fails, beginning with its most abominable form, human sacrifice. But attempts to abandon the sacrificial system too abruptly deprive the society in question of its only effective ritual for curing itself of the tensions to which mimetic desire inevitably lead. When the Bible says that Abel's blood sacrifice was pleasing to God, it means that it was religiously and socially effective, whereas Cain's bloodless sacrifice was not.

There is, I feel, a tragic aspect to the story of Cain, similar in many ways to the tragedy that surrounded the life of the biblical Moses. Cain renounced the sacrificial underpinnings of religious and cultural life too casually. His ritual innovation was driven by no discernible moral or religious scruple. Lacking that motivation, his renunciation of sacrifice was accompanied by no heightened sense of moral and religious responsibility. To dispense with sacrificial systems without accepting greater moral and religious responsibility is to follow Cain down a dark road that, in the Bible, led in five generations to Lamech, who declares:

> I killed a man for wounding me,
> a boy for striking me.
> Sevenfold vengeance for Cain,
> but seventy-sevenfold for Lamech.
> (Gen. 4:23–24)

The story of Cain shows what the history of the twentieth century shows, namely, that if we dispense with the sacrificial structures upon which religion and culture have for so long depended without at the same time renouncing the mimetic passions that made these structures necessary in the first place, then sooner or later we will become murderers. Does this mean that we must tolerate existing sacrificial structures that we find morally offensive? Emphatically not. It was Nietzsche who argued — against the biblical tradition — that we must summon the resolve to perform acts of sacrificial violence for which we may feel a moral repugnance. It is crucial to note that Cain does not renounce the sacrificial conventions of his day as morally repugnant and religiously meaningless, as do the later Hebrew prophets. There is ample biblical warrant for believing that humanity *can* learn to live without its sacrificial apparatus, and it seems to me that the pace at which we should try to do so ought always to be determined by genuine moral or religious promptings. Only in light of such promptings can we be reasonably confident that the effort required to live with fewer sacrificial structures will be made. For if we are to live without such structures, we will have to be able to renounce conflictual desires and abstain from the kind of social melodramas whose worst consequences the sacrificial system averts.

As obvious as it is, it has often been overlooked that the story of Cain revolves around the anthropological problem of sacrifice, just as the story of the fall revolves around the anthropological issue of mimetic desire and mimetic rivalry. Like many of the Bible's major themes, however, it is only as these themes recur ever and again throughout the Bible that one begins fully to realize their centrality. The story of Cain, for instance, doesn't really become fully intelligible until we get to the story of Abraham and Isaac. So let me turn to that.

Abraham and Isaac

Far more than we moderns generally realize, human sacrifice was a fact of life among the peoples of the ancient Near East in tension with whom Israel first achieved cultural self-definition. Israel's renunciation of the practice of human sacrifice took place over a long period of time, during which intermittent reversions to it occurred. No biblical story better depicts how the Bible is at cross-purposes with itself on the subject of sacrifice than does the story of Abraham and Isaac. Like the fall story, the story of Abraham's (non)sacrifice of Isaac can easily be obstructed by the story's narrative armature. And in the same way that the author of the Suffering Servant Songs in Second Isaiah remained too enmeshed in the sacrificial logic to give a perfectly lucid account of the fate of the Suffering Servant, so in one glaring instance that same logic obscured the insight of the author and redactors who gave us the story of Abraham's non-sacrifice of Isaac. As a result, the religious emphasis is just slightly off center, but in a way that makes all the difference. We are told that God bestowed the blessing and promise on Abraham after the "test" on Mount Moriah because Abraham had been willing to do what God had intervened to keep him from doing — sacrificing his son. This understanding may have had a certain coherence in the dark world of human sacrifice to which it hearkens back, and it may have some psychological pertinence, but the true biblical spirit has little nostalgia for the sacrificial past and almost no interest in psychology. What we must try to see in the story of Abraham's non-sacrifice of Isaac is that Abraham's faith consisted, not of almost doing what he didn't do, but of *not* doing what he almost did, and not doing it in fidelity to the God in whose name his contemporaries thought it should be done.

The central issue of the story of Abraham's substitution of a ram for Isaac is precisely that, the issue of substitution. Abraham renounces human sacrifice and "inaugurates" the ritual substitution of animals for humans. Anthropologically, attempts like that of Cain to substitute non-blood sacrifices for blood sacrifices obviously occurred long after the substitution of animal for human victims such as occurs in the story of Abraham and Isaac. Nevertheless, the existing sequence of the two stories is extremely propitious.

Cain's ritual innovation is too casually made. His alternative to blood sacrifice was inspired by neither a moral nor a religious imperative. This, in my opinion, is how the failure of Cain's sacrifice is best understood. The sacrificial innovation undertaken for neither moral nor religious reasons fails, and the failure results in fratricide. Since Cain's alternative sacrifice had no moral mandate, it had no religious effect. By contrast, the story of Abraham's renunciation of human sacrifice is suffused with moral concerns, and it proved to be both religiously and anthropologically effective. It was Abraham, and not Cain, who took the Bible's first great step toward the renunciation of sacrifice. Seemingly more modest by comparison with Cain's complete rejection of blood sacrifice, Abraham's substitution of a ram for the human victim represents a more "realistic" step in humanity's historic dismantling of its sacred systems of sacrificial violence.

The Bible's way of acknowledging the significance of what Abraham did is to regard him as the father of faith and to declare that in due course the whole human race ("all the nations") would become the "heirs" of Abraham, his religious descendants. For Abraham performed the quintessentially biblical act: he renounced a form of sacrifice that had become morally intolerable, *and* he did so in the name of the God whom his contemporaries thought was requiring them to perform the outmoded sacrifice. In sharp contrast to Cain, Abraham's alteration of the sacrificial system was driven by both moral and religious imperatives. Those who renounce sacrificial arrangements for more superficial reasons run the risk that Cain ran, and those who refuse to renounce them even after a moral and religious aversion for them has awakened risk succumbing to the morally numbing nihilism that Nietzsche espoused.

The biblical narratives don't merely insist on abandoning the use of human victims in favor of animal victims. They insist, as the Abraham and Isaac story does, on calling attention to the fact that the animal is a surrogate victim slain on behalf of a designated human victim. The presence of designated human victims, for whom animals were no doubt sometimes substituted only at the last minute (as in the Abraham and Isaac story), significantly heightened the intensity of the rite of animal sacrifice. At the same time that the proximity of the designated human victim was lending the ritual its riveting power, the substitution of an animal surrogate was reminding Israel of its moral superiority over its historical contemporaries, whose sacrificial fires smoked all too regularly with the flesh of human victims. Paradoxically, the fact that the liturgy *might* revert to human sacrifice lent the ritual the degree of intensity necessary to insure that it would conclude *without* reverting to human sacrifice.

As more resilient and durable cultural institutions evolved, virtually every ancient culture sooner or later began replacing human sacrifice with animal sacrifice. What is unique about the Hebrew experience is that this transition from human to animal sacrifice occurred in response to *moral* and *religious* imperatives. In Israel, as elsewhere, other social rituals whose effect was human sacrifice — such as wars and public executions — continued, as they do, of course, today. But if the biblical mill grinds slowly, it grinds exceedingly well. Sooner or later these ritual vestiges of human sacrifice will become as morally incomprehensible as those ancient ones upon which we now look with such horror and bewilderment. As these residual sacrificial systems break down and lose their moral and political legitimacy, if we do not learn to live without their protection, we will have dismantled them only to stand naked before the catastrophe they existed to ward off.

In the background of virtually every biblical narrative is a cultural crisis — latent or full-blown — associated with a sacrificial system whose mythological power was waning and whose rituals were malfunctioning. This is the real greatness of the biblical literature. Since we are living in the later stages of the same epochal process whose first stages the biblical literature so vividly portrays, we have every reason to try to understand the nature and overall direction of the anthropological revolution these texts both launched and documented. Obviously, a thorough and detailed review of the Bible is beyond the scope of this book. In what follows I will try to highlight the nature of the historical and religious process in relation to which the individual biblical texts take on their greatest significance. Inasmuch as the anthropological and religious backdrop against which biblical literature becomes intelligible is essentially the same backdrop against which our own cultural crisis is being played out, the following excursion into the Bible is just another way of taking a closer look at our own perplexing dilemma.

Moses and the Commandments

The fall story, Cain's murder of Abel, Abraham's discovery that the God who had beckoned him to a strange land was not to be worshiped in blood — these are the legends that serve as an overture to the grand and grating symphony of the Hebrew Scriptures. The rest of the book of Genesis recounts the lives of Israel's ancestral figures. It is with the figure of the biblical Moses, however, that the story of Israel's historical journey really begins. The Bible not only assumes that such a man existed; it tells much about him. I don't know if he existed, but there can be little doubt that the stories of him in the Hebrew Bible are rooted in historical experience and that that historical experience has unparalleled anthropological and religious significance. If by quibbling over the *exact* historicity of these texts, we devalue the incomparable anthropological chronicle they represent, our historical scrupulosity will have backfired, and our determination to discover the human past will have served only to bury it again, this time under exegetical details. In an effort to remain loyal to the paramount anthropological task, I will in general accept the biblical texts — even those that are obviously legendary — as historically reliable.

The Exodus story is both rich in detail and pregnant with implications for our own time. And yet there is an internal tension within the story, a tension between Israel's determined effort to emancipate itself from the stifling world of the primitive sacred and its inability to sustain its own cultural cohesion without some vestiges of the sacral system. Just as the story of the "fall" and the murder of Cain in the book of Genesis highlights the essential anthropological issues of mimesis and sacrifice and hints at their interrelationship, so the dramatic story in the book of Exodus of the founding events that brought biblical Israel into existence encapsulates the historical and religious struggle the Bible documents.

Just as Abraham glanced up to see a ram caught in a thicket, Moses glanced up and saw Egyptian society caught in a violent sacrificial crisis. Many people were dying. The specter of death was palpable. Moses seized the interpretive possibilities this situation provided as deftly as Abraham seized the ram on Mount Moriah. If the "Passover" meal inaugurates Israelite culture under Moses, then Israel's founding event was not an act of sacrificial violence, but an act of Mosaic interpretation. Just as the biblical God created the world, not violently, but by speaking, the Bible's first political leader created culture, not by sacralizing his own community's mob violence, but by interpreting violence unleashed by others. Whatever the nature of the violence from which the Hebrews in Egypt cowered in dwellings whose doors were marked in blood to ward it off, and whatever might have kept that violence from taking its anticipated toll of Hebrew lives, the violence that accompanied Israel's initial act of cultural self-consciousness was not committed by those who discovered their religious identity under its pall. The fact that Moses interpreted the violence as the work of Yahweh is a "myth" in one sense, but it is not mythological in the way in which I am using that term. It was not an attempt to camouflage *Hebrew founding violence.* Rather, it was a way of giving Yahweh the credit for the fact that some of the Hebrews managed to escape from the violence of their oppressors.

When Moses and the former Egyptian slaves reached Sinai, they had only the most rudimentary sense of common purpose. With nothing but a reinterpreted harvest festival for a ritual and with little more than campfire stories for a common heritage, Moses first tried to give social coherence to the refugees whose leader he had become by fashioning a code of ethical behavior, the ten commandments. These commandments, listed in Exodus 20, are lofty, original, and morally demanding. They are strikingly lacking in ritual prescriptions. In terms of mimetic desire, this set of commands is remarkably sophisticated.[8] So sophisticated is it, in fact, that in its final injunction it forbids not only rivalrous and violent behavior but the covetousness that gives rise to the rivalry and violence. The last commandment is this:

> You shall not covet your neighbor's house. You shall not covet your neighbor's wife, or his servant, man or woman, or his ox, or his donkey, or anything that is his. (Exod. 20:17)

H. L. Ellison wrote of this injunction against covetousness that "it is not wanting more that is condemned, but wanting it *at the expense of others.*"[9] In a perceptive comment about covetousness, C. K. Barrett shows that while the last commandment explicitly prohibits only the forms of mimetic desire most likely to lead to violence, it is easy enough to recognize beneath these specified transgressions the larger and looming problem of mimetic desire itself. Barrett says:

> It is of course wrong to desire one's neighbor's wife; but behind this guilty desire, shown to be guilty by its object, lies a desire which is guilty *in itself,* independently of its object, and sinful though quite possibly respectable.[10]

Rabbinical interpretations of the Hebrew Scriptures frequently give special attention to the first and last items in a sequence of texts or a list of proscriptions. When this interpretive procedure is applied to the ten commandments, the two commandments highlighted are the injunction to have only God as a god — "I am Yahweh your God . . . you shall have no other gods" — and to forswear conflictual or rivalistic mimesis — "Thou shalt not covet." For the most part, the intervening commandments address the social and religious repercussions of failing to obey the first and last commandments. Were the commandments insisting on true transcendence and condemning mimetic rivalry to be universally obeyed, the social order would be relieved of those aggravated passions that lead to social deterioration, to a demand for victims, and, eventually, to sacrificial religion. The New Testament summation of the commandments — to love God and to love one's neighbor as oneself — expands, in effect, the first and last commandment in Exodus 20 in such a way that the intervening commandments are subsumed in them. We are mimetic creatures, of course, and so eliminating mimesis is impossible. Without it, humanity would not exist. But the humanity that does exist has soaked the earth with blood, and the prohibition against the most destructive forms of mimetic desire is a worthy attempt to reduce the violence. But we haven't a prayer of eliminating the worst of the mimetic passions unless we find a truly transcendent focus for our deepest imitative urges, our deepest "desires." I suppose one could say: without prayer, we haven't a prayer. That's why the first commandment must be taken into consideration in trying to come to grips with the last one. It is also why it *is* the first one. It is an insistence that we "desire" and have as our ultimate model the One in whose image and likeness we are made, to use the biblical idiom for expressing something almost too profound for expression.

The Demand for Ritual

The Moses we first meet in the biblical accounts is a man morally incensed by the plight of the slave laborers with whom he feels an affinity. After many years of compelled and demeaning drudgery in an alien culture, whatever common religious and cultural traditions these dispirited Semites might have once shared have been almost completely lost. For his part, Moses initially seems little interested in religious matters. It is moral concerns he has. The first act in what would later become his role as liberator was to kill a cruel Egyptian slave driver. It was a clumsy and futile attempt to counter violence with violence, and it was clearly motivated, not by religious concerns, but by social justice ones. According to the biblical account, then, it was only when Moses fled from Egypt to Midian and married a woman whose father was a Midianite priest that he was first exposed to the semi-nomadic religiosity of the kind that he was later to fashion into the Yahwist tradition of biblical Israel. I think it is not without significance for our understanding of Moses, therefore, to note that his empathy for victims and his passion for liberation existed prior to his exposure to and interest in cult religion.

Furthermore, the cultic aspects of Midianite religiosity seem to have made little impact on Moses. He encountered the divine, not at Jethro's Midian shrine, but as a voice calling to him in the wilderness from a burning bush. It was in solitude, far from the shrine and rituals of Jethro, that Moses experienced the God he spent his life trying to place at the center of Israel's cultural enterprise. Asked to reveal his identity, the divine voice said simply: "I am who am." It was not the god of mountains or thunder or rain or fertility that Moses met, nor was it the local god of the Midianites. The God whom Moses came to know in the wilderness was a God whose name is an emphatic form of the verb "to be." This was a God heedless of worldly power, who chose as agents in history the social underclass. The greatness and the tragedy of Moses consist, I feel, in the fact that he strove to put the elusive God who empathized with losers at the center of a culture that would have to win in order to survive. He gave the Hebrew people a God with an empathy for the lowly and downtrodden, a God whose most defining feature was a refusal to be defined, a God openly hostile to the kind of cult idolatry that was synonymous with the conventional religious life of the age.. Moses' God was a God wary of religion.

Be that as it may, however, when Moses had distilled his burning bush experience and his Mount Sinai experience into the religious and moral code and proposed that code to his followers, he had enough respect for the power of sacrificial religion to commemorate their ratification of it sacrificially. The sacrificial ritual he performed, however, was little more than a method for insuring obedience to the commandments by endowing them with religious solemnity. Clearly, the moral code Moses proposed did not emerge from the ritual; rather the ritual was the afterthought with which the code was clumsily ratified. It was a crude ritual in which copious amounts of blood from the sacrificed animals were splashed on the altar and the people.

Moses made the same mistake that Cain made, but he didn't make it in exactly the same way. Whereas Cain had discarded blood sacrifice, Moses seems originally to have simply performed careless and unconvincing versions of it. Moses' sacrificial rite amounted to very much what Cain's amounted to. Its cathartic effect was only temporary. When Moses withdrew to the mountain to consult Yahweh, the demand for cult rituals quickly surfaced, and Moses' brother Aaron accommodated the demand. Before the effigy of the Canaanite fertility god the people bowed down and then ate and drank and "amused themselves," a euphemism for the sort of sexual orgy that typically accompanied rituals dedicated to fertility gods. Descending the mountain, Moses heard the chants of pagan religion. Cain had tried to renounce blood sacrifices too prematurely. In his own way, by taking blood sacrifice for granted, by resorting to it casually, Moses had underestimated the power and meaning of sacrificial religion as much as Cain had. Cain became a murderer, and Moses had made Cain's basic mistake.

> When Moses saw the people so out of hand — for Aaron had allowed them to lapse into idolatry with enemies all round them — he stood at the gate of the camp and shouted, "Who is for Yahweh? To me!" And all the sons of Levi rallied to him. And he said to them, "This is the message of Yahweh, the God of Israel, 'Gird on your sword, every man of you, and quarter the camp from gate to gate, killing one his brother, another his friend, another his neighbor.' " The sons of Levi carried out the command of Moses, and of the people about three thousand men perished that day. "Today" Moses said "you have won yourselves investiture as priests of Yahweh at the cost, one of his son, another of his brother; and so he grants you a blessing today." (Exod. 32:25–29)

Three thousand people killed in a violent mêlée. This is an example of the astonishing candor of scriptural literature. The candor of the text is candor about the *failure* of Moses, and to read it otherwise is to reinforce the feeble myth of sacred violence that the Bible undermines in spite of itself. Just as Aaron had accommodated the people's demand for an idol by insisting that the idol be called Yahweh, Moses took control of the sacrificial frenzy of the golden calf episode, channeled its violence, deputized the executioners, and proclaimed the violence that brought the riot to an end to be Yahweh's violence. It is extremely important to notice that the violence accompanying the golden calf episode ended with the inauguration of an Israelite priesthood, whose task thereafter would be the maintenance of the cult of animal sacrifice, but whose priestly initiation consisted of slaughtering "one his son, another his brother." To kill one's brother is to repeat Cain's crime, and to kill one's son is to rescind Abraham's religious innovation.

Moses had tried to launch a cultural enterprise by enunciating a lofty religious ideal—a God so wary of idolatry that his first prohibition was against "graven images"—and by issuing a demanding set of moral admonitions. By way of what seems more or less a cultic afterthought, the ritual he used to ratify the covenant with Yahweh and the new moral code was one that combined an ancient Semitic ritual with a few clumsy and gratuitous sacrificial gestures. Moses' God was the God of the burning bush, a God wary of religion. The moral code Moses espoused was one that might dampen the mimetic passions of its adherents to the point where they might able to recognize this God. But the cultic vacuum he left was filled in due course with a Canaanite fertility ritual. Moses' violent reaction against revival of pagan idolatry was accompanied by the informal institution of an Israelite cult, and the priests who were given control over the cult rituals were the Levites who had played the key role in the violence that ended the Canaanite revival.

When Moses had first realized that the Israelites had lapsed into pagan idolatry, he threw down the tablets of the original covenant and smashed them. The casual assumption is that the breaking of the original code was impetuous and inadvertent, but that is not what the text says. Especially in light of later developments, Moses' act seems to have represented a *decision,* a very practical one. The breaking of the tablets on which the original commandments were written leads to the creation of a second covenantal code, which is delineated in Exodus 34.[11] The second set of commandments is introduced this way:

> Yahweh said to Moses, "Cut two tablets of stone like the first ones and come up to me on the mountain, and I will inscribe on them the words that were on the first tablets, which you broke." (Exod. 34:1)

The original code is now to be replaced, and there is every indication that the replacement will be a facsimile of the original. By asserting the identity between the two codes, the authors and redactors of the text have made it all but impossible for the reader to miss the obvious fact that they are utterly different. The new set of commandments is completely preoccupied with the maintenance of rituals and cultic procedures.

> All that first issues from the womb is mine... You must not offer the blood of the victim sacrificed to me at the same time as you offer unleavened bread, nor is the victim offered at the feast of Passover to be put aside for the following day... You must not boil a kid in its mother's milk. (Exod. 34:18, 19, 25, 26)

"All that first issues from the womb is mine," is a sweeping demand that the first-born be sacrificed. It is a demand that sometimes occurs, ominously, without qualification, but in this text the all-important exception is duly noted: "You must redeem all the first-born of your sons." This redemption involved a double substitution. First, the sacrificial priest took the place of the first-born, and then the sacrificial animal he offered on the altar took his place. Not only was the priest the divine executioner, but he was also the designated victim in whose place the actual victim died as his substitute. Should the sacrificial ritual break down, however, the substitution might be abrogated and the priest himself die. The priest was, therefore, Abel as well as Cain, Isaac as well as Abraham. That the system of sacrificial substitutions was a delicate one is clear from the intense scrupulosity with which the ritual procedures were followed. Any little mistake might lead to a collapse of the intricate system of replacement and result in a human death or in a ritual meltdown, giving way to social crisis. For a textbook on how to take liturgical care under such precarious circumstances, the book of Leviticus is available.

The Institution of the Scapegoat

The journey from the careless ritual afterthought with which Moses tried to ratify the first covenant to the mind-boggling sacrificial apparatus that gradually became Israel's religious preoccupation is not exactly edifying. It is of tremendous anthropological significance, however, because it helps document the slow and painstaking process by which the sacrificial system must be repudiated. The elaborate proscriptions and prescriptions that grew up around Israel's sacrificial cult played a role in the life of ancient Israel comparable in many ways to the role of legislative and political reform in the history of Western culture. That is to say, Israel's religious system was as unstable as the West's social and political system has been, and for the same reason: neither ever found a sacrificial formula that was both morally tolerable and riveting enough to have sustainable social benefits. The unstable nature of Israel's cult of animal sacrifice made it even more imperative that the ritual prescriptions be carried out with meticulous care, lest the priest lose control of the ritual violence. The danger the priests faced is easily deduced from the texts that describe the precautions Aaron and his sons had to take before approaching the altar. Note, for instance, the fastidious care required of Aaron and the priests as they vested themselves prior to a sacrificial ritual.

> And you shall make the robe of the ephod all of blue... On its skirts... bells of gold.... And it shall be upon Aaron when he ministers, and its sound shall be heard when he goes into the holy place before the LORD, and when he comes out, *lest he die.*
>
> And you shall make a plate of pure gold, and engrave on it, like the engraving of a signet, "Holy to the LORD." And you shall fasten it on the turban by a lace of blue; it shall be upon Aaron's forehead, and *Aaron shall take upon himself any guilt* incurred in the holy offering which the people of Israel hallow as their holy gifts; it shall always be upon his forehead, that they may be accepted before the LORD.
>
> And for Aaron's sons you shall make coats and girdles and caps; you shall make them for glory and beauty. And you shall put them upon Aaron your brother, and upon his sons with him, and shall anoint them and ordain them and consecrate them, that they may serve me as priests. And you shall make for them linen breeches to cover their naked flesh; from the loins to the thighs they shall reach; and they shall be upon Aaron, and upon his sons, when they go into the tent of meeting, or when they come near the altar to minister in the holy place; *lest they bring guilt upon themselves and die.* (Exod. 28:31, 33, 35–38, 40–43 RSV; emphasis added)

Surely such precautions would not have been taken had experience not dictated the need for them. If the Hebrew priests vested themselves for the sacrificial liturgy like members of a bomb squad preparing to defuse a ticking bomb, it was for good reason. It was the priests who would "bring guilt upon themselves and die" should the ritual get out of control. Nor were precautions taken against such a dire outcome always successful. There are a number of Old Testament texts that suggest that ritual meltdowns led to violence. Perhaps the most dramatic of these texts is the story of the death of Aaron's two sons, both of whom died in the course of their priestly duties. The passage describing the event is as brief as it is pregnant with innuendo:

> Aaron's sons Nadab and Abihu took their censers, put fire in them and added incense; and they offered unauthorized fire before the LORD, contrary to his command. So fire came out from the presence of the LORD

and consumed them, and they died before the LORD. Moses then said to Aaron, "This is what the LORD spoke of when he said:

> 'Among those who approach me
> I will show myself holy;
> in the sight of all the people
> I will be honored.' "

Aaron remained silent.

(Lev. 10:1–3, NIV)

Says one earnest biblical scholar, referring to the liturgical indiscretion of Aaron's sons, "It is difficult to determine the exact nature of their sin."[12] Indeed it is. Even when it tries to mythologize its violence, the Hebrew Bible is inadvertently frank about the arbitrariness of the violence and remarkably clumsy at establishing the victim's guilt. The only hint of the priests' culpability that the text offers is a vague suggestion that they lit their censers from the wrong source. There has been a historical tendency to read such enigmatic passages allegorically. As well-intentioned as it might be, however, an allegorical reading of texts such as this is a betrayal of their true biblical significance.

"Aaron remained silent," the text tells us. The haunting encounter between Moses and Aaron is a study in the tension between biblical revelation and mythological mystification, but symbolically and structurally it represents an immensely important moment in the anthropological experiment Moses had launched. Aaron's silence — whether an act of deference for the sacred or an act of social realism — made it possible to preserve the sacrificial system, early Israel's only bulwark against chaos and violence. But by remaining silent, Aaron in effect abrogated the religious revolution inaugurated by Abraham's substitution of an animal for his son. At this ritual, in place of the animal victim — or in addition to it — the priest's sons have been slain, and no word was spoken in rebuttal. The voice that Abraham heard on Mount Moriah was silenced. The voice that would have spoken on behalf of victims was squelched. The hush of myth hovers for a moment over the biblical world.

After this episode, and as a telling example of its likely effects on the religious cult, the text abandons its narrative structure in favor of a catalogue of cultic recipes and prescriptions for discerning the clean from the unclean. At the conclusion of this section of Leviticus (chapters 11–16) the institution of the "scapegoat" ritual occurs. In this rite, two goats are chosen, lots are cast to determine which of them will be dedicated to Yahweh — sacrificed in atonement for sin — and which will be sent into the desert, the haunt of the demon Azazel. In the Latin translation of the

Bible, "the goat sent out" became *caper emmissarius,* in the vernacular languages, "the scapegoat." The significance of this ritual can be fully comprehended only when we take note of the first verse of the passage that describes it:

> *After the death of the two sons of Aaron* who died through offering unlawful fire before Yahweh, Yahweh spoke to Moses. (Lev. 16:1–2a)

We do not need this verse to tell us that the death of the sons of Aaron has happened prior to this; the textual sequence is all we need on that score. This verse alerts the reader to a cause-and-effect relationship between the death of the two priests and the scapegoat atonement ritual. The scapegoat ritual is a liturgical innovation specifically designed to avoid the kind of sacrificial frenzy that led to the death of the two priests. The ritual in which they died was itself an atonement ritual in which copious animal sacrifices were offered in what seems to have been a desperate effort to appease Yahweh and avoid divine punishments that would otherwise come due. Any ritual innovation aimed at preventing a recurrence of such a crisis would have to relieve the community of part of its sense of impurity and the load of guilt associated with it. This is precisely what the scapegoat ritual does. A ritual innovation is required because, beyond a certain point, religious scrupulosity becomes a counter-productive response to anxiety and guilt. The greater Israel's scrupulosity, the greater the number of prohibitions. The greater the number of prohibitions, the greater the chances of violating them inadvertently, and therefore the greater the anxiety and the more determined the scrupulosity. It is a vicious cycle in which sacrificial religious systems are forever being caught. St. Paul's linking of the Law with death in his New Testament letters is an amazing untangling of precisely this vicious cycle.

Chapter 8

Crossing the Jordan Opposite Jericho

> There is a foundational violence behind every sacrificial cult. After a certain period of time, a foundational murder loses its binding power and a mimetic crisis is kindled that sacrifices cannot assuage; ultimately, that crisis generates a new foundational murder. Each new foundational violence begins a new sacrificial cycle that endures until the sacred power of the foundation has evaporated.[1]
>
> René Girard

The prologue to John's Gospel says something apropos of the Bible as a whole when it says that "the light shines in the darkness." This does not simply mean that the light has managed to successfully fend off the darkness. Rather, it means that the crucifixion has actually turned the world's darkness into an agent of revelation. "The light shines *in* the darkness." Once we understand this, it is clear how misplaced are the efforts to apply the tar brush and the gold leaf to biblical texts. These texts impugn themselves and redeem themselves so much more powerfully than do their detractors and defenders that the task of being one or the other is always a little comic.

Israel's historical experience was that failure and defeat were neither impediments to a relationship with its God nor fatal to its historical mission. Though it took Israel's religious geniuses centuries to draw out the profound implications, it is clear enough in retrospect that Israel's God was a God who saw the world upside down, a God who had a special regard for those reckoned as worthless in terms of wealth, prestige, and power. Obviously, a people with this particular heritage will operate the mechanisms of sacrificial or scapegoating violence at something of a disadvantage, and the text suggest that Israel's sacrificial apparatus was under constant strain. Typically, the first sign that a sacrificial system is losing its effectiveness is the existence of social tensions that the ordinary sacrificial rituals are unable to resolve. As Israel groped for sacrificial solutions to its social tensions, and as its ritual forms of sacrifice proved either too volatile to be confined within ritual boundaries or insufficiently cathartic to drain away social tensions, Moses and then Joshua found it necessary to augment ritual sacrifice with violent quasi-ritual purges of dissidents and holy wars against external enemies. The texts that describe this shift in Israel's sacrificial center of gravity are invaluable for understanding the relationship between violence, religion, and culture.

One of the most revealing of these accounts is the story in the book of Numbers of a breakaway group of Levites, led by Korah, who challenge the leadership of Moses and Aaron. Specifically, their challenge is directed to the exclusive rights and privileges of the ordained priesthood under Aaron. To decide the matter, Moses orders a liturgical showdown. Moses says to Korah:

> "Tomorrow morning Yahweh will reveal who is his, who is the consecrated man that he will allow to come near him. The one he allows to come near is the one whom he has chosen.... You and all your followers, come tomorrow into the presence of Yahweh, you and they, and Aaron too. Let every man bring his censer, put incense in it, and carry his censer before Yahweh — two hundred and fifty censers. You and Aaron also, each of you bring a censer." So every man took his censer, filled it with fire, and put incense in it. (Num. 16:5, 16–18)

Astonishingly, this story makes clear that the controversy within the Israelite community over leadership will be settled according to which of the contending parties manages to shroud the liturgical scene with the thickest cloud of incense. Anthropologically, the underlying question Moses and Korah are raising is who can more persuasively lend religious legitimacy to the violence that each is prepared to unleash. This is one of those priceless texts that allow us to see how intimately religion, violence, and culture are bound together.

Of the opposing forces, the one that will eventually control the political life of Israel is the one able to choreograph the most intoxicating liturgical spectacle. From a symbolic point of view, it is fitting that so much emphasis is placed in this and many of the surrounding texts on the smoke of incense and its role in the rituals. The censer is one of those amazing symbols that allows us to see the key feature of the cultural and religious problematic. Like the cloud of Yahweh's glory that so often accompanies divine epiphanies in these stories, the cloud of incense — with which it is somewhat synonymous — stands as a marvelously apt symbol for the mystifying concealments of sacred violence. Without such mystifications, the violence they envelop could not have been religiously distinguished from the violence it countermanded.

The rebels, of course, lose the liturgical contest. At first, even biblical history is written by the winners.[2] Just before the story reaches its climax, Moses solemnly assures the assembly that what is about to happen was not his doing but Yahweh's. He then warns everyone to stand clear of the dwelling of Korah. This "dwelling" translates the Hebrew word *miskan,* the usual term for the sacred tabernacle. It may indicate that Korah and his followers had set up a rival shrine and performed rituals that conflicted with those presided over by the Aaronic priesthood. Almost every verse in these texts confronts the attentive reader with the fact that, in the world into which he is peering, religion and violence are indistinguishable. Moses passes solemn religious judgment on the dissidents and interprets the violence they are about to suffer as having Yahweh's warrant—two dramatic announcements whose effect on an agitated crowd an experienced leader might have predicted:

> The moment he finished saying all these words, the ground split open under their feet, the earth opened its mouth and swallowed them, their families too, and all Korah's men and all their belongings.
>
> They went down alive to Sheol, they and all their possessions. The earth closed over them and they disappeared from the midst of the assembly. At their cries all the Israelites around them ran away. For they said, "The earth must not swallow us!"
>
> A fire came down from Yahweh and consumed the two hundred and fifty men carrying incense. (Num. 16:31–35)

The lines blurred by the rebellion have now apparently been redrawn. At this point it would seem that matters have returned to normal, with the leadership of Moses and Aaron once again secure. But "as early as the next morning," the liturgical spell seems to have worn off.

> On the following day, the entire community of the sons of Israel grumbled against Moses and Aaron, saying, "*You* have brought death to the people of Yahweh." As the community was banding together against Moses and Aaron, these turned toward the Tent of Meeting, and there was the Cloud covering it, and the glory of Yahweh appeared. (Num. 16:41–42)

Before the killing began, Moses had insisted that "Yahweh himself has sent me to perform all these tasks and that *it is not my doing.*" (Num. 16:28) Only as long as that assertion remains plausible can Moses unleash violence without arousing the spirit of revenge. *Sacred violence is violence that leaves no spirit of revenge in its wake.* All merely human violence fascinates, scandalizes, spins out of control, or provokes a vengeful response. If the violence he orchestrates is to restore order, Moses must appear to be but the human instrument and not the human initiator of it.

A striking contemporary parallel to this caught my eye as I read a July 31, 1992, newspaper account of the Serbian campaign of "ethnic cleansing" undertaken by Serbian nationalists in areas the Serb army had conquered.[3] What caught my eye and reminded me of Moses telling the people that the violence was Yahweh's doing and not his was the following:

> Asked if the Serbs ever explained their motivation, one Muslim who had been on the train responded: "They told us nothing. They just said this is politics doing things to you, it is not us."

"Politics" is a very poor substitute for "Divine Wrath," but, alas, it is all most perpetrators of sacred violence have left. And it isn't enough. It cannot envelop the violence it tries to justify in a thick enough mist. Whether it is called politics or the wrath of Yahweh, whether in the ancient records of Israel's wilderness wanderings or in the pages of the *New York Times,* the system of sacred violence strives fervently to exempt certain violence from the moral scrutiny that it righteously insists must be applied to all other violence.

In spite of all that Moses had done to surround the violence with ritual and liturgical reassurances and to bestow sacred status on it, dissatisfaction within the Israelite community returned *with a vengeance.* The day after the violence that crushed the rebels, the *entire* community was grumbling. It is the community's unanimity, even more than its murderous mood, that indicates how close Moses had come to becoming its victim. Rebuking Moses, the community said: "*You* have killed the people of the LORD" (RSV). Here is the biblical literature at its paradoxical best. In the midst of a dark episode of sacred violence, the spell is broken. This is the myth of sacred violence publicly confessing its insubstantiality in the midst of a text that, on the surface, seeks to substantiate the myth. It is the biblical revelation outflanking the pious intentions of its own authors and most of its readers. But not quite. This is still very much a text in travail. In the inverted world of biblical anthropology, unanimity inspires suspicion of, rather than confidence in, the unanimous point of view. The fact that the "entire community" accused Moses of killing the dissidents and that it then "banded together against Moses and Aaron" shows how thoroughly the community was caught in the grip of a mimetic contagion, and therefore how predisposed to scapegoating they had become.

Holy War

Like that of every other society of the time, Israel's cultural existence was dependent upon its sacrificial system. What distinguished Israel, however, was the existence of rudimentary but growing moral misgivings that, as they grew, began to undermine the capacity of its sacrificial system to turn social tensions into camaraderie. The institution of the scapegoat ritual described in Leviticus 16 was a particularly striking and carefully designed ritual innovation, but it was only one of many that occurred as Israel began groping for socially effective and religiously compelling sacrificial routines. Most of these innovations seem to have emerged more or less spontaneously out of their accompanying social and religious circumstances. Some were sacrificial possibilities that had existed in a latent form for some time prior to emerging as a familiar part of Israel's sacrificial options. For instance, when Moses descended the mountain and heard the Israelites loudly worshiping the golden calf, we are told that he grew angry because "Aaron had allowed them to lapse into idolatry with enemies all round them." The usual interpretation of this passage is valid, but it doesn't exhaust its meaning. If Moses was exclusively concerned about the Israelites' lack of military preparedness, the speed with which he was able to muster the Levites to arms suggests that his concern was misplaced. Is there another innuendo in this text? I think there is. The text can be read to mean that Aaron had overlooked, not the threat of enemy forces, but the sacrificial opportunities these enemies presented. "The surest, and often the only, way by which a crowd can preserve itself lies in the existence of a second crowd to which it is related," writes Elias Canetti.[4] When such a "crowd" can no longer generate its social solidarity by internal means alone, says Canetti, a counter-crowd may be found against which the first crowd can unite. By "crowd" Canetti simply means any social or cultural entity. What he calls the "two-crowd structure" of social life has been the structural centerpiece of the anthropological epoch to which I have referred as "history" (with quotes).

There was in ancient Israel a predictable tendency to deflect the violence, and whatever proto-violent tensions the priestly rituals were unable to dissolve, toward external enemies. And yet, there comes a point in the biblical narrative when war, and more specifically Holy War, began to serve a sacrificial function augmenting and complementing the more formal rituals with which the priesthood chiefly concerned itself. At this point, the wars that Israel begins to wage are to a considerable extent elaborate sacrificial orgies serving cultic as well as political and military ends. The texts in which this shift occurs allow us to glimpse one of the most important moments in human anthropology, the moment when the faltering religious cult discovers the almost limitless sacrificial possibilities that nearby alien cultures provide. It is the moment when the structures and assumptions we call "history" began to provide Israel with an important sacrificial outlet.

If we need a threshold for distinguishing a predominantly cultic phase of Israel's sacrificial system from a predominantly "historical" phase, then Joshua's crossing of the Jordan river serves remarkably well. The Jordan crossing is a cultural watershed, just as the crossing of the Red Sea on which it is modeled had been an earlier one. One need only look at the first salient episodes in the book of Joshua to see that what has taken place is something far more fundamental than merely a geographical shift from one side of the Jordan river to the other.

Scholars have long noted that the story describing the Jordan crossing and the battle that followed is actually a liturgical text describing a ritual reenactment of the crossing and the destruction of Jericho. From an anthropological point of view, this convergence of original event and ritual reenactment enhances rather than diminishes the text's historical reliability, for it shows how culturally galvanizing the ritualized memory of violent events can be. The most essential phrase in these texts, however, is perhaps the most inconspicuous one of all: "The people crossed opposite Jericho" (Josh. 3:16b). Exegetes, who detect no intentional double entendre here, generally give this phrase scant attention. The word "opposite" translates the Hebrew word *neged,* meaning not just "in front of," but also "in the sight of" or "in the presence of." Beyond whatever spatial reference it might have, the term can also connote that which has become one's focus, the "ground of one's being," one's "ultimate concern," or, in this case, a society's ordering principle. Second Isaiah for instance, in calling Israel back to God, uses a form of this word, *neged,* when he writes:

> All the nations are as nothing *in his presence,*
> for him they count as nothingness and emptiness.
> (Isa. 40:17)

Had the people crossed "opposite" Yahweh, in other words, had they crossed "in the presence of" or "in the sight of" Yahweh, rather than becoming fixated on their historical adversaries, they would have realized that the basic units of history, "the nations," count as nothing in God's sight. All the air would have gone out of their sacred ethnocentrism.

Gerhard von Rad commented upon the shift in Israel's historical focus that occurs at roughly this point in the Bible's chronicle. He drew attention to the "large part which the consideration of other peoples plays" in the texts that treat of events after the wilderness period. He noted that in these texts: "The being and duty of Israel are constantly brought into relation with the existence of other peoples, and with the judgment passed upon them, and their customs and sins."[5] In other words, cultural self-identity becomes indistinguishable from, as von Rad puts it, "a very pressing concern with Israel's existence *over against* foreign nations."[6]

Even the attempts made to retell the story of the invasion of Canaan in terms reminiscent of the exodus from Egypt serve only to underscore the religious sea change it involved, a change brought about by the increasing preoccupation with historical adversaries. When, for instance, the text tries to supply Joshua with something of a Mosaic profile, certain glaring discrepancies are revealed. Especially striking is the comparison between the theophany to which Joshua is privy and the appearance of Yahweh to Moses in the burning bush, on which it is modeled.

> When Joshua was near Jericho, he raised his eyes and saw a man standing there before him, grasping a naked sword. Joshua walked toward him and said to him, "Are you with us or with our enemies?" He answered, "No, I am captain of the army of Yahweh, and now I come. . . . " Joshua fell on his face to the ground and worshipped him and said, "What are my Lord's commands to his servant?" The captain of the army of Yahweh answered Joshua, "Take your sandals off your feet, for the place you are standing is holy." And Joshua obeyed. (Josh. 5:13–15)

The author clearly intends for the reader to notice the parallels between Joshua's vision and Moses' experience at the burning bush. Once attention is called to these parallels, however, they serve only to dramatize how fundamentally different Joshua's vision is from Moses' encounter. Moses had been told, "Set my people free." Here the talk is not of liberation, but of being "with us or with our enemies." The true religious enigma of "I am Who Am," is here replaced by the sphinx-like ambiguity of the primitive sacred. Asked if he is "with us or with our enemies," the angel answers, "No. . . . " And yet, he is armed for battle, his naked sword ready to vanquish Joshua's adversaries. The very fact that the attempt is made to liken Joshua's vision to Moses' encounter at the burning bush, therefore, has the effect of calling attention to the huge spiritual gulf that separates them. The voice from the bush had reverberated with genuine transcendence. The armed angel of Joshua's vision is purely and simply a specter of sacred violence expressed militarily.

It is not coincidental that it is at this stage in Israel's cultural history that the sundry Israelite tribes began the gradual process of merging into a single political unit. In fact, the book of Joshua describes the *simultaneous* emergence of two new institutions: Holy War and Tribal Confederation. This simultaneous emergence could not have been merely fortuitous. The federation of the Israelite tribes apparently required the existence of common external enemies and communal rituals for expelling them. Glaring directly at such enemies, crossing the Jordan "opposite" them, Israel enters "history." The new form that the sacrificial system takes is that of "Holy War," and the new form of cultural organization that accompanies it is the tribal confederacy or amphictyony. The fact that the narrative brings the relationship between these two innovations into view is, itself, extraordinary. Here is how Gerhard von Rad put the matter:

> The amphictyony was not, in the last analysis, a religious union assembling simply for the communal performance of sacrifice and for hearing the rules which God gave it for its life. Rather was it a band of tribes which, besides engaging in cultic activities in the narrower sense, also safeguarded and defended its whole political existence, sword in hand. Now, of course, this second side of its activity was not secular, but cultic just like the other, and subject to definite laws and ideas. We refer to the institution to which we give the name, the Holy War. Perhaps it was in the Holy War even more than the Covenant Festival at Shechem that ancient Israel really first entered into her grand form.[7]

What does it mean to say that a multitribal cultural enterprise only first enters into its grand form when its combination of religious and social circumstances creates the possibility of Holy War? It means simply that Holy War provided a sufficiently generic and sufficiently compelling ritual in which all the tribes could join and, in doing so, share an *esprit de corps* that was effective across tribal lines.

The Ban

What distinguished Holy War from the lesser forms of belligerence was the element of the *ban*. The Hebrew word is *herem,* which means to "set apart." In the Greek Septuagint, this word was translated as "anathema." The ban meant the total annihilation of all life and all objects of value and tokens of wealth or prestige in the city under assault. Once it was introduced, enforcing it with "religious" scrupulosity became a primary concern, another indication that it was fundamentally a ritual tool, and not a military or political one. And yet, as I have mentioned, beyond a certain point scrupulosity is a sign of cultural weakness, not strength. The hyper-scrupulosity often associated with the ban is, I think, a symptom of how fragile the cultural system convened and reconvened by Holy War actually was.

Why would the ban require that everything be destroyed? In antiquity the obvious result of a war was the booty it yielded, including slaves and concubines, herd animals, and plundered material wealth. The practical effect of the ban was to prohibit the bringing of such plunder back into the camp of the victors. Why would such booty have been forbidden? Once again, the obvious answer is even more obvious in light of Girard's explication of mimetic desire. The booty cannot be brought back into the victorious camp because it would all too easily arouse the mimetic desires and generate in turn the mimetic rivalries that it was the task of the war or sacrificial ritual to drain away. What this means is that the imposition of the ban, which is such a glaring and savage version of the sacrificial system, is really a sign of its weakness, for it is based on the fear that the social solidarity engendered by the war is too fragile to survive the envy and acrimony likely to be provoked by an influx of plundered goods.

The ban Joshua imposed during the campaign against "Jericho" was subsequently discovered to have been violated, and what makes this story so extraordinary is the almost perverse candor with which it tells of the violation and its consequences. At first, we learn only that a man named Achan has "laid his hands on something that fell under the ban, and the anger of Yahweh flared out against the Israelites" (Josh. 7:1). The discovery that the ban had been violated was made, in my view, by inference and in retrospect.

The conquest of "Jericho" is followed immediately by an attack on Ai, a nearby Canaanite town. In this campaign, Israel was defeated, and it is only after this defeat and, in my judgment, in response to the social disarray that must have accompanied it that the violation of the ban on Jericho was discovered. Once Israel began to think of its God as the invincible patron of military victory, defeats at the hands of enemies could be explained only on the assumption that this all-powerful god had found fault with his people and abandoned them. The central requirement of the Holy War ritual, the only one weighty enough to have had such serious repercussions if flouted, was the ban. So, just as Moses scrambled to find prior transgressions that would explain the violence that killed Aaron's sons, so here the failure of the campaign against Ai was retroactively blamed on a violation of the ban placed on Jericho.

The "evidence" that a violation of the ban had occurred wasn't the discovery of war booty in the belongings of those returning from the war. The "evidence" was that a military venture had failed. It was only in the *aftermath* of the defeat that Yahweh announced that "Israel has sinned."

> ...they have taken what was under the ban, stolen and hidden it and put it into their baggage. *This is why the sons of Israel cannot stand up to their foes;* why they have turned their backs on their enemies, because they have come under the ban themselves. I will be with you no longer unless you *remove what is under the ban from among you.* (Josh. 7:11–12)

According to this text, what was lacking in Israel's campaign against Ai was not military might but military *morale.* The Israelites lost heart, Yahweh declares. There is only one remedy for this lack of *esprit de corps,* namely, a cathartic sacrificial ritual that would regenerate it. The cure for the problems associated with a failed sacrificial rite is another sacrificial rite. Yahweh instructs Joshua as to how to proceed:

> In the morning therefore you will come forward tribe by tribe, and then the tribe that Yahweh marks out by lot will come forward clan by clan, and the clan that Yahweh marks out by lot will come forward family by family, and the family that Yahweh marks out by lot will come forward man by man. And then the man taken with the thing that is banned is to be delivered over to the fire, he and all that belongs to him, because he has violated the covenant with Yahweh and committed an infamy in Israel. (Josh. 7:13–15)

As we are learning so painfully in our own time, once the sacrificial apparatus of a culture under biblical influence has begun to malfunction, almost anything done to repair it has the effect of further exposing the ropes and pulleys of its scapegoating apparatus. This is what happens here. The culprit/victim is selected in a completely arbitrary way. *Lots are cast* to determine who has offended Yahweh. If we imagine some rather casual and minor pilfering by the combatants to have widely occurred, then we can see how dreadful the phrase "the ban is now among you" must have sounded, how liturgically intense the casting of lots must have been, and how readily those exonerated by the process would have been willing to close ranks against those selected as culprits.

There in an almost infinite number of possible variations on the basic recipe for solving social crises sacrificially. Key to them all is transference of the community's religious terrors and guilt-ridden anxieties onto the victim. Of course, the most successful sacrificial resolutions are those in which the mimetic polarization is complete, the consensus unanimous, and the sacrificial zeal utterly uncontested. So great is the power of the mimetic avalanche that produces such unanimity, in fact, that sometimes the result exceeds even the one Girard calls "unanimity-minus-one." Though certainly the victim is the least likely of those present to be swept into the unanimity, and even though we must remain suspicious of the sacrificial crowd's penchant for fabricating the victim's consent, there are cases in which the victim himself is caught up in the firestorm of sacrificial contagion. He professes his guilt. In the case of Achan, as I have just indicated, he may well have been guilty, but if he was, and if casting lots proved a reliable way of locating him, it is highly unlikely that he was the only guilty one. Where widespread looting has taken place and where equal enforcement of the prescribed punishment would decimate the army, casting lots is quite an ingenious solution to the problem of designating the lone law-breaker on whom divine wrath is to fall and the prohibition he violated reasserted. Once so inscrutable a method has designated the guilty party, the accused himself joins in the accusation. Achan publicly confesses.

> Then Joshua took Achan son of Zerah, with the silver and the robe and the ingot of gold and led him up to the Vale of Achor—and with him his sons and daughters, his oxen and donkeys and sheep, his tent and everything that belonged to him. All Israel went with him.
>
> Joshua said, "Why did you bring evil on us? May Yahweh bring evil on you today!" And all Israel stoned him. (Josh. 7:24–25)

Vox populi, vox dei—the voice of the people is the voice of god. The one selected by lots is killed by what seems to have been a combination of spontaneous mob violence and an orchestrated and ritualized execution. Though Yahweh sentences the violator of the ban to be delivered over to the fire, in point of fact, Achan is stoned to death. Such discrepancies are not likely to occur for no reason. Of the two forms of killing, stoning is much more likely to have taken place spontaneously than is the burning of the victim. In other words, at some point, the controlled mob violence of the "judicial proceedings" seems to have given way to mimetic mob violence, and "*all* Israel stoned him." We are back at square one, unanimity-minus-one. Once again, Israel's moral aversion to human sacrifice has been overwhelmed. Nevertheless, the fact that we who are the beneficiaries of the biblical tradition read this story with a sense of moral discomfort proves that the efforts to sacralize the killing have not prevailed after all. When we find these stories morally offensive, we do so because of an empathy for victims and a skepticism about the judgment of mobs that the biblical tradition itself awakened in us.

Stone Shrines

I have chosen the crossing of the river Jordan as the moment when Israel's sacrificial center of gravity shifts from a predominantly cultic one to one in which wars against "historical" enemies and the public executions of transgressors and apostates take their place in Israel's sacrificial repertoire. After the Jordan crossing, intertwined versions of them became a common feature of the social and religious landscape in the biblical narrative. For instance:

> Joshua . . . dealt with all the dwellers in Ai as with men under the ban. For booty, Israel took only the cattle and the spoils of the town, according to the order Yahweh had given to Joshua. Then Joshua burned Ai, making it a ruin for evermore, a desolate place even today. He hanged the king of Ai from a tree till evening. (Josh. 8:26–29a)

With the city of Ai smoldering in the background and the corpse of its king swinging from a tree, the "military" and "judicial" rudiments of Israel's sacrificial system are vividly represented, and the link between them is explicit. If a link could be found connecting these two forms of sacred violence with the purely cultic form, then this text could be regarded as a miniature anthropological encyclopedia. We are not disappointed. The text provides, in fact, three related cultic references. The first occurs just after Achan has been stoned: "A great cairn was reared over him, which is still there today" (Josh. 7:26). The second occurs after the public hanging of the king of Ai:

> Joshua ordered his body to be taken down from the tree. It was then thrown down at the entrance to the town gate and a great cairn was reared over it; and that is still there today. (Josh. 8:29)

A cairn is a mound of stones used as a marker or memorial. There is little doubt that the first cairns were the result of collective stonings. Metaphorically at least, and probably often enough in actual fact, culture begins with a *lapidation,* a stoning. The most frenzied sacrificial violence occurs like an avalanche, and it does not abruptly come to a stop with the victim's death. As we saw in the Aztec myth of Tezcatlipoca, the presence of a recognizable human corpse seriously impedes the process of divinizing or demonizing the victim and mythologizing his murder. In the most primitive settings, when the victim dies under the knife, dismemberment often followed. A similar process no doubt occurred when the victim was stoned. The stones kept coming until the victim's corpse was completely enshrined beneath them. Not only did the act of victimization help engender social solidarity, therefore, but the solidarity was extended in time and made physically memorable by the continued existence of a shrine standing at the spot where the victim was slain. In each of the passages I have quoted, we are told that the mounds of stone still existed at the time the author was relating the more ancient event. Such mounds of stone were where murders were turned into memories and memories into beautiful obligations. The cairn as shrine therefore symbolizes a sort of "missing link" in the transformation of mob violence into cult religion.

Since, however, the "shrine" to which Joshua 8:29 refers appears to have no religious standing, is it not a little farfetched to regard it as a "missing link"? Once again, the biblical texts astound us with their anthropological perspicuity. Immediately after the verse referring to that cairn raised over the body of the king of Ai, a text taken from an independent literary tradition is inserted into the narrative. The resulting textual sequence is an anthropological masterpiece thanks precisely to the kind of editorial tampering biblical scholars usually regard as evidence of literary unreliability. The next verses of the text read:

> Then Joshua built an altar to Yahweh the God of Israel on Mount Ebal, as Moses, Yahweh's servant, had ordered the sons of Israel, as is written in the Book of the Law of Moses, "an altar of undressed stones that no iron tool has ever worked." On this they offered holocausts to Yahweh and offered communion sacrifices as well. (Josh. 8:30–31)

Following the public murder of the king of Ai, the Israelites enjoy a moment of cultural harmony and coherence that hearkens back to an earlier and less complicated phase of Israel's spiritual journey. The obvious question is, What is the relationship between these three stone monuments: the mounds of stone beneath which the two human victims are buried and the *altar of undressed stones* on which animal sacrifices are now once again being offered? The question almost answers itself. The ritual taking place at the newly reconstructed altar commemorates the restoration of the very system of animal sacrifice whose waning efficacy led to Israel's cultural and religious destabilization in the first place. Israel seems for the moment to have restored its traditional system of animal sacrifice and thereby to have recaptured its religious poise. It has come full circle. As crude as the primitive shrines described in these texts must have been, they were the sacrificial prototypes and the architectural precursors of the great Jerusalem Temples of later times.

It is striking, in this regard, that both times in John's Gospel when the crowd threatens to stone him, Jesus is *inside* the Temple precinct. Symbolically speaking, where would the stones have come from if not from the Temple walls, floors, and altars? *Symbolically,* then, even before the crucifixion, the scapegoating zeal that led to it had already begun to compromise the structural integrity of the hallowed sacrificial shrine in whose name the zealous were arming themselves. They were entering a world that would one day become the world in which we live, where every act of sacrificial violence (lapidation) contributes to the further di-lapidation of the sacrificial structures that lend legitimacy to violence. This di-lapidation has become as relentless in human history as it is in biblical history, and it will not cease until not one stone of the old sacrificial structure is left upon another (Matt. 24:2).

Ultimately, then, it was another Joshua — the *Yehosua* about whom the Gospels were written — who stepped into the Jordan in a truly decisive way, not "opposite" (*neged*) his hated enemies, but "in the presence of" (*neged*) his God. This Joshua/Jesus became the victim of the kind of sacrificial violence over which his ancestral namesake presided, and, to make the parallel complete, he left behind him no "cairn" that might be turned into yet another sacrificial shrine. They went to the tomb and found it empty.

Chapter 9

The Prophets

What the story of the conquest illustrates is that, had the story ended there, it could never have become the Bible at all.[1]

ERIC GANS

Greek tragedy and the prophetic tradition in Judaism appeared at a moment...when no sacrificial system seems to work, when all sacrifices lead only to more violence and all victimage leads only to more victimage and therefore to the need for more sacrifice....Judaism and to a lesser extent Greek tragedy formulate a response to the following question: How can I live in a world in which there are no longer any gods of the sacrificial kind?[2]

SANDOR GOODHART

With Cain's inept and superficial rejection of sacrifice, and then Abraham's faithful act of animal substitution, the Bible begins the world's most remarkable account of the world's most daunting, morally compelling, and religiously daring enterprise: the gradual extrication of the human race from the grip of sacred violence, cult sacrifice, and scapegoating — undertaken in almost blind fidelity to the God who chose slaves as historical agents and a hanged man as the messiah. Because we humans are so socially and psychologically adapted to sacrificial arrangements, however, the renunciation of sacrifice has proceeded — and is still proceeding — by fits and starts. Except for the astonishing moment when Jesus looked down from the Cross and prayed, "Father forgive them for they know not what they do," every rejection of sacrifice has taken place *within* the sacrificial system, albeit a system whose power is waning. Some may manage through grace, devotion, conversion, or selflessness to free themselves from mimetic compulsions and sacrificial reflexes, but they continue to inhabit a world — like the biblical one — that rejects sacrifice sacrificially.

With the emergence of Israelite national institutions and especially with the building of the Temple of Jerusalem under Solomon, Israel entered an entirely new historical phase. To a considerable degree, it still saw itself vis-à-vis its enemies, and waging war against them was still a religious as well as a patriotic duty. But the impressive Temple at Jerusalem, the locus for Israel's cult of animal sacrifice, became the new center of religious life. With varying degrees of cooperation and tension, the kings and the Temple priesthood played their respective roles as leaders of Israel's political and religious life. Eventually, a third force emerged, one destined to change the moral and religious landscape of Israel: the prophetic movement. The kings, the priests, and the prophets — these were the central forces in Israel's cultural dynamism from the time of Samuel to the Babylonian exile.

The term "prophet" — in Hebrew *nabi* — can be used to refer to so diverse a group of ancient religious enthusiasts that it almost loses any specificity. Standing head and shoulders above all those to whom the term was applied, both in Israel and among its neighboring cultures, are Israel's great prophets whose lives, words, and deeds are recorded in the books of the Bible that bear their names — Amos, Hosea, Isaiah, Jeremiah, Ezekiel, and so on. These strange and striking men are easily distinguished from those prophets who were part of the prophetic guilds or brotherhoods that were active in many cultures of the time, Israel included. Though their writings are placed at the end of the Hebrew Bible and the Christian Bible's Old Testament, it was very largely their influence that brought the Bible as we know it into existence.

The Bible's supreme anthropological value is that it allows us to see the structures and the dynamics of humanity's conventional cultural and religious life and to watch as these structures give way under the weight of a revelation incompatible with them. It was a slow, historical process. Even though many of the early prophets possess only faint hints of the greatness of those who were to come after them, one can nevertheless see in their ministry the seeds of what was to come. Part of what we have to learn from Israel's prophets, therefore, we can learn only by understanding how they emerged as the living embodiment of the antisacrificial impulse that had been incubating in Israel's cultural history since its inception.

In what follows I will briefly discuss four episodes involving prophets from widely varying historical stages in biblical Israel's spiritual and anthropological journey: Elijah, Micaiah, Jeremiah, and Daniel. As ancient as the events depicted in these episodes are, if all that could be achieved by reviewing them was the satisfaction of some historical curiosity, the exercise would not be warranted. On the contrary, however, by comparing and contrasting these texts, I think we can catch a vivid glimpse of the spiritual, historical, and anthropological issues that are at the heart of our own cultural crisis.

Elijah: Anti-sacrificial Sacrifice

One of the most famous of the early prophets was Elijah, a man who lived during the reign of king Ahab, one of the most notoriously wicked kings in the Scriptures. Under the influence of his wife, Jezebel, Ahab built altars to Baal, the Canaanite fertility god, and, as the text says rather euphemistically, "committed other crimes as well" (1 Kings 16:33). To better grasp the overall religious atmosphere of Ahab's reign and the probable nature of the "other crimes," the next verse in the First Kings narrative can be taken as a clue. It reads:

> It was in his time that Hiel of Bethel rebuilt Jericho; he laid its foundations at the price of Abiram, his first-born; its gates he erected at the price of his youngest son Segub. (1 Kings 16:34)

This is an explicit reference to what are called foundational sacrifices. Common enough in the Canaan of biblical times, these rituals sacrificed humans, typically children, to the patron god of the city or building being erected, and placed the bodies of these victims into or under the foundations or walls of the structure. By referring to this notorious practice in the verse following the reference to Ahab's "other crimes," the author of this text infers by innuendo that the Baal cult that thrived under Ahab could be expected to eventually tolerate sacrifices such as these. The text assumes that a drift toward such things was inevitable. Human sacrifice was often seen, not only as the most shocking of the Canaanite religious customs, but as the one toward which all the others ineluctably led. A later passage, for instance, says of Ahaz, king of Judah, that:

> He followed the example of the kings of Israel, even causing his son to pass through fire, copying the shameful practices of the nations which Yahweh had dispossessed for the sons of Israel. He offered sacrifices and incense on the high places, on the hills and under every spreading tree. (2 Kings 16:3–4)

Causing a child to "pass through fire" was the standard euphemism for child sacrifice in the ancient world. The "high places" were sacrificial cults that had grown up in the countryside. Since human sacrifice was the most horrendous of the religious perversions that occurred at these shrines, the term "high places" became a synonym for shrines engaged in human sacrifice. Another reference to Ahab's pagan ways occurs in the Second Kings account of the loathed king of Judah, Manasseh.

> He did what is displeasing to Yahweh, copying the shameful practices of the nations whom Yahweh had dispossessed for the sons of Israel. He set up altars to Baal and made a sacred pole as Ahab king of Israel had one.... He built altars to the whole array of heaven in the two courts of the Temple of Yahweh. He caused his son to pass through the fire. (2 Kings 21:35–36a)

The condemnation of Ahab's apostasy seems to be based on the understanding that, unless it is remedied, his pagan predilections would lead (or perhaps had already led) to the same abominable human sacrifices to which Hiel and Manasseh resorted. Among the "other crimes," in other words—and most abhorrent of them all—was human sacrifice. In fact, since Ahab's Syrian wife, Jezebel, had begun "butchering the prophets of Yahweh," a non-ritual form of human sacrifice was already occurring. The question of course is: With what religious and moral resources will the anti-sacrificial forces under Elijah respond to this abomination? Will the sacrificial outrages be ended by sacrificial means? Will the outrageous behavior exert such a mimetic fascination that it becomes the model for the campaign aimed at eliminating it? All one has to do is look around to see that this question remains one of the most burning questions of our time.

Elijah confronted Ahab and accused him of apostasy. He demanded a showdown on Mount Carmel between himself, as the true Yahwist prophet, and the 450 prophets of Baal. Once "all Israel" was assembled on the mountain, Elijah, as Yahweh's sole spokesman, insisted on a contest between two rituals, one performed by all the prophets of Baal and the other by Elijah, the prophet of Yahweh. Both he and the prophets of Baal were to build sacrificial pyres, slaughter a bull, dismember it, and lay it on the wood. Neither was to set fire to the pyre. Then the 450 prophets of Baal and the one prophet of Yahweh were to engage in a ritual contest to see whose god was the real God.

Elijah said to the prophets of Baal: "You must call on the name of your god, and I shall call on the name of mine. The god who answers with fire is God indeed" (1 Kings 18:24). *The god who answers with fire is god indeed.* What a central tenet of primitive religion this sentence is. In the Old Testament, as elsewhere, fire is a frequent synonym for sacred violence. When Aaron's sons died as a result of a ritual meltdown, the text said: "from Yahweh's presence a flame leaped out and consumed them, and they perished in the presence of Yahweh" (Lev. 10:3, NJB). In these and many other instances, fire is a synonym for sacred violence, but sacred violence is not something performed by metaphysical agents. It is human violence performed in a religious frenzy. If fire is to come down from Yahweh, or if a god is to answer with fire, the ardor of religious firebrands must be kindled. The contest between Elijah and the 450 prophets of Baal is a contest to determine who can "fire" "all Israel" with the more convincing quotient of primitive religious zeal. The ritual showdown begins with prophets of Baal:

> [The prophets of Baal] took the bull and prepared it, and from morning to midday they called on the name of Baal. "Baal, answer us!" they cried, but there was no voice, no answer, as they performed their hobbling dance around the altar they had made. Midday came, and Elijah mocked them. "Call louder," he said.... So they shouted louder and gashed themselves, as was their custom, with swords and spears until blood flowed down them. Midday passed, and they ranted on...but there was no voice, no answer, no attention given to them. (1 Kings 18:26–29)

By mocking the prophets of Baal with such audacity and hurling insults at them, Elijah injects precisely that discordant voice which is so destructive of primitive religious unanimity. When it came his turn to invoke the fire, Elijah would pour water on the carcass to dramatize the awesome power of his deity. It was really, however, his mocking catcalls that had the effect of pouring cold water on the religious frenzy of his opponents and keeping the spectators from being caught up in it. The Baalist prophets responded to the dampening effect of Elijah's mockery with wilder and more flamboyant ritual excesses, culminating in a frenzy of ritual violence during which the prophets "gashed themselves, as was their custom, with swords and spears until blood flowed down them." The function of this "custom," a familiar one in archaic societies, is clear. The mind enthralled in religious frenzy is a mind so mimetically excited that ritual gestures — especially violent ones resulting in bloodshed — can set in motion an orgy of violence of precisely the kind that its perpetrators interpret in retrospect as the violence of the gods. In other words, the behavior of the Baalist prophets makes perfect sense in light of their underlying goal of conjuring into existence a convincing display of sacred violence.

The story purports to demonstrate the prophet of Yahweh's moral and religious superiority over the prophets of Baal. Elijah's superiority, such as it was, may have consisted of his clever exploitation of the mimetic frenzy that his religious opponents were able to whip up. It is a mistake to think that the contest between Elijah and the prophets of

Baal involves first the Baalist ritual and then the Yahwist one under Elijah. The ritual that Elijah orchestrated began the moment the ritual set in motion by the prophets of Baal began to exert its mimetic fascination of its onlookers. Elijah simply turned their ritual into the prelude to his own. In fact, what makes the conclusion to Elijah's ritual so anthropologically convincing is that it was preceded by the wild and violent one performed by the prophets of Baal. When their ritual ended without having coaxed the god to "answer with fire," it was Elijah's turn. It is with a palpable sense of pride that the text notes that Elijah needed none of the crude ritual excesses in order to get his god to answer with fire, but the pride is misplaced. It is not that Elijah invoked divine fire without ritual, but that he invoked it by exploiting the mimetic power and cathartic potential that his opponents' ritual excesses made available.

The prophets of Baal may well have understood, as ancients often did, that the god who answers with fire was a god whose worshipers became so filled with the god's fiery zeal that they became enthusiastic instruments of it. (The word "enthusiasm" comes from the Greek *en-theos* and referred originally to a form of possession that typically accompanied ritual ecstasies.) Yet the prophets of Baal seem not to have understood the workings of this contagious phenomenon well enough to have consciously aimed their ritual at those assembled to observe it. Their liturgical focus was on their god and the sacrificial animal whose carcass they implored him to consume. Elijah, however, seems to have understood that the real locus of the religious violence he sought to conjure was not the pyre and the carcass but the people. He began his ritual invocation of the god who answers with fire by fanning the smoldering embers of the failed Baalist ritual. He turned to the *people.*

> Then Elijah said to all the people, "Come closer to me," and all the people came closer to him. He repaired the altar of Yahweh which had been broken down. Elijah took twelve stones, corresponding to the number of the tribes of the sons of Jacob . . . and built an altar in the name of Yahweh. (1 Kings 18:30–32)

"Come closer to me," Elijah said. To fully appreciate the ritual significance of this phrase we have to perceive its psychological as well as its physical reference. Elijah then poured water on the carcass of the slain bull, an almost comic antic that drew his opponents' attention back to the altar. His attention, meanwhile, remained on his audience, the dry tinder on which the embers from the pagan spectacle of ritual violence were falling. His ritual consisted of blowing on those embers. If there was to be an epiphany of holy wrath, this was where the god who answers with fire would appear. Once the fire was kindled, Elijah insisted that what was about to happen was not his doing, but Yahweh's.

> At the time when the offering is presented, Elijah the prophet stepped forward. "Yahweh, God of Abraham, Isaac and Israel," he said, "let them know today that you are God in Israel, and that I am your servant, that I have done these things *at your command.*" (1 Kings 18:36)

Elijah wanted it to be known that he was functioning as Yahweh's representative and acting at Yahweh's command. As with Moses, his ability to successfully assert that claim was critical to the outcome of the ritual he was choreographing. In such a sacrificially surcharged situation, the solemn declaration that the spectacular events to follow were sanctioned by the god enraged by pagan idolaters would, by itself, probably be enough to set these spectacular events in motion.

> Then the fire of Yahweh fell and consumed the holocaust and wood and licked up the water in the trench. When all the people saw this they fell on their faces. "Yahweh is God," they cried, "Yahweh is God." Elijah said, "Seize the prophets of Baal: do not let one of them escape." They seized them, and Elijah took them down to the wadi Kishon, and he slaughtered them there. (1 Kings 18:38–40)

It is not enough to see the obvious: that Elijah has resorted to human sacrifice. That may be a moral abomination, and it may shock the pious reader of the Bible to see it without rose-colored glasses, but human sacrifice in one form or another was a common enough phenomenon in antiquity. What makes this story unique is that Elijah's dramatic act of human sacrifice was performed in an effort to root out the cult of human sacrifice and the religious delusions that led to it.

Micaiah

Another element in the contest between Elijah and the prophets of Baal is the obvious one that the true prophet of Yahweh stood alone facing 450 of the prophets of Baal. Though, as we shall soon see, prophetic guilds existed in Israel as well, by its very nature, the prophetic vocation that was so unique to Israel was a solitary one, while the prophetic traditions of Israel's surrounding cultures consisted for the most part of schools of ecstatics whose prophetic incantations were little more than a frenzied form of mimetic contagion. And so while the religious mood of ninth century B.C.E. Israel is still fresh in the reader's mind, I want to discuss briefly another encounter between the wayward king Ahab and a prophet. It is also the story of a contest between a prophetic brotherhood and a solitary prophet, though in this case both the prophetic brotherhood and the individual prophet were, ostensibly at least, prophets of Yahweh.

The story begins when Jehoshaphat, king of Judah, the southern Israelite kingdom, visits Israel, the northern kingdom. Ahab, king of Israel, took the opportunity to seek an alliance with Jehoshaphat for the purpose of recapturing the disputed town of Ramoth-gilead from the Aramaeans. The mimetic influences are palpable from the moment the drama begins.

> The king of Israel said to his officers, "You are aware that Ramoth-gilead belongs to us? And yet we do nothing to wrest it away from the king of Aram." He said to Jehoshaphat, "Will you come with me to fight at Ramoth-gilead?" Jehoshaphat answered the king of Israel, "I am as ready as you, my men as your men, my horses as your horses." (1 Kings 22:3–4)

Ahab seems to have been unhappy with the lack of zeal among his officers for reclaiming Ramoth-gilead. Nor did Jehoshaphat evince much interest. Almost like some Shakespearean figure, Ahab toys with the latent rivalry between the officers of Israel and the king of Judah by dangling Ramoth-gilead between them and conspicuously displaying his own desire for the Aramaean city. Once glistened with Ahab's desire, Ramoth-gilead becomes more desirable to all concerned. The mimesis hardly ends there, however; it suffuses Jehoshaphat's response to Ahab. "I am as ready as you," he says, "my men as your men, my horses as your horses." This sounds remarkably like schoolyard chants familiar the world over. In response to the invitation to join in a military campaign, Jehoshaphat immediately begins comparing himself, not to his potential foe, but to his future comrade. Underlying the alliance between Ahab and Jehoshaphat is a preexisting rivalry between them that their joint campaign against the Aramaeans, if successful, will help to dissolve. The pattern is the familiar one: mimetic rivalry turned into camaraderie at the expense of a common victim or enemy.

Before committing himself to war, however, Jehoshaphat insists that the two kings consult the word of Yahweh. For the purpose, Ahab has four hundred court prophets ready. Like their Canaanite contemporaries, Israel's prophetic guilds often produced their oracular utterances out of a collective frenzy. Born as they were of such mimetic contagion, the divine mandates they uttered were predictable enough. Ahab had at his behest a prophetic guild, and at the sign of reluctance on Jehoshaphat's part, he summoned his court prophets.

> So the king of Israel called the prophets together, about four hundred of them. "Should I march to attack Ramoth-gilead," he asked, "or should I refrain?" "March," they replied, "Yahweh will deliver it into the power of the king." (1 Kings 22:6)

With the help of his four hundred court prophets, especially the more zealous among them, and with the further advantage of the impressive display of regal authority, Ahab's proposed campaign against Ramoth-gilead seems to be taking on the aura of a great and noble cause. Certainly no one could fault Ahab for not arranging the symbols and social furniture to the best advantage. Nor did the prophets do anything unpredictable.

> The king of Israel and Jehoshaphat king of Judah were both sitting on their thrones in full regalia, at the threshing floor outside the gate of Samaria, with all the prophets raving in front of them. Zedekiah son of Chenaanah had made himself iron horns. "Yahweh says this," he said. "With these you will gore the Aramaeans till you make an end of them." And all the prophets prophesied the same. "March to Ramoth-gilead," they said, "and conquer. Yahweh will deliver it into the power of the king." (1 Kings 22:10–12)

Group rapture being essentially the sacrificial machine in neutral gear, all that's needed to get it rolling is for a Zedekiah to say the right thing and let the clutch out. Eagerly, he goes on to offer what is essentially a parody of the prophetic signs the later prophets will occasionally perform. He both dramatizes his lust for blood and provides a divine license for indulging it. His act parallels that of the prophets of Baal on Mount Carmel when they "gashed themselves, as was their custom, with swords and spears until blood flowed down them."

Jehoshaphat seems to sense that a single prophetic voice is a more reliable conduit for Yahweh's truth than is a chorus of ecstatics. Consequently, he asks if there is no other prophet from whom a second opinion might be elicited. Grudgingly, Ahab admits that another prophet does exist, Micaiah, but Ahab quickly adds that he despises Micaiah, for he never provides favorable prophecies. Mildly chastised by Jehoshaphat, Ahab grudgingly agrees to hear Micaiah's opinion on the matter.

The messenger sent to fetch Micaiah alerts the prophet and the reader to the fact that an irresistible unanimity is forming. With a wink and nod, he invites Micaiah to take the prudent path and enter into the mimetic vortex that is gathering its vertiginous energies in the royal hall. The scene is set for a dramatic showdown. Remarkably, however, when

Micaiah is asked by Ahab whether he should march against Ramoth-gilead, Micaiah responds exactly as the court prophets had. "March and conquer," he said. "Yahweh will deliver it into the power of the king." Either the mimetic vortex was at first too much for Micaiah, and he was actually drawn into it, or he was uttering the exact words of the court prophets with such a sarcastic tone that even those who wanted most to believe the words could not ignore the irony with which they were spoken. The latter may have been the case, inasmuch as Ahab seems to have realized that Micaiah had not spoken the truth. He demands that Micaiah respond again. Micaiah replies: "I have seen all Israel scattered on the mountains like sheep without a shepherd" (1 Kings 22:17).

What is to be noted is not just that the prophetic mind is lucid, but that the prophetic personality is sufficiently grounded in something other than the shifting sands of the social order to withstand the contagious power of social consensus. The clearest proof that Micaiah has managed to stay outside that vortex is that when he looks at the Israelite gathering, it isn't a nation firmly united for combat with its enemy that he sees. What he sees, and what Zedekiah and the raving prophets in his entourage cannot even imagine, is "Israel scattered like sheep without a shepherd." The ability to see *that* under *those* social circumstances is the prophet's chief social distinction and what makes his existence so anthropologically extraordinary.

Independence from the obligatory social seizures of one's culture must be paid for, however, and now Micaiah, like his descendants, the later prophets, begins to pay. Zedekiah "came up and struck Micaiah on the jaw" (1 Kings 22:24). At that, the sacrificial system contracts for a moment around the man who spoke a judgment on it.

> The king of Israel said, "Seize Micaiah and hand him over to Amon, governor of the city, and to Prince Joash, and say, 'These are the king's orders: Put this man in prison and feed him on nothing but bread and water until I come back safe and sound.'" Micaiah said, "If you come back safe and sound, Yahweh has not spoken through me." (1 Kings 22:26–28)

This is a major turning point. We might designate it as the point of transition in the biblical narrative between the early and the later prophets. As early as Micaiah appears in the history of Israel's prophetic movement, having earned and suffered social opprobrium, he represents the next stage in the prophetic vocation. In occasionally championing the *cause* of victims, the early prophets may have challenged the mighty and suffered their intermittent scorn, but it fell far more often to the later prophets to actually suffer the *plight* of victims. The prophet's victimary status, so unmistakable in certain passages in Jeremiah and Deutero-Isaiah, emerged only gradually, but in the blow to Micaiah that Zedekiah struck one can recognize the direction that the prophetic vocation would inevitably follow.

Before taking a quick glance at the later prophets and in order to better understand them, let us stop to ask how and where the prophet Micaiah acquired the mental and spiritual ballast that made it possible for him to resist being drawn into the social vortex of those caught up in a sacrificial frenzy. Though he was surrounded by a prefabricated mob in the full heat of its enthusiasms, Micaiah managed to hold his ground. How? Where did he find the Archimedean point outside the social mood from which to see its delusions and its social insubstantiality? Micaiah himself provides the answer. With all Israel's pomp and regal show in front of his eyes, what Micaiah saw was "Yahweh seated on his throne; all the array of heaven stood in his presence." Here we have an early glimmer of what would become so prominent with the later prophets and what was unquestionably Jesus' most distinguishing personal characteristic, namely, God-centeredness. Those who think immunity from the mimetic vortex can be achieved without some measure of it flatter themselves and miss the great spiritual opportunity our frenzied age is offering us.

Jeremiah

The prophet's unpopularity, his God-centeredness, and the clarity of his social insight were not isolated and unrelated aspects of his strange vocation. On the contrary, the prophet's social misfortunes were as responsible for the depth of his insights as the unpopularity of these insights was responsible for his social rejection. These insights were unpopular because "God's ways are not man's ways." Whereas the experience of his contemporaries was mediated primarily by their social and religious surroundings, the prophet was psychologically constituted by his personal relationship to his God. The prophets as a group were particularly prone to unpopularity because social ignominy was a necessary ingredient in the formation of the prophetic mind. Not only was the prophet's insight into the social and religious delusion one vouchsafed to the victims of such delusion, but the prophet was God-centered because the biblical God is the God of victims and the dispeller of the myths that shroud their faces and silence their voices.

The revelatory power of the prophet depended on how close he was to "the still point in the turning world," the point of lucidity in a frenzied world, namely, the place occupied by the victim of the frenzy. The prophet's enigmatic position in history and in the Bible has to do with the paradox of the victim, namely, that the victim is socially marginal and anthropologically central. The victim is the stone the builders of cultural consensus reject in the process of generating that consensus. As the ostracized outsider sitting at the shimmering center of the social vortex, it is the victim who, at least potentially, can see what can be seen only from his or her unenviable position. The convergence of victim and prophet is one of the most dramatic and unmistakable signs of the uniqueness of biblical revelation.

Though none of the sacrificial rituals escaped the condemnation of the early prophets, these were men who had just begun to free themselves from sacrificial thinking. Abraham had repudiated one sacrificial modality in favor of a more morally tolerable one. But, like Elijah, many of the early prophets sought to crush morally and religiously offensive forms of the primitive sacred with sacrificial acts that could hardly be distinguished at all from those they strove to destroy. Like these earlier prophets — Samuel, Elijah, and others — Israel's great writing prophets still lived in a world made morally intelligible by the idea of *divine wrath.* And yet it is in their lives that we see the first faint outlines of a world made morally intelligible by *divine empathy.* Their lives were living crucibles in which the early stage of a great anthropological transformation occurred, a transformation in whose later stages we are now living.

As I have already stressed, what made the prophet able to withstand the scorn of others was his experience of intimacy with his God. Most prophets recalled the moment when this experience germinated, when they first felt compelled to speak prophetically to their people, the moment of their call. They wrote of this moment as though with it their lives were begun anew. The prophet's call involved not merely a new "vocation" but a new life, a new self. The call was a conversion. Once they heard this call, however, the prophets often found themselves deprived of the social and psychological resources upon which those who remained in the social envelope could still depend. Again, von Rad expresses it well:

> The importance which the prophets attached to their call makes it quite clear that they felt very much cut off from the religious capital on which the majority of the people lived.... So deep is the gulf which separates the prophets from their past that none of their previous social relationships are carried over into the new way of life.[3]

The prophet Jeremiah epitomizes the prophet's plight. In him, the prophetic vocation took a decisive turn, and he and his literary executor left us the most detailed biblical account of a prophet's life that we have. Jeremiah carried on his multifaceted prophetic mission for forty-five years. He foresaw historical disaster, which culminated in 587 B.C.E. with the destruction of Jerusalem and its Temple. Legend has it that he was stoned to death by his fellow Jews in Egypt.

Jeremiah's call dramatically and unmistakably anticipates the social misfortune Jeremiah would later suffer. Clearly, even as he was being called, Jeremiah was being specifically prepared to withstand social scorn. In calling him, Yahweh said to Jeremiah:

> So now brace yourself for action.
> Stand up and tell them
> all I command you.
> Do not be dismayed at their presence,
> or in their presence I will make you dismayed.
> I, for my part, today will make you
> into a fortified city,
> a pillar of iron,
> and a wall of bronze
> to confront all this land:
> the kings of Judah, its princes,
> its priests and the country people.
> They will fight against you
> but shall not overcome you,
> for I am with you to deliver you—
> It is Yahweh who speaks.
>
> (Jer. 1:17–19)

As the prophet began to experience the world as one of its victims, his insight into social and historical dynamics increased, and his dependence on God grew. But the relationship between the social contempt the prophet suffered and his divine call is an even more profound one. Especially in the extraordinary cases of Jeremiah and Second Isaiah, the suffering of the prophet at the hands of his society *was* his prophetic message. In order for those of his day and those of later ages to understand the real significance of his spoken or written words, they would have to reckon with the fact that they were words uttered *by the victim.*

Given the historical span of the prophetic age and the widely varied social circumstances to which the prophets responded, it is striking how uniformly and similarly the prophets condemn the most prevalent and respected religious rituals of their time. "The men who speak to us in these accounts," wrote Gerhard von Rad, "were men who had been expressly called upon to abandon the fixed orders of religion which the majority of people still considered valid—a tremendous step for a man of the ancient East to take."[4] Men as thoroughly committed to interpreting the divine will as were the prophets cannot be characterized as anti-religious. And yet, by the conventional religious standards of their day, their message seemed to many, if not most, to amount to precisely that. "Not one of the pre-exilic prophets says a single word in favor of ritual sacrifice," writes Samuel Sandmel. "When they speak of ritual and ceremony, they speak in opposition to it."[5] The vehemence with which the prophets challenged this most central feature of the religion of their time is truly astonishing. For instance, Yahweh, speaking through Amos, the first of Israel's later prophets, makes no mistake about the contempt with which he regards what was for the people of Amos's time the very essence of religion:

> I hate and despise your feasts,
> I take no pleasure in your solemn festivals.
> When you offer me holocausts, . . .
> I reject your oblations,
> and refuse to look at your sacrifices of fattened cattle.
> Let me have no more of the din of your chanting,
> no more of your strumming on harps.
> But let justice flow like water,
> and integrity like an unfailing stream.
>
> (Amos 5:21–24)

Isaiah condemns the cult of animal sacrifice with equal severity. Speaking through him, Yahweh spurns the sacrificial rituals on which so much of Israel's religious life depended:

> "What are your endless sacrifices to me?"
> says Yahweh.
> "I am sick of holocausts of rams
> and the fat of calves.
> The blood of bulls and of goats revolts me. . . .
> Bring me your worthless offerings no more,
> the smoke of them fills me with disgust. . . .
> When you stretch out your hands
> I turn my eyes away.
> You may multiply your prayers,
> I shall not listen.
> Your hands are covered with blood,
> wash, make yourselves clean."
>
> (Isa. 1:11, 13, 15–16)

As outraged as Jeremiah's contemporaries were by what seemed his political betrayals, his condemnation of the rituals of animal sacrifice constituted what surely must have seemed to them a frontal attack on religion itself. Jeremiah saw the emptiness of the cult of animal sacrifice, but he did not for one minute think that the sacrificial appetite that the Temple priests assuaged with animal blood could be renounced by merely walking away from religion. If Cain had abandoned animal sacrifice only to descend into fratricide, Jeremiah had seen the terrible consequences that a casual rejection of Israelite religion could sometimes have.

> "It is long ago now since you broke your yoke,
> burst your bonds
> and said, 'I will not serve!'
> Yet on every high hill
> and under every spreading tree
> you have lain down like a harlot....
> How dare you say, 'I am not defiled,
> I have not run after the Baals?'
> Look at your footprints in the Valley,
> and *acknowledge what you have done.*"
> (Jer. 2:20, 23; emphasis added)

What was true in Judah in the seventh century B.C.E. is still true today. In the West, the bursting of bonds has been the chief business of social life for the last couple of centuries. Today the last of the weary and progressively nihilistic avant-garde try in vain to simulate the gusto with which their ancestors burst the bonds of convention during skepticism's golden age — when iconoclasm still had its religious aura. No doubt many of the methods used in the past to enforce our social and moral conventions were sacrificial. No doubt social taboos, once violated, trigger some form of scapegoating on the part of the offended society. But cavalierly dispensing with these taboos, while flaunting the mimetic passions they exist to curtail, is hardly a recipe for leaving behind sacrificial or scapegoating violence. Jeremiah saw his people breaking the bonds by which they had collectively maintained at least formal religious and social decorum. He listened to their modern-sounding prattle about being free: "I will not serve." But then he watched as all this rhetoric collapsed into pagan idolatry and eventually into child sacrifice.

When Jeremiah mentions harlotry under spreading trees on high hills he is referring to sacrificial shrines of the sort that he and other prophets condemn for being too tolerant of human sacrifice. Likewise, when he urges his people to look at the footprints in the Valley, he is speaking of the Valley of Ben-hinnom, a place notorious for the occasional rituals of human sacrifice that occurred there. He calls attention to the footprints and insists that his people acknowledge what they have done. In places like the infamous Valley of Ben-hinnom, Israelites were rescinding the moral and religious revolution begun by Abraham on Mount Moriah.

> "They have filled this place with the blood of the innocent. They have built high places for Baal to burn their sons there, which I had never ordered or decreed; which had never entered my thoughts. So now the days are coming — it is Yahweh who speaks — when people will no longer call this place Topheth, or the Valley of Ben-hinnom, but the Valley of Slaughter." (Jer. 19:5–6)

This is an important prophecy, one with profound historical implications. Jeremiah was saying that the day would come when it would no longer be possible to veil the violence of Ben-hinnom cults with religious mystification. When that day came, the word "slaughter" would be used and the myth that formerly camouflaged the terrible truth of human sacrifice would be shattered once and for all.

As I have said, however, one needn't have been a moral paragon to condemn human sacrifice even in a world where instances of it were still not far to seek. Israel's great prophets were able to register moral objections to much more subtle and mystifying forms of sacrificial behavior. They found the most respected religious rituals of their day to be spiritually contemptible, little more than pagan non-sense under a Yahwist label. They found the routine callousness toward widows, orphans, strangers, and the poor to be signs of apostasy when their contemporaries thought of ritual scrupulosity as the only real touchstone of religious orthodoxy.

During Jeremiah's life, and very likely with Jeremiah's initial encouragement, King Josiah had instituted a Temple reform. Josiah's reform involved the systematic elimination of Canaanite religious influence and the methodic destruction of the cult apparatus associated with it. There is a lengthy and remarkably detailed catalogue of Josiah's religious purges, which prominently includes a reference to his elimination of vestiges of the ultimate abomination: human sacrifice:

> [Josiah] desecrated the furnace in the Valley of Ben-hinnom, so that no one could make his son or daughter pass through the fire in honor of Molech. (2 Kings 23:10)

Disconcertingly, however, these reforms began to take on certain features of the perversions they sought to eradicate, most notably when

Josiah took his reformation north. First, he destroyed the sacrificial altar at Bethel, and then he swept into Samaria, his anti-sacrificial passion burning with such intensity that it ended in sacrifice.

> Josiah also did away with all the temples of the high places that the kings of Israel had built in the towns of Samaria, provoking the anger of Yahweh; he treated these places exactly as he had treated the one at Bethel. All the priests of the high places who were there he slaughtered on the altars, and on those altars burned human bones. Then he returned to Jerusalem. (2 Kings 23:19–20)

Like Joshua and Elijah before him, Josiah crushed the cult of ritual human sacrifice with an act of quasi-ritual human sacrifice. The end result of his religious purges was a revival of Temple-centered orthodoxy in Jerusalem that, by Jeremiah's reckoning, soon grew smug about its newfound religious rectitude. Jeremiah's moral compass was not stuck in one position. Before long, he strode to the gate of the Temple and challenged those entering:

> Put no trust in delusive words like these: This is the Temple of the Lord, the Temple of the Lord, the Temple of the Lord! But if you do amend your behavior and your actions, if you treat each other fairly, if you do not exploit the stranger, the orphan and the widow (if you do not shed innocent blood in this place), and if you do not follow alien gods, to your own ruin, then here in this place I will stay with you. (Jer. 7:4–7)

His claim that the Temple cult was incapable of assuring divine favor was a radical one to be sure. Jeremiah's challenge at the Temple is retold with some additional detail in a later passage, from which we learn more about the reaction of those who heard his reproach:

> When Jeremiah had finished saying everything that Yahweh had ordered him to say to all the people, the priests and prophets seized hold of him and said, "You shall die!"...And the people were all crowding around Jeremiah in the Temple of Yahweh. Hearing of this, the officials of Judah went up from the royal palace to the Temple of Yahweh and took their seats at the entry of the New Gate of the Temple of Yahweh.
>
> The priests and prophets then addressed the officials and all the people, "This man deserves to die, since he has prophesied against this city, as you have heard with your own ears...." (Jer. 26:8, 9b–11)

Here is the prophet as critic of religion becoming the prophet as the victim of religious righteousness. Here is Jeremiah as the spiritual descendant of Micaiah and the spiritual ancestor of Jesus of Nazareth.

Perhaps the prophet earned the wrath of his contemporaries by seeing and saying things they found offensive. Perhaps someone on whom a society had turned its wrath found himself the unexpected beneficiary of what Andrew McKenna has called "the victim's epistemological privilege"[6] and tried to tell his contemporaries what this privilege had made clear to him. In either case, there is a biblical affinity between the vocation of the prophet and the fate of the victim. This relationship, in fact, is the heart and soul of biblical literature. The victim, finally, is the Bible's truth-telling agent par excellence.

Chapter 10

Repenting of the Violence of Our Justice

Those whom we would banish from society or from the human community itself often speak in too faint a voice to be heard above society's demand for punishment. It is the particular role of courts to hear these voices, for the Constitution declares that the majoritarian chorus may not alone dictate the conditions of social life.

JUSTICE WILLIAM J. BRENNAN

Sacred violence provides the state with its legitimacy and fuels the optimism and idolatry of the patriot. It sanctions the judiciary, justifies class distinctions, bestows prestige on the "best people," and dignifies the executioner.[1]

ROBERT HAMERTON-KELLY

"Can you name a single prophet your ancestors never persecuted," says Stephen to the Jewish high priest and the Sanhedrin in the Acts of the Apostles. Heir to the prophets as he was, Stephen soon suffered their fate. It is a familiar New Testament portrait of the biblical prophet. It is one painted in broad brush strokes, but its basic insight is essentially valid. Nevertheless, some prophets, for example, Samuel and Elijah at the moment of his victory over the prophets of Baal, enjoyed wide support. The key to their popularity is also the key for understanding how and why so many prophets failed to achieve it. As embodiments of the fundamental biblical imperative, the prophets challenged idolatry and railed against its worst consequences. To see Elijah mocking the prophets of Baal as they fell into their collective trance is to witness one of the Hebrew prophets' quintessential acts. Whether such acts eventually lead to the prophet's popularity or unpopularity depends in large part on whether, having abruptly interrupted a sacrificial frenzy prior to its cathartic finale, he then provides those caught up in it with an alternative sacrificial climax, one for whose religious orthodoxy he vouches.

The victim's anthropological centrality is necessarily linked with his or her social marginality. It is the stone that the builders rejected that becomes the cornerstone of biblical revelation. It is perhaps appropriate, therefore, that the final story to which I want to turn attention, and which I think fairly sums up the issues raised by the biblical stories thus far reviewed, is one whose scriptural standing is in dispute. It is a text not found in the Jewish Bible and relegated to the apocrypha in Protestant Bibles. Only in the Catholic Bible does the book of Daniel include the story of Susanna with which I would like to conclude our review of the Hebrew Scriptures. It is a text that is marginal, not only because of its questionable canonical status, but also because of its very late date. Composed in the middle of the second century before Christ, it might serve as much as an introduction to the New Testament as an epilogue to the Old, and to some extent, I am using it in both these ways. I have chosen to conclude our reflections with a look at the story of Susanna, however, because, like a miniature Shakespearean masterpiece, it brings together in one narrative all the essential social and spiritual issues that this book is an attempt to comprehend.

The story begins this way:

> In Babylon there lived a man named Joakim. He had married Susanna daughter of Hilkiah, a woman of great beauty.... Joakim was a very rich man, and had a garden attached to his house; the Jews would often visit him since he was held in greater respect than any other man. (Dan. 13:1–2, 4)

The story that will soon focus on the beautiful Susanna begins by focusing on her prosperous and greatly admired husband, Joakim. Much of the story's deeper meaning is lost, however, if we pass too quickly over this brief portrait of Joakim. To be "held in greater respect than any other man" is to be the natural object of envy and jealousy, should these mimetic passions emerge. For envy and jealousy are simply the radioactive isotopes into which admiration decays in a world whose myths, rituals, and taboos are losing their ability to keep mimetic rivalries in check.

The author of this priceless story clearly has an understanding of the social and psychological dynamics of mimetic desire, but the author's psychological sophistication and literary genius should not blind us to the fact that his story is a *biblical* one. That is to say, it is a story best understood against the background of a historically emerging revelation, a story of people suffering from the destabilizing effects of that revelation. There is hardly a story in the Old Testament that is not being played out against a backdrop of cultural and religious upheaval, and the story of Susanna in the book of Daniel is no exception.

No sooner do we learn of Joakim's economic and social preeminence and of his wife's great beauty than the author of this story introduces two elders, themselves prominent members of the community, but clearly Joakim's social inferiors. These two elders have been serving as judges, passing judgment on wrongdoers and adjudicating disputes between members of the community. And so another piece of the story falls into place. Mimetic desire is always kindled in those whose social situations most closely approximate that of the one whom they envy. Joakim is, of course, without peer in his community, but these elders would no doubt be his closest social rivals. The author misses no opportunity to alert a careful reader to the fact that the two keys to this story are: (1) the relationship between Joakim and the two elders, and (2) the relationship between the two elders themselves. We are told, for instance:

> These men were often at Joakim's house, and all who engaged in litigation used to come to them. At midday, when everyone had gone, Susanna used to take a walk in her husband's garden. The two elders, who used to watch her every day as she came in to take her walk, gradually began to desire her. (Dan. 13: 6–8)

The emotional engine of this story is *mutual desire,* and it is operating at two levels: the covetousness of the elders for Joakim's wife, a covetousness driven more by envy of Joakim than by the beauty of his wife, and, second, the desire for Susanna awakened in each elder by the other elder's desire for her. As I said, the "Shakespearean" quality of the narrative is quite remarkable.

> They threw reason aside, making no effort to turn their eyes to heaven, and forgetting its demands of virtue. Both were enflamed by the same passion, but they hid their desire from each other, for they were ashamed to admit the longing to sleep with her, but they contrived to see her every day. (Dan. 13:9–12)

So much is compressed into these few verses. Having made *no effort to turn their eyes to heaven,* the elders were enflamed by the *same passion,* which they immediately tried to *hide from each other.* Mimesis cannot and should not be eradicated. It is essential to human existence as we know it. But if we are to remain sane and civil, we must keep our mimetic propensities from degenerating into the kind of "desire" that causes us to "throw all reason aside," kick over every trace of civility, and descend into spiritual squalor and social chaos. The author of this story makes an explicit link between the descent into irrationality and immorality and the failure to "turn one's eyes to heaven," clearly a metaphor for the experience of genuine religious transcendence. To the degree that one's existence is grounded in the experience of religious transcendence, one is able to resist, as Micaiah did, the otherwise intoxicating power of the mimetic passions. In a world where the social and legal structures capable of restraining these passions are dissolving, there may be no more urgent task than that of fostering and nourishing this experience of religious transcendence. If, like the elders in this story, we "make no effort to turn our eyes to heaven," there is little hope of turning them *away* from the tawdry spectacles of mimetic fascination that, if allowed to run their course, end in the kind of violence from which the biblical revelation is trying to deliver us.

It's hardly coincidental, of course, that the two elders are "enflamed by the same passion." Mimetic passions are *aroused* by models and *enflamed* either by obstacles or by rivals. The elders are enflamed by the same passion because they *share* a single passion between them. Short of the scurrilous solution they finally arrive at, each represents an obstacle to the other's desire. When the story tells us that they hid their desire from each other because they were "ashamed," we have reason to be skeptical. To be ashamed of covetousness implies moral qualms, and moral qualms don't seem to be the elders' strong suit. Each elder hides his desire from the other because he knows that, were he to flaunt it, it would only enflame the more his rival's desire, thus making him into an even more formidable rival. Shakespearean drama is full of plots in which "friends" become "rivals" and then "doubles," and our story, too, provides a humorous little metaphor for the process that has a Shakespearean ring to it:

> One day, having parted with the words, "Let us go home, it is time for the midday meal," they went off in different directions, only to retrace their steps and find themselves face to face again. Obliged then to explain, they admitted their desire and agreed to look for an opportunity of surprising her alone. (Dan. 13:13–14)

Mimetic rivals always go off in different directions, only to end up face to face in the end. The encounter between them is a critical moment. The truth about their identical desire is now out in the open. They are at a crossroads. One option is to openly declare their antagonism and become mimetic doubles, ready to destroy one another for the prize they both desire. Were this option exercised and one were to kill or eliminate his rival, he would have effectively killed the goose that laid the golden egg of his passion. In this story, however, the friends/rivals come to another solution. It is more depraved and cynical, but it is anthropologically more ancient. In a twinkling, their *rivalry* is relieved of its latent violence and their *desire* is laden with violence. The antagonism between the two rivals is transferred to the one they both desire. They become co-conspirators in a rape. Whether by rape or by falsely accusing Susanna of adultery, they are now willing to destroy the one whom both profess to desire. She is sacrificed for the sake of their "friendship," a term that loses its meaning as the mimetic passions take over. The contemporary implication of this story comes out when we notice that what has occurred here is a strange and perverse intermingling of violence and sexuality. In contemporary popular culture the fact that the line separating violence and sexuality is increasingly blurred is one of the most significant and alarming symptoms of our present crisis.

Susanna Accused

Soon, of course, the two elders find Susanna alone. They demand that she submit to them, telling her that if she refuses they will give false evidence, accusing her of adultery, for which the penalty is death. Rather than submit to them, Susanna cries out, and, as they had vowed, the two elders loudly claim to have caught her in the act of adultery. The formal accusation is scheduled for the following day. At the appointed time, Susanna arrives, accompanied by her mourning family.

> Susanna was very graceful and beautiful to look at; she was veiled, so the wretches made her unveil in order to feast their eyes on her beauty. (Dan. 13:31–32)

Those who think Susanna's great beauty the key to the desire of the two elders must be flabbergasted by their unveiling of her. If desire is a spontaneous and unalterably benevolent response to that which is intrinsically desirable, then the elders' unveiling of the beautiful Susanna is so obvious a blunder that no one in his right mind would think of making it. Has our narrator suddenly lost the gift for social verisimilitude that he so vividly displayed earlier in the story? Hardly. The author of this text knows better than we, not only how destructive mimetic desire can be, but also how socially volatile and morally capricious it is. The explanation for what the elders do here is to be found in what they did earlier in the story: they turned their own covetousness into a conspiracy to destroy the object they mutually coveted. By making her unveil, the elders are simply beginning the process by which the whole community might be lured into doing likewise. If myths are any indication, extraordinary physical beauty is just as likely to be the marker by which a mob designates its victim as is physical deformity of some kind. In either case, the all-important initial task is to cause the entire community's mimetic fascination to focus on the extraordinary one. Once the fascination is unanimous, changing the valence of that fascination, if need be, from positive to negative is easy. In a twinkling, the one whom all have found desirable can become the most undesirable one of all.

As the elders formally accuse her before the assembled community, Susanna "tearfully turned her eyes to heaven, her heart confident in God." She does exactly what the elders "made no effort" to do. Again, unless we acknowledge the pertinence of these two references to turning one's eyes to heaven, we miss the story's religious significance. Like Micaiah in the Jewish Scriptures and Stephen in the New Testament, Susanna remains grounded in the experience of transcendence at exactly the moment when her community begins toying with the idea that killing her may be God's will. For one vivid moment in the story, true religious transcendence stands face to face with the false transcendence of sacred violence. Susanna is condemned to die, and upon hearing her sentence, she cries out to God. The biblical God hears the cry of the victim and does so in a way that prefigures the moral imperative at the heart of Western civilization.

> The Lord heard her cry and, as she was being led away to die, he roused the Holy Spirit residing in a young boy named Daniel who began to shout, "I am innocent of this woman's death!" At which all the people turned to him and asked, "What do you mean by these words?" Standing in the middle of the crowd he replied, "Are you so stupid, sons of Israel, as to condemn a daughter of Israel unheard, and without troubling to find out the truth? Go back to the scene of the trial: these men have given false evidence against her." (Dan. 13:44–49)

As I have already pointed out, the Jesus of John's Gospel refers to this Holy Spirit as the Paraclete, the advocate for the accused. Here Daniel falls under the influence of the Holy Spirit gradually, as most who fall under its influence do. At first, he simply proclaims his own innocence, sounding like so many of us moderns. When the crowd replies, demanding that he explain himself, he is drawn further into the work of the Spirit. He stands "in the middle of the crowd," symbolically taking the victim's place. From that *crucial* spot, Daniel is able to speak with an authority that neither he nor his contemporaries could explain. This is the authority about which Jesus spoke in Matthew's Gospel when he said:

> "Be prepared for people to hand you over to sanhedrins and scourge you in their synagogues. You will be brought before governors and kings for my sake, as evidence to them and to the gentiles. But when you are handed over, do not worry about how to speak or what to say; what you are to say will be given to you when the time comes, because it is not you who will be speaking; the Spirit of your Father will be speaking in you." (Matt. 10:17–20)

Mistaking the inspiration with which Daniel has just spoken for human wisdom, the elders say, "Come and sit with us and tell us what you mean, since God has given you the gifts that elders have." Having spoken the "gospel truth" in defense of an innocent victim, Daniel is asked to lead the community in finding a guilty one. He faces a conundrum that, in one form or another, historical Christianity has faced for fifteen hundred years. Daniel then begins to preside over the trial of the two elders for having given false witness against Susanna. The defender becomes the prosecutor.

Corresponding to this shift, Daniel is soon animated by an accusatorial spirit, not an exonerating one. Both are necessary and valid in the world of criminal justice, but *anthropologically* the accusatory one is foundational, and the exonerating one, unless it is followed immediately, as it is here, by the accusatory one, is destabilizing. Daniel's transition from the exonerating to the accusatory spirit involves only one brief interim stage. With the air of a Solomon, he gives instructions: "Keep the men well apart from each other for I want to question them." I suppose one could call this the birth of due process. The circumstances in which it is born remind one of a memorable remark Girard has made. We didn't stop burning witches because we invented science, Girard insists; we invented science because we stopped burning witches. Here, of course, Daniel is inventing judicial due process under the same circumstances. We have no right to expect it to be a highly refined form of due process, but nevertheless something more troubling begins to enter the story at this point. Once the two elders are separated, Daniel brings them before him one at a time. To the first he said, "The sins of your earlier days have overtaken you, your acquittal of guilty men, when the Lord has said, 'You must not put innocent men to death.'"

As we have seen, the author of this story is fully in control of this narrative, and fully capable of dropping hints about underlying motivations that, for reasons of his own, he chooses not to make explicit. One such hint is the remark about the sins of the elders' earlier days. It suggests that in arraigning the elders Daniel is exploiting longstanding resentments members of the community have harbored against the elders. In making vague public reference to these "sins" of the past, Daniel is, as we say, "working his audience" in a way that parallels Elijah's handling of the crowd on Mount Carmel. When Elijah told the people to "come closer to me," he was encouraging the same social consolidation that Daniel is bringing about rhetorically with his accusation and innuendo.

What the text tells us about the unspecified misdeeds of the elders, the memory of which Daniel is reviving, is hauntingly ambiguous. He mentions the Mosaic Law that forbids both the putting to death of the innocent and the acquittal of the guilty. The former admonition is, of course, extremely pertinent to the issue Daniel is adjudicating, but publicly reminding the assembly of the law against acquitting the guilty could be expected, under the circumstances, to have a predictable effect on the assembly. Clearly, acquitting guilty men is not a sin that Daniel intends to commit.

Since the elders have both accused Susanna of committing adultery under a tree in her garden, Daniel now demands that the first elder specify under which tree he found the couple lying. "Under a mastic tree," the man replies. Anticipating with remarkable perspicuity the as yet unsolicited testimony of the second elder, Daniel greets the first elder's response as tantamount to final conviction. "Your lie recoils on your own head," he tells the man; "the angel of God has already received your sentence from him and will slash you in half." Daniel is the prophetic hero of this story, but in his growing sacrificial enthusiasm, he seems to have more in common with the false prophet Zedekiah than with the faithful prophet Micaiah. In fact, Zedekiah's frenzied assertion that "With these [iron horns] you will gore the Aramaeans till you make an end of them" bears a remarkable resemblance to the ardor with which Daniel publicly accuses the two elders of their crime.

The second elder is brought into the assembly and, before he has spoken a word of his testimony, Daniel greets him with a racial slur. "Spawn of Canaan, not of Judah!" he says. There is nothing elsewhere in the story to suggest that the elder is not a Jew, but, of course, the purpose of a racial epithet is hardly to report objective reality. Rather, the purpose of a racial epithet is to alter *social* reality by uniting those hearing the charge against the one against whom it is made. Once the racial pejorative has been introduced, Daniel uses it like a bellows to fan the embers. "This is how you have been behaving with the daughters of Israel and they have been too frightened to resist," Daniel asserts, "but here is a daughter of Judah who could not stomach your wickedness!" The elder, of course, *is* guilty of the crime of which he is accused, and his testimony shows that this is so. But Daniel's inflammatory rhetoric has to be analyzed for its social, not judicial, effects. Judicially, he has an airtight case, and he knows it. One needn't accuse Daniel of feigning his righteous indignation in order to point out that it is judicially superfluous. Its social effects, however, are not.

Daniel the Accuser

Just as we tend not to notice the cultural and psychological instability for which the emergence of mimetic desire is a symptom, so, when desire has run its course and an accusing crowd gathers around those on whom all the resentments are being focused, we tend not to notice the anthropological significance of the drama that is being played out in the background of the judicial one. In the former case, we become fascinated by the drama or melodrama that desire sets in motion; and in the latter case, we tend to focus only on the veracity of the charge brought against the accused. In each case, we focus on the *themes* of the social drama. They are not without significance. In the tangle of desire, some are more sinned against than sinning, and deciding which is which is not an empty exercise. And, of course, determining the innocence or culpability of an accused is extremely important. What lies behind the *themes* generated by desire and its social repercussions, however, is the mimetic process that generates them. Robert Hamerton-Kelly calls it the Generative Mimetic Scapegoating Mechanism, and he perceptively observes that the *themes* it generates have the effect of eclipsing the most important thing about it, namely, its generativity. In the story of Susanna and the two elders, for instance, the *theme* of lust (which is really covetousness — mimetic desire) with which the story begins, and the *theme* of criminal culpability with which it ends, are fascinating enough to draw attention away from the process — the Generative Mimetic Scapegoating Mechanism — that first generates the fascination and then exploits its thematic potential.

As I have said, the drama of mimetic desire with which the story begins is a symptom of the waning effect of the cultural structures whose function is to keep the mimetic crisis at bay. Jean-Michel Oughourlian has remarked that "desire . . . flourishes within a society whose cathartic resources are vanishing — a society where the only mechanism that could renew these resources functions less and less effectively."[2] If this is the anthropological backdrop to the *beginning* of the story of Susanna, and if the story *ends* with an act of unanimous collective violence, we must not miss the forest for the trees. For a society like the one described in this story to restore itself sacrificially, the "Generative Mimetic Scapegoating Mechanism" must be given a local habitation and a name. As soon as Daniel gives it a name — "the angel of God with sword in hand" — the crowd gives it a local habitation. "The whole assembly shouted, blessing God...and they turned on the two elders...." The elders were put to death, and justice was done.

In the Bible, the angel of God is a busy figure. Just as Abraham raised his hand to slay his son on Mount Moriah, the angel of Yahweh called out and turned his attention toward a ram caught in a thicket. So, the members of Susanna's community stood ready to perform a grim ritual for which they had no appetite. This time it was the prophet Daniel in the role of the angel. He turned their attention to a sacrificial substitute: two wretched old men, once the leaders of the community, whose guilt was beyond doubt. It is an outcome few would lament. Our criminal system, without which we would quickly sink into barbarism, is designed to produce versions of this happy outcome. A huge number of films and television dramas are simply variations on this *theme.*

The mimetic interplay involved in every crowd endows all crowds with a latent scapegoating predilection. How often we hear of crowds *turning,* sometimes turning on those who fancied themselves to be their leaders. The term suggests, correctly, that the crowd is driven by a preexisting motivation that has simply changed its focus. Lackluster though it was, the sacrificial mandate that hovered over Susanna as she awaited execution cannot be separated from the wholehearted sacrificial zeal that was suddenly *turned* upon her false accusers. Just as Elijah exploited the ritual frenzy the prophets of Baal had aroused and *turned* it toward those who had aroused it in the first place, so Daniel tapped into an already existing sacrificial appetite, one that had been evoked by the men on whom it fell with a vengeance. At the level of criminal justice, it's hard to improve on the outcome. But at a deeper level, larger issues loom.

The last verse in the story of Daniel and Susanna is this: "From that day forward, Daniel's reputation stood high with the people." The story begins and ends, therefore, on the theme of social prestige. The word "prestige" originally meant the power to dazzle, connoting something magically conjured by slight of hand. Originally and anthropologically, prestige is the by-product of collective violence, bestowed on those who give the violence direction, logic, and legitimacy. "Prestige is a subcategory of vengeance," writes Robert Hamerton-Kelly. "It is the aura of threat that emanates from violence."[3] A community capable of resolving its mimetic crisis by enthusiastically focusing its accumulated resentment and latent violence on a victim whose culpability is beyond doubt may be — in fact must be — profoundly unconscious of the process that has brought about its social renaissance. Such societies may have no concrete idea about the social catastrophe they have been able to avoid at their victims' expense, but they are usually vaguely enough aware of these things to be in an almost giddy mood when the drama has reached its sacrificial climax. Such societies are notoriously generous to those, like Joshua and Daniel, who have helped to choreograph the sacrificial denouement. Our story began when the old hierarchy of prestige dissolved into mimetic rivalry between Joakim and those whose social prestige was closest to his. It ended with a "new world order," at the top of which stood the man whose accusing gesture had been the galvanizing key to the happy ending of the crisis. Inhabiting, as he did, a world under the influence of the biblical revelation, his prestige was all the greater inasmuch as he was recognized as the defender of victims.

When Susanna cried out to her God in the presence of her accusers, her cry was heard, and the Holy Spirit residing in the heart of Daniel was roused. This Holy Spirit is the Bible's legacy to the world. It is the Spirit of which the Jesus of John's Gospel says that it will "show the world how wrong it was about sin, about who was in the right, and about judgment" (16:8). And, the same source tells us, the world will be shown this truth only gradually because it "would be too much for you now" (16:12). Whether the social effects of this Spirit of revelation are positive or negative will, of course, depend on whether those no longer able to resolve mimetic crises sacrificially can learn to live in ways less likely to lead to such crises in the future. That, in turn, will depend on whether, like Susanna and the prophet Micaiah, they have learned to "turn their eyes to heaven." For ultimately, it is with religious reality, and not with social and historical improvements, that this biblical Spirit is primarily concerned. Its beneficial social and historical effects are the by-product of its religious effect: the gradual awakening of humanity from the spell of the primitive sacred so that the Living God it conceals and impersonates can get through to us.

Since, as I have tried to show, the moral revolution the biblical Spirit is bringing about is necessarily a very gradual one, we have no right to look back with smug contempt on those who may have perceived this Spirit, so to speak, through a glass darkly. There is no doubt that the biblical Daniel felt the call of this Spirit. Nor have we reason to question the story's assertion that the two elders were guilty as accused of a perfidious crime. What we *should* recognize, however, is that the moral and social rectitude with which the story concludes occurs within the orbit of the sacrificial system and with the aid of its mimetic illusions. Like so many of us moderns, Daniel felt the spiritual power and emancipatory imperative of the Holy Spirit, and he stepped bravely and boldly into the breach to champion the cause of the victim. But as his ardor for justice swelled and his community enthusiastically rallied to his message, another darker social force came into play. The innocence of Susanna was gradually eclipsed in his mind by the moral perversity of the men who had accused her. Imperceptibly, the man who had been the tool of the Holy Spirit became the tool of the Accuser. The result was that instead of a community, remorseful and racked with moral misgivings, carrying out a legally prescribed punishment on an innocent victim, a wildly unanimous mob killed two morally despicable old men in a fit of righteous indignation. Given only those two options, who would have it otherwise? But if these are the only two choices, the human race is condemned to the sacrificial system forever and forever enthralled to the god of sacralized violence.

Space does not permit a detailed comparison, but the story of Susanna is most profitably read in the light of the Gospel story of the woman caught in adultery (John 8:3–11). In that story, of course, the woman caught committing adultery is guilty. Her accusers, having caught her in the act, are clearly eager to stone her to death in accord with the law Moses had laid down. The scribes and Pharisees, Jesus' religious opponents, clearly appreciate mob phenomena well enough to realize how readily those prepared to kill as Moses had commanded would turn their murderousness on anyone who tried to stop them by quibbling with the Law of Moses. Jesus does not redirect the crowd's sacrificial fury, nor does he directly challenge its central premises — which would only have had the effect of redirecting its fury toward himself. He dissolves the crowd and frees those swept up into it from the grip of its sacrificial passions. He destroys the anonymity of the crowd by inviting the first to cast a stone to *step out of the crowd* in order to cast it. They went away one by one, beginning with the eldest.

Conventional culture begins with a mob murder, and walking away from the spell of the crowd and its social consensus *one by one* is the only nonsacrificial alternative to it. Neither in this story nor in human history does it happen spontaneously, as we are learning to our chagrin today. The master thinkers of the Enlightenment inherited a Europe that had been buoyed up by the moral ethos of Christianity for so long that they thought they could scuttle the ark and wash ashore on the next tide. They were sure that reasonable people, with a wink from Voltaire and Rousseau, would walk away from crowds in droves. When, by the grace of God, we are able to walk away from a crowd in the grip of a mimetic contagion, it is not because we are the sturdy individualists we fancy ourselves to be. Rather it is because we, like the members of the mob accusing the adulterous woman, have been moved by a moral force of even greater power than that which the old system of sacred violence has been able to muster. As infrequently as we actually walk away from the consensus reality, we live in a world in which doing so is as universally extolled as it was universally abhorred in the ancient world. The moral shift from the latter to the former is a symptom of an enormous anthropological revolution whose initial psychological effects we underestimate and misinterpret as "individuality" precisely because we refuse to recognize under whose subtle spiritual influence our fledgling acts of social independence are taking place.

The Blood of the Prophets

The saving power of the biblical revelation will not be stopped, nor will its liberating effects be long arrested by those whom it has only partially liberated. If we have been able to see something in the story of Susanna that our forebears were unable to see, it is because the Spirit that God roused in Daniel at the cry of the victim has been at work in history for an additional two thousand years, and we are the inheritors and moral beneficiaries of its work. Kierkegaard said we must live life forward but understand it backward. To this I would add, the Bible is our scrapbook. So beguiling are the melodramas spawned by envious and rivalistic desire that the truth these spectacles eclipse is almost always recognized only in retrospect. But recognize it we will, for the myths that make our misrecognitions possible are slowly dissolving under the revelatory power of biblical tradition. We are members of that "generation" to which Jesus referred in Luke's Gospel:

> "This generation will have to answer for every prophet's blood that has been shed since the foundation of the world, from the blood of Abel the just to the blood of Zechariah, who was murdered between the altar and the sanctuary." (Luke 11:50–51)

If the full significance of this passage is to get through to us, we must appreciate the anthropological ramifications of the word "generation." The Greek word translated here as "generation" is a cognate of the word *genesis*. It occurs widely in the New Testament and has many layers of meaning. It is often translated and understood as a synonym for "this *age*." The anthropological significance of the passage just quoted comes fully into focus, however, if we allow one of the latent innuendoes in the word "generation" to come to the fore. Earlier, I referred to Robert Hamerton-Kelly's discussion of what he calls the Generative Mimetic Scapegoating Mechanism, and especially to his emphasis on that mechanism's *generativity*. If we interpret the word "generation" in the passage above in terms of a particular *kind* of cultural and religious *generativity*, then, I think, the full import of the passage reveals itself. So, I would understand "this generation" as referring to something beginning with the first culture-founding bloodshed and lasting up through the last "prophet." This "generation" would therefore mean all cultural and religious systems for which scapegoating violence is the underlying *generative* mechanism — in other words, to one degree or another, all conventional cultures, including our own. This passage is, therefore, both logically consistent and equitable. Those who have enjoyed the social and psychological benefits of the Generative Mimetic Scapegoating Mechanism will have to answer for the blood of the "prophets" on which conventional cultural and religious systems have depended.

But what does that have to do with the story of Daniel and Susanna? No prophets' blood is shed in that story. If we had to look closer to see the anthropological meaning of "this generation," we must likewise try to discover the deeper meaning of the term "prophet" as it is used in the Lucan passage. Heading the list of "prophets" is Abel. Was Abel a prophet? Well, yes, this text tells us that he was. It comes as something of a surprise. Of what exactly did Abel's prophetic role consist? What makes him a prophet? If the logical coherence of this passage is to be preserved, whatever Abel's prophetic status consists of, it must be the same thing that endows Zechariah and all the unnamed prophets with their prophetic status. What did they have in common? Not a lot. Abel wasn't even a Jew. What they had in common was that they were all slain. Each in at least some rudimentary way was the embodiment of the Lamb slain since the foundation of the world. What, then, does "prophet" finally mean in the quoted passage? It means someone against whom collective violence has had a *generative* effect.

When Jesus says that this generation must answer for all that blood, the clear implication is that it has not heretofore answered for it. It has never recognized what it has done. "Forgive them, for they know not what they do." And so there is one more criterion for the "prophet" in the passage. The prophet is someone who has suffered at the hands of those who discovered their social camaraderie in turning their violence on him *without realizing what they were doing*. In other words, in the special way the term is used in this passage, the "prophet" is discovered to have been a prophet only in retrospect. "Prophet," then, means someone misunderstood, persecuted, victimized, and recognized as an agent of biblical revelation only in retrospect. By this definition, who is the real prophet in the story of Daniel and Susanna? If we look for prophets only among the moral paragons, the only candidates in the story are Susanna and Daniel. But if the prophets for whose blood we must answer are those whose violent deaths revived the social consensus of the people who killed them, then the "prophets" in the Daniel and Susanna story are the two despicable old elders. We who belong to this "generation" must answer for it all.

To Repent of Our Violence

On April 29, 1955, a Paris radio station carried a broadcast by the Jewish philosopher Emmanuel Levinas. During the broadcast, Levinas quoted from an article written from the perspective of a survivor of the Warsaw ghetto massacre in 1943. The purported author of the article was Yossel ben Yossel. We might draw our reflections on the Hebrew Scriptures to a conclusion by quoting one of the comments Yossel makes in the article that Levinas found so powerful. He said:

> "Our God is a God of vengeance," says Yossel ben Yossel, "and our Torah is full of death penalties for venial sins. And yet it was enough for the Sanhedrin, the highest tribunal of our people in its land, to sentence a person to death once in seventy years to have the judges considered murderers. On the other hand, the God the Gentiles has commanded to love every creature made in his image, and in his name our blood has been poured out for almost two thousand years."[4]

The God *depicted* in the Bible is not always synonymous with "the biblical God," and sometimes the two are profoundly incompatible. When the former is vengeful and violent, the latter begins undermining the myths of sacred violence that endow such violence with religious legitimacy. The struggle between these two religious realities is what the Bible is all about, and the anonymous creator of Yossel ben Yossel refers to that struggle. Earlier I quoted the poet Howard Nemerov: "murders become memories, / And memories become the beautiful obligations." But what the text Levinas quoted is describing is carefully adjudicated and solemnly sanctioned violence — Jewish or Christian — becoming "murder." It is the Valley of Ben-hinnom becoming "the valley of slaughter" (Jer. 19:6). That is the biblical God at work, gradually obliging the human race to answer for all the blood of all the "prophets." And, of course, not even those most committed to the tradition that is breaking the spell of the primitive sacred are immune to its residual spellbinding power. Perhaps the theologian Frans Jozef van Beeck expressed the situation best in a book in which he refers to Levinas's radio broadcast. "In the name of God," van Beeck writes, "Jews and Christians must learn how to challenge each other to repent of the violence of their justice and refer each other back to the transcendent mystery of the God they worship so as to have their feet guided into the way of peace."[5]

I said there are no simple solutions to the moral dilemma we face, but if it is not a formula that van Beeck provides, it is nevertheless a lapidary reminder of our dilemma: to repent of the violence of our justice *and* to remind one another of the transcendent mystery of God. Our challenge is to do this in a world where half our contemporaries — the "conservatives" — do not think our justice is cause for repentance, and where the other half — the "liberals" — think that we can tinker our way out of the crisis that is upon us without being touched anew by the transcendent mystery of God.

Chapter 11

"His Snares Are Broke"

> ...and Satan bowing low
> His grey dissimulation, disappear'd
> Into thin Air diffus'd...
>
> JOHN MILTON,
> *Paradise Regained*

> Christ came so directly from silence into the word...that the whole world between silence and language — the world of mythology — was exploded and bereft of its significance and value. The characters in the world of myth now became demons stealing language from man and using it to cast demonic spells. Until the birth of Christ they were the leaders of men, but now they became the mis-leaders, the seducers, of men.[1]
>
> MAX PICARD

From an anthropological point of view, the uniqueness of the Gospels is structural. They perfectly *reproduce* and then *decode* the "Generative Mimetic Scapegoating Mechanism" by which human cultural systems have been structured since "the foundation of the world." The Gospels show, for instance, the underlying relationship between the conviction of the crowd and the "convict" at its center, between adulation and accusation, between violence and religion, and so on. At the narrative level, the level at which Christian believers revere the texts, the Gospels present us with a man whose relationship with God was so utterly profound, unique, and mysterious that the ordinary meaning of the word "relationship" broke down under the weight of it; a man whose incomparable understanding of the human dilemma could in no way be explained by reference to learning or genius or wisdom or experience. In this chapter, I will reflect on the issue of Jesus' understanding of his own mission and the forces against which he had to contend in trying to share that understanding with the rest of us.

John the Baptist, one of the most charismatic figures of his age, slammed into first-century Palestine's cauldron of religious and social agitation with shattering force. The role he played in the onset of Jesus' ministry was profound. John's effect on Jesus' awareness is summed up in the first words John speaks in the New Testament. Preaching in the outlying regions of Judea, John proclaimed: "Repent, for the kingdom of heaven is close at hand." Upon his own return from a period of desert solitude, one probably modeled on John's, Jesus repeated these words virtually verbatim.

When Pharisees and Sadducees came to John for baptism, he rebuked them: "Do not presume to tell yourselves, 'We have Abraham for our father,' because, I tell you, God can raise children for Abraham from these stones" (Matt. 3:7–9). For John, the religious pedigree was next to worthless as an amulet for warding off the historical reckoning he sensed was about to occur. Just as Israel's great prophets of an earlier age had appeared at a time of crisis to challenge the religious and social routines of their age, so John stood as an unmistakable rebuke to the conventional Judaism of his day. "Implicit... in John's whole movement," writes Edward Schillebeeckx, "is an unprecedented disavowal of the Jerusalem Temple cult and propitiatory sacrifices."[2] To pious fellow Jews — whether of the Temple cult, the sectarian, or the politically zealous variety — John's dismissal of Jewish distinctiveness represented a vehement attack on the centerpiece of their religious lives.

In the physical isolation of the desert, John had been far enough removed from the routine social fascinations to see how ultimately meaningless were the social and religious melodramas for which these fascinations served as the thematic warp and woof. Immediately after his baptism by John, Jesus headed straight for the lonely wilderness from which John had so recently returned with his vision of another reality.

The Devil and Satan

There can be little doubt that the most profound religious experience of Jesus' early ministry — the one that brought that ministry into existence and into public view — was Jesus' baptism by John at the Jordan. As embarrassing as it was for the early Christian community to have to admit that the man they claimed to be the messiah had so publicly deferred to another popular religious reformer, we can be sure that the story was not fabricated. Most likely, Jesus later reminisced with his friends and followers about the baptism and how it figured in his subsequent mission, and the evangelists worked these reminiscences into the narrative accounts of Jesus' baptism as they now appear in the Gospels. Were Jesus to tell his listeners that it was at the Jordan baptism that he first felt the power of God's call, it would be quite natural for Matthew to express it the way he did:

> As soon as Jesus was baptized he came up from the water, and suddenly the heavens opened and he saw the Spirit of God descending like a dove and coming down on him. And a voice spoke from heaven, "This is my Son, the Beloved; my favor rests on him." (Matt. 3:16–17)

Practically while these words calling him God's son were still echoing, the Gospels tell us that Jesus went to the desert to be alone, to pray, and to struggle with the practical implications of the profound experience that accompanied his baptism in the Jordan. Since Jesus was alone during his desert retreat, had he not later spoken of it to his friends and disciples, nothing would be known of it. Furthermore, both Jesus and his disciples would have tended to understand his desert experience in terms of its religious and scriptural reverberations. Jesus' forty-day period of trial, for instance, obviously parallels the Israelites' forty years of Exodus wanderings and the numerous scriptural echoes of it. And yet, as we shall now see, it is as much with the book of Genesis as with the book of Exodus that the wilderness story coincides. Matthew's version of Jesus' trials in the wilderness begins:

> Then Jesus was led by the Spirit out into the wilderness to be tempted by the devil. (Matt. 4:1)

According to the synoptic accounts, at his baptism Jesus experienced being called "God's son." The devil begins each of his temptations with the words: "*If* you are the Son of God. . . ." The devil tempts Jesus in precisely the same way that the serpent tempted Eve in the Genesis story. Just as Adam and Eve — made in God's image — were lured into envying God and striving to acquire that which would make them God's equal, Jesus is tempted to "grasp at divinity" by a dazzling display of messianic power. The devil in the wilderness and the serpent in the garden both advertise their alluring offerings in the same way. In both stories, the "tempter" tempts by mimetic suggestion, and both stories revolve around whether or not one can remain God-centered enough in the presence of these mimetic decoys to be able to resist them.

In the desert, Jesus was tempted by the devil, the *diabolos* in Greek. This was a fairly common term for the demonic force in New Testament times, but it is a particularly apt one for understanding the forces against which Jesus contended throughout his public ministry. The prefix *dia* means *across,* and *bollo* means to throw or cast. It means one who maligns, or slanders, or sows discord and division. The devil breeds animosity; he sows resentment. The New Testament personifies the diabolic force, and there is a good argument for doing so. By personifying the *diabolic,* we can better appreciate the autonomous way in which it actually functions. Since, however, demonizing is one of the devil's most devious tricks, the mere fact that we personify the demonic involves certain dangers. Care must be taken. If, according to André Gide, the greatest ruse of Satan is to convince us that he does not exist, according to René Girard his *second* greatest ruse is to convince us that he does. In any case, one gets closer to the reality of this strange and compelling force by speaking and thinking of "the devil," as the New Testament often does, than by trying to account for it in abstract terms or by invoking the familiar sociological or psychological idioms of our time. I will therefore follow the New Testament and personify the demonic force.

There is an unmistakable link between the call Jesus experienced at his baptism and his solitude in the desert that immediately followed the baptism. The story of the "temptations" is a story about Jesus wrestling with the nature of his vocation. It is as valid an affidavit as we will ever have for the mental and moral breakthrough that was to set Jesus' ministry apart from that of other religious reformers of the time. In the desert, he rejected the temptations to turn his vocation into a religious sideshow, or to undertake yet another campaign of social or religious reform. He was tempted to turn stones into bread, to throw himself down from the parapet of the Temple, and to worship the devil in return for "all the kingdoms of the world."

Matthew and Luke relied on the same source in constructing their respective accounts of the wilderness temptations. In Luke's version of the temptations, we read that "leading him to a height, the devil showed him in a moment of time all the kingdoms of the world" (4:5). Luke understood that what appears as a "very high mountain" in Matthew's Gospel was a metaphor, not for a panoramic vista, but for a *moment* of lucidity. He used the Greek word *stigme,* which comes from the verb meaning "to prick" or "to pierce," and is often translated as "in a moment of time." I feel that Luke provides the better account of the *moment* of clarity with which the trial by diabolic suggestion was brought to an abrupt end, while Matthew provides the better account of the reply that explodes out of the mouth of Jesus at that moment.[3]

If it is not just a frivolous figure of speech, what might the gospel mean when it says that Jesus saw *all* the kingdoms of the world *in an instant?* Since Luke has replaced a spatial reference with a temporal one, the reference to "all" kingdoms implies all that have ever existed and all that ever will. To see *all* such kingdoms in an instant of time can refer only to one thing, namely, a flash of insight into the *nature* of these kingdoms, a revelation about the nature of human culture itself. With the sketchy accounts of the wilderness temptations as a hint and with the whole of Jesus' public ministry as a ramification of that hint, one can say that in the desert Jesus decoded the metaphysics of power and came to understand the demonic mechanisms by which culture itself is convened and perpetuated. Please note: this revelation need not have been a conceptual one in order to have been decisive for the life of the man to whom it was revealed. It wasn't so much that Jesus *had a concept,* but rather that he apprehended the illusory and beguiling nature of the *pre-*conceptions upon which all cultures depend. All that the Gospels tell us of this revelation is that the kingdoms with which Jesus was "tempted" were at the disposal of the devil. Whatever the "kingdom of God" meant—and it was Jesus' central proclamation—it did not mean a more magnificent or more Jewish version of the kingdoms of "this world."

There was nothing in Jesus' subsequent ministry to suggest the kind of Gnostic contempt for the material order that some later Christian sects adopted, but neither did Jesus concede any ultimate significance to conventional human culture. As Marcus Borg writes, "the Teaching of Jesus is world denying; indeed, the world of culture *as the center of existence* comes to an end."[4] According to Borg, "Jesus called his hearers to a life grounded in Spirit rather than one grounded in culture."[5] The poet W. H. Auden remarked wryly that culture was one of the things that belong to Caesar. Like nature, it is to be given its due, and one ought to be grateful for its blessings, but the worship of culture is just as pagan as the worship of nature, and just as likely to lead to the sacrificial altars.

What was really at stake in the wilderness comes to the surface at the end of the temptations. In Matthew's version, the last temptation evoked from Jesus a powerful repudiation:

> Then Jesus replied, "Be off, Satan! For scripture says:
>
> You must worship the Lord your God
> and serve him only."
>
> Then the devil left him, and angels appeared and looked after him. (Matt. 4:10–11)

This is the first use of the term *Satan* in Matthew's Gospel. Until this moment, the tempter was referred to only as "the devil," the *diabo-*

los. The fact that the terms *satan* and *diabolos* are used interchangeably in the New Testament has tended to obscure the structural significance of their interplay in Matthew's account of the wilderness temptations. The force with which the exclamation "Be off, Satan!" exploded from Jesus cannot be explained merely as moral exasperation. For that matter, one could argue that morally exasperating temptations hardly qualify as temptations at all. The force of Jesus' "Be off, Satan!" is not the result of exasperation or moral revulsion alone. It is the result of a sudden *recognition.* It is spoken by one who has just fully recognized the identity of his interlocutor.

As I said earlier, *Satan* is a Hebrew term that means "the accuser." The two terms — *diabolos* and *satan* — can be seen as the two complementary manifestations of the forces of delusion, despair, and violence. The *diabolos* sows discord by arousing mimetic passions and then exacerbating the social tensions and the psychological apprehensions that accompany such passions. The *diabolos* produces all the psychosocial complications for which Girard's mimetic theory so ably accounts. The fundamental tool of the *diabolos* is what the author of the book of Wisdom called "the devil's envy," the mimetic incentives that generate the delusions and distractions of the social melodrama. At the critical moment, when these passions have sown enough frenzy and reduced a society to pandemonium, the *diabolos* changes its modus operandi. The *diabolos* becomes the *Satan.* Suddenly, the accusing finger points, and a violent avalanche is set in motion, the end result of which is a pile of stones, a glorious memory, and the rudiments of yet another of the kingdoms of "this world." What Hamerton-Kelly calls the Generative Mimetic Scapegoating Mechanism — a synonym for *diabolos/satan* — "generates" such kingdoms, but if its spellbinding myths were ever shattered, "this generation" would have to account for all the blood it shed since the foundation of the world.

What the *diabolos* divides, *satan* unites, minus the victim that makes the union possible. It makes sense, then, to say that in the desert Jesus discovered that social division and social unanimity had the same source, and that it was demonic. By recognizing both the essential link between the *diabolos* and *satan* and the subtle difference in their roles, Jesus of the synoptic Gospels accomplished an unparalleled anthropological breakthrough, and much of his ministry can be understood in light of it.

The English poet John Milton wrote of Jesus' temptations in the wilderness in his *Paradise Regained.* For Milton, it was in renouncing the temptations in the desert that Jesus destroyed the satanic power. For

Milton the crucifixion was the public exposé of the perverse truth of human sinfulness that Jesus had deciphered and conquered in the wilderness. After Jesus renounces Satan, the narrator in Milton's poem simply adds: "his snares are broke."

As I said, however, the breaking of these snares is by no means an intellectual feat. It was not Jesus' superior understanding that made it possible for him to repudiate the tempter and his gaudy lures; rather it was his God-centeredness. Girard's groundbreaking examination of the central role of mimesis in human experience may be the most important contribution to our understanding of the doctrine of "original" or universal sinfulness since Augustine, but the mimetic hypothesis does not replace the traditional idea that sin is alienation from God; rather it demonstrates the anthropological validity of that notion.

When the Christian tradition insists that Jesus was like us in all things but sin, what are we to think? As I have said, Jesus was no doubt a moral paragon, but as long as we understand the sinlessness of Jesus only on the level of behavior, we do not go to the heart of his uniqueness, which was his God-centeredness. As the story of the wilderness temptations shows, the essence of his sinlessness was his immunity to the contagion of desire. His triumph over demonic snares in the wilderness was a triumph over the glamour of mimetic suggestion, but it was an achievement made possible, not by Jesus' strength of will, but by the superior strength of *another* mimetic desire: the desire "to do his Father's will," to become the image and likeness of the One in whose image and likeness he knew himself to have been made. The temptation to emulate another's desire — the devil's — was unable to lure him away from his desire to imitate the God of powerless love in rapport with Whom he lived and moved and had his incomparable Being.

Scandal

As I have shown, throughout the Old Testament the renunciation of sacrifice always took place sacrificially. If we are to take seriously the New Testament's proposal for a *new anthropos* — an alternate way of engendering social and psychological stability — the text that proposes it will have to teach us how to avoid the trap into which the prophetic tradition fell from Moses to John the Baptist. It will have to decode and decommission the mechanism by which the *old anthropology* of sacrifice turned its fieriest critics into its most faithful perpetuators.

As illuminating as it is, it is not enough to recognize how the same mimetic forces that breed discord — the *diabolos* — restore social harmony at a later stage of the crisis — *Satan* — by transferring all the social poisons onto one scapegoat victim. We must better understand how even those who have begun to recognize this process and raise moral objections to it still get caught up in the social contagions choreographed by the *diabolos* and *Satan*. The New Testament cannot be humanity's revelatory text par excellence unless it can show us how to keep from turning our moral outrages into newfangled versions of the thing that outraged us.

If the fiery beginning of John's prophetic career set in motion Jesus' own vocation, another important factor in Jesus' growing understanding of his mission seems to have been John the Baptist's fatal collision with the court of Herod, the Jewish client monarch who ruled Judea at the time. Both personally and politically, Herod was a repulsive figure embroiled in endless plots and murderous intrigues, and John openly condemned him. Soon John was in Herod's prison, and not long after that, dead. John's fate seems to have had an effect on Jesus' ministry comparable in many ways to the effect of the desert temptations. While in Herod's prison, John sent his followers to Jesus to ask about the nature of Jesus' mission:

> Now John in his prison had heard what Christ was doing and he sent his disciples to ask him, "Are you the one who is to come, or have we got to wait for someone else?" Jesus answered, "Go back and tell John what you hear and see: the blind see again, and the lame walk, lepers are cleansed, and the deaf hear, and the dead are raised to life and the Good News is proclaimed to the poor; and happy is the man who does not lose faith in *me*." (Matt. 11:2–6)

John took his spiritual challenge right to the core of Jewish apostasy and moral decay. With admirable courage, he challenged raw power and exposed himself to its cruelties. And what had Jesus done upon hearing of John's plight? Had he been as bold to challenge? Had he faced the powers-that-be? Was he prepared to become, if need be, the resurrected John the Baptist, as Herod had feared at one point? Seen from the perspective of Herod's dungeon, Jesus' innocuous behavior left some doubt in the minds of John and his followers.

John urged contrition on his listeners and railed against their sinfulness. By contrast, it was Jesus' conspicuous indifference toward his listeners' prior moral failures that caused certain righteous elements in Jewish society to regard his mission as socially pernicious. Contrary to John, Jesus seems to have understood that the only real and lasting contrition occurs, not when one is confronted with one's sins, but when one experiences the gust of grace that makes a loving and forgiving God plausible. John warned of the approach of the kingdom and passionately enjoined his listeners to renounce their evil ways. Jesus *inhabited* that kingdom and made it a palpable reality for others by forgiving sins, restoring faith and hope to those around him, and bringing people he touched fully alive. What the encounter between Jesus and John's disciples makes explicit, however, is that Jesus had consciously chosen *not* to do what John had done. John had raged at the shamelessness of the Herodian court in so bellicose a manner that the predictable reactions and counter-reactions were set off. Soon, John's life and ministry became consumed—first morally and then literally—by the very thing he railed against.

When John's disciples asked if Jesus was the one "who is to come," using the words of the prophet Isaiah, Jesus spoke of his ministry of healing and reconciling, and he concluded by saying: "Happy is the man who does not lose faith in me." In the literal Greek, he says: happy is he who is not *scandalized* by me. It is in this phrase that we find Jesus' rebuttal to the critique of his ministry implied by John's question. The Greek word *skandalon* is often translated as "stumbling block" or "offense." There is as well, however, an implication in the word of an almost irresistible compulsion, an obsession.[6]

When Jesus told John's disciples that "happy is the one who is not scandalized by me," he was responding to John's implied critique of his more reticent missionary work. John had allowed himself to be scandalized by the moral and religious shamelessness of the Herodian court. The passion of his contempt eventually entangled him in the very delusions he was condemning. In his well-meaning attempt to usher in the kingdom he sensed was imminent, John had become a player in the same melodrama whose insubstantiality and moral shabbiness he was condemning. Scandalized by Herod's depravity, John merely became the occasion for another depraved act. He accused Herod of the awful things that Herod did, but when the "diabolical" charade became "satanic," it was John at whom the Accuser pointed. John's accusations were certainly just, but they just as certainly gave the inevitable counter-accusations a thread of plausibility. John embroiled himself in the kind of sordid melodrama that destroys the moral coherence even of its despisers. If in the wilderness Jesus had come to appreciate something about the diabolical dynamic of mimesis, conflict, accusation, and scapegoating violence, John's fate would have confronted him with a vivid and horrifying example of exactly that dynamic.

I feel, therefore, that there is in the Gospels a structural link between the *diabolos,* the *skandalon,* and the *satan.* They constitute what we might think of as a demonic trinity by which we humans are forever being drawn into the mimetic scenarios that blind us and lead eventually to violence.

The Fires of Hell

One episode in the Gospel of Matthew helps bring into focus what the New Testament means when it speaks of "scandal" and the need to avoid it if possible. In this story, Jesus' disciples demonstrate how poorly even they understand his message by jockeying for position among themselves. Jesus rebukes them with what seems to be an extended non sequitur on the subject of scandalization:

> At this time the disciples came to Jesus and said, "Who is the greatest in the kingdom of heaven?" So he called a little child to him and set the child in front of them. Then he said, "I tell you solemnly, unless you change and become like little children you will never enter the kingdom of heaven. And so, the one who makes himself as little as this little child is the greatest in the kingdom of heaven. Anyone who welcomes a little child like this in my name welcomes me. But anyone who scandalizes one of these little ones who have faith in me would be better drowned in the depths of the sea with a great millstone around his neck. What terrible things will come on the world through scandal. It is inevitable that scandal should occur. Nonetheless, woe to that man through whom scandal comes! If your hand or foot is a scandal to you, cut it off and throw it from you! Better to enter life maimed or crippled than be thrown with two hands or two feet into the endless conflagration. If your eye is a scandal, gouge it out and cast it from you! Better to enter life with one eye than be thrown with both into the fire of hell." (Matt. 18:1–9)

The first thing to notice is how the disciples' lapse into mimetic rivalry evoked from Jesus a discourse on scandal and scandalizing. As I said, it seems at first a non sequitur. From the mimetic point of view, however, it is the perfect response. Jesus recognized his disciples' anxiety about their relative social standing for what it was: an indication that they were becoming "stumbling blocks" for one another. They were becoming envious and rivalrous.

Ironically, Jesus here uses imagery that is scandalous in the conventional sense of being shocking in order to stress the dangers of scandal in the scriptural sense of something that arouses envious, covetous, or rivalrous desire. The image of gouging out one's eye or crippling oneself in order to avoid a dangerous possibility is so hideous, in fact, that there is no chance that it would be taken literally. At the same time, it dramatically underscores the scope of a danger of which Jesus' disciples remain oblivious. Here, however, it is only Jesus who understands the depth of the problem of mimetic rivalry. Only he had been to the desert. Only he had realized that the sower of discord dispenses satanic forms of camaraderie, and that all the kingdoms of this world owed their coherence to this satanic alchemist and his accusatory recipe for turning discord into harmony.

In the passage, Jesus uses two terms in speaking of the result of scandalization. In one verse he speaks of "endless conflagration" (my translation). Like all conflagrations in which the Bible takes an interest, this conflagration is no doubt a metaphor for violence. It is endless, obviously, because the violence cannot be effectively terminated. In other words, it is apocalyptic violence. The sacralized violence that had always been humanity's instrument for terminating the deadly reciprocities of ordinary violence would be undermined by the Cross, and, during his lifetime, the man who was murdered on it implored his followers to avoid the scandals that led to reciprocities of rivalry and violence. What Jesus realized was that the only alternative the world would one day have to "endless conflagration" would be the renunciation of the highly flammable mixture of envy, rivalry, jealousy, and resentment for which the word "scandal" is a virtual synonym.

The other term Jesus used in this passage to warn against the effect of scandal was the Greek term here, as elsewhere, translated as "hell." The Greek word is *gehenna.* The word has a literal as well as a symbolic reference. It refers to the garbage dump located in New Testament times southwest of Jerusalem. For better or worse, the smoldering fires that burned there "endlessly" gave the later Christian notion of "hell" its most enduring metaphor. The deeper meaning of this passage surfaces, however, when we learn that *gehenna* was the Greek term that translated the Hebrew "valley of *ben-hinnom*" (the place where idol-worshiping Israelites had engaged in child sacrifice), the term that Jeremiah has used as a synonym for cults of human sacrifice generally. Seen against this larger scriptural backdrop, therefore, Jesus' warnings become anthropologically intelligible. He sees rivalry leading to scandal, and scandal leading either back into the worst forms of cult sacrifice (*gehenna*) or, in a world whose sacrificial resources have been exposed and destroyed, to the endless conflagration of apocalyptic violence. In this passage, astonishingly, Jesus responds to the most familiar and seemingly innocuous forms of scandal — the disciples' petty rivalry for social status — with the direst of warnings about the dangers of human sacrifice and catastrophic violence. Either the passage is illogical or it is coherent at a level deeper than the one at which human behavior and its consequences are usually reckoned. Deciding whether it is one or the other is not a matter of idle curiosity. We live in an age in which we are encouraged from cradle to grave to maneuver for social or economic advantage vis-à-vis others. If Jesus' rebuke to his disciples is not a clumsy mistake on his part or on the part of Matthew, then we flout his warnings about the need to avoid scandal at our peril.

Avoiding Impurity

There is abundant evidence suggesting that both during Jesus' life and at the time the New Testament was written the flash point of Jewish religious orthodoxy was the dietary laws. These proscriptions were an elaboration of the passages in the book of Leviticus whose original function had been to regulate the selection, preparation, and consumption of animals used for ritual sacrifice. The dietary laws to which the Pharisees and other orthodox Jews carefully adhered prescribed meticulous ritual washings deemed necessary to avoid contamination, and they carefully regulated how food was to be prepared and eaten and with whom it might be safely shared. Scrupulosity about defiling contact with sinners and the fear of ingesting unclean food combined to make the sharing of meals a particularly touchy issue. For observant Jews of the time, it was a perilous thing to share a meal with those about whose moral and religious status they were uncertain. Conscious intention had nothing to do with the all-important matter of avoiding impurity. Contact with sinners or the ingestion of forbidden or unsanctified foods would defile one and make it necessary to submit to ritual cleansings, regardless of how inadvertent the exposure to the impurity might have been. The safest course, under the circumstances, was to avoid all contact with outcasts and sinners and with pagans and nonobserving Jews. For those who strove to observe every detail of the elaborate dietary regulations, meals shared with anyone other than one's most intimate kin and co-religionists were occasions fraught with moral and religious dangers.

In the first century, Greek and Roman influence in Palestine was pervasive, and mingling with non-Jews became a fact of life for Jews living in the cities of Judea and Galilee. Consequently, orthodox Jews found the task of adhering to the dietary proscriptions more challenging, while at the same time they felt adherence to these customs more than ever essential for the preservation of Jewish cultural identity. It is only by understanding the *moral* significance of sharing meals for the Jews of Jesus' time, therefore, that one can fully appreciate what was one of the distinguishing features of his ministry: table fellowship. Again and again, the Gospels show Jesus and his disciples sharing meals, and Jesus' eagerness to share these meals with "sinners" and the "outcasts" may have been the most conspicuous feature of his ministry.

By simply sitting at table with those widely regarded as morally contemptible, Jesus earned the scorn of the Pharisees and other strict observers of Jewish custom. By sharing meals with those considered by the religiously righteous to be outcasts and sinners, Jesus challenged "the central ordering principle of the Jewish social world."[7] As Geza Vermes put it, Jesus "took his stand among the pariahs of the world, those despised by the respectable. Sinners were his table-companions and the ostracized tax collectors and prostitutes his friends."[8] The meals Jesus shared with the outcasts were not, therefore, simply the occasion for the delivery of his message. They *were* the message. They served as "prophetic signs" meant to manifest the meaning of Jesus' ministry. They involved what Borg speaks of as a "radical relativizing of cultural distinctions."[9] It is in this context of Jewish dietary concerns that I think one can best understand the miracle of loaves and fishes.

The Miracle of Loaves and Fishes

It seems clear to me that Jesus' burning passion was to free those he encountered from the grip of religious mystification and scandalous delusion whose effects were to harden the human heart and turn people into accomplices in cruelty and lovelessness. In trying to bring about this liberation, Jesus seems to have found the popular appetite for miracles exasperating. At times he fled from crowds looking for a miracle worker, and he resolutely refused to perform miracles simply for the purpose of demonstrating his ability to perform them.

It is important, therefore, to remember that for a miracle to have genuine religious significance it must transform the human heart and that it was a transformation of the heart that Jesus brought about in those he deeply touched. Curing a crippled leg is not as miraculous as curing a hardened heart or a despairing soul. In approaching the miracles, therefore, we should look to their spiritual effect primarily and strive to understand them on that level first. The great miracle of Jesus' ministry was reconciliation — with God and with others. This, I think, is the starting point for understanding the miracle of the loaves and fishes, and the other miracles as well.

The various Gospel accounts of Jesus feeding large crowds from scant supplies may be versions of one memorable event for which several accounts survived. In the present form, the accounts presuppose that those who had come to hear him, some from considerable distance, brought no food with them. Jesus' audience would have been almost exclusively made up of Jews, and, as I pointed out, most religious-minded Jews of the time would have taken the precaution of bringing with them enough bread or dried fish to insure that they would not be forced to eat food whose ritual purity was in doubt. But taking the precaution of bringing a supply of ritually clean food would have been only one hurdle, and perhaps not the largest one. For eating these provisions while in the company of others of uncertain moral and religious character would have placed one in jeopardy of moral contamination from sinners and pagans. The fact that Jesus had a reputation for attracting and tolerating the socially marginal would have added to the anxiety of observant Jews in this regard. Not knowing the moral and religious status of those sitting nearby would have made many reluctant to bring out whatever provisions they had with them.

In all the accounts of Jesus feeding the multitude, it is Jesus who takes the initiative and invites the people to sit down and prepare for a meal. Sharing a meal together was *his* idea, not theirs. For reasons I have already stated, Jesus' audience probably found the idea unsettling. This wariness, on the other hand, would have been symptomatic of the niggling religious apprehensions from which Jesus was trying to liberate them. Given the role of table fellowship in Jesus' ministry, it is my view that it was not primarily the lateness of the hour that made the unexpected sharing of a meal necessary, but rather that Jesus decided to drive home the points he had been making in his preaching by inviting his audience to sit down then and there for the purpose of sharing a meal with those around them. The point of the feeding, in my opinion, was not food; it was the breaking down of religious and social barriers that Jesus had been challenging as spiritually inconsequential in his preaching. It was hands-on learning. It was practice for living in the kingdom.

All the Gospel accounts speak of Jesus praying a blessing before the miracle occurred. In other words, he didn't just go to the few loaves and dried fish and cause them to multiply; he gave thanks to God in words *to which the people listened carefully.* It was *then* that the miracle occurred. By now the reader will have guessed what I think the miracle was. Jesus opened their hearts, and they, in turn, opened their satchels, and the greatest miracle of all occurred. Following a pattern that is still today embedded in the Catholic Mass, Jesus preached of a God of love and forgiveness and then invited those who heard his message to sit down together and live for a moment in the "kingdom" about which he was preaching. Changing the human heart and liberating those trapped in religious superstition is simply a greater miracle than pulling loaves and dried fish out of a basket. The feeding of the multitude was a *real* miracle. The miracle was a new kind of community, one generated by prayer and inclusion, a "new generation." Transitory as it may have been, it remains a model for a new community, one on which all human culture will one day have to be based. The social bond that gave the community that Jesus inspired its coherence had one conspicuous feature: the breaking down of religious prejudice.

Exorcisms

Jesus performed other miracles. He cured the sick and cast out demons from those possessed by them. Just as in the case of the feeding of the multitude, however, we must not allow the greater — sometimes subtle — miracle to be eclipsed by more blatant but lesser miracles. Nothing deserves the name of miracle that does not renovate the human heart, and anything that does, deserves the name. Miraculously restoring a blind man's sight is surely a most startling thing, inasmuch as it happens in defiance of what we think of as natural laws. But in and of itself simply making a blind man see may have little spiritual significance. In *King Lear,* old Gloucester, his eyes gouged out, says, "I stumbled when I saw." On the other hand, Elias Canetti attributes the elation and conviction of a mob turning on its victim to "the excitement of blind men who are blindest when they suddenly think they can see."[10] This is the blindness that Jesus strove to cure.

Jesus cured those thought to be possessed by "demons," but these cures were all features in his overall mission of exposing the perversities and ending the reign of "prince of this world" — the "Diabolos-Satan." In New Testament times, to be diseased — whether physically or mentally — implied sinfulness. The good prospered materially and were rewarded with robust health, while the sinners, outcasts, and religious backsliders were fated to suffer for their apostasy and wickedness. The logic of the underlying moral principle easily worked in reverse. A physical affliction was thought to be a divine punishment, perhaps for some sin that remained undetectable but that could be deduced from the fact of the affliction. A person in poverty or in ill-health or mentally ill or psychologically distraught was thought to be marked by sin. Those with psychological or physical disorders suffered from a social stigma that may have been a greater source of distress than the physical or mental affliction and that almost certainly placed the afflicted one in at least some social jeopardy.

Just as designation of a social crisis as a "plague" is often an early sign that a scapegoating episode is in the making, so the diagnosis of demonic possession indicates that those who have arrived at this diagnosis are slipping into the grip of the uncanny forces of primitive religion, forces whose eventual manifestation will be accusatory and violent. When Jesus expelled the demon from the madman of Gerasene, the demon revealed his real name: *Legion.* The real demonic force under whose sway the "possessed" one begins to fall the moment his community designates him as "possessed" is the mob, which will eventually form to rid itself of the contaminated one. What is demonic is not the person suffering from this or that distress. What is demonic is the *diagnosis* of demonic possession. In healing the one possessed, Jesus effectively overrules the diagnosis or cancels its social consequences. He disarms the satanic (accusatory) power by restoring the dignity and social standing of those most in danger of becoming scapegoats.

Jesus' whole life, ministry, and death had the effect of restoring to their senses those who had eyes but could not see and ears but could not hear. If the healing of disease or the curing of afflictions involves a suspension of the "laws" of nature, softening the human heart or refashioning the human self requires that social and psychological reflexes relied upon and reinforced "since the foundation of the world" be overridden. So tenacious are these reflexes that they have often enough been thought synonymous with "human *nature.*" Transcending these reflexes, or suppressing their influence, is at least as arduous a feat as manipulating objects in the material order, and vastly more spiritually significant.

Chapter 12

"It Is Accomplished"

By the time of his trial and passion Jesus had succeeded in uniting an improbable, indeed unprecedented, coalition against him: the Roman authorities, the Sadducees, the Pharisees, even Herod Antipas. And in destroying him, this unnatural combination appears to have acted with a great measure of popular support. What conclusions can we draw from this?[1]

PAUL JOHNSON

Jesus was a real victim, but so were the two "thieves" and countless other Jewish patriots of his period. Jesus' cultural importance did not come from being a victim, but from being *the* victim.[2]

ERIC GANS

Jesus is not there in order to stress once again in his own person the unified violence of the sacred; he is not there to ordain and govern like Moses; he is not there to unite a people around him, to forge its unity in the crucible of rites and prohibitions, but on the contrary, to turn this long page of human history once and for all.[3]

RENÉ GIRARD

Ultimately, it was Jesus' public execution and not his public ministry that consummated the biblical revelation, inspired the New Testament, launched the Christian movement, and eventually led to the anthropological crisis in which we now find ourselves. As the first Christians moved beyond the Jewish cultural orbit into the wider Greco-Roman world, they found people bewildered by the idea that the world had been saved by a young Jew condemned by his co-religionists and publicly executed as a political nuisance by the Romans authorities. There was an understandable tendency to make the gospel more intelligible to the Greek world by downplaying the crucifixion and stressing instead the *teachings* of Jesus. Paul reacted vigorously to this, and he adamantly insisted on "preaching Christ crucified." Almost two millennia later, the historian Paul Johnson would observe that the central paradox of Jesus' mission was that it could have been fully vindicated only by its failure.[4]

If, as Paul insisted, the Cross is at the center of the Christian message, both Christianity's emancipatory claims and its claim of universal relevance would seem to depend on whether or not collective violence of the kind structurally indistinguishable from that involved in the crucifixion is *the* linchpin of human delusion. Moreover, seen through the eyes of open-minded nonbelievers, it's difficult to think of how else such claims could be sustained. Of course, one of the main reasons we have missed the gospel's universality and tarnished its universal claims in the eyes of others is that we have tended to appropriate it in such parochial ways. The surest way to miss the link between the cure (the crucifixion and its aftereffects) and the disease (the structures of scapegoating violence upon which all human social arrangements have depended) is to read the passion story with an eye to locating and denouncing those most responsible for it. There is a deep irony in this. The fact that we automatically search the text—or the world outside the text—for culprits on whom to blame the crucifixion is proof that we are one of the culprits, for the crucifixion was demanded by those determined to find a culprit to blame or punish or expel. Responsibility for the crucifixion—and the system of sacred or scapegoating violence it epitomizes—is to be borne either by all of us or by only some of us. If the responsibility belongs only to some of us, those who bear responsibility deserve the contempt of those who do not, and we are back in a world of religious categories and sacred violence. The crucifixion's anthropological significance is lost if responsibility for its violence is shifted from *all* to *some.* To lay the blame on the Pharisees or the Jews is to undermine the universal meaning of the crucifixion in favor of the familiar finger-pointing theory of human wickedness.

The fact, however, that religious zeal played such a decisive role in Jesus' death is both historically true and structurally essential to the revelation for which the Cross stands. The fact that it was Jewish religious zeal is not entirely without significance, but it has precisely the same significance that historical Christianity's anti-Jewish pogroms have, namely, that the people who should have known better didn't. And so, one of the great ironies is that historical Christianity's willingness to blame the Jews for the crucifixion has often kept it from appreciating the role Jews played in recognizing the meaning of the crucifixion. The Cross became the revelation it is largely because it occurred in a Jewish setting. Only in a culture predisposed to empathize with victims could the crucifixion have had its full effects. If the forces that militated for Jesus' crucifixion were Jewish, so were the men and women whose lives were fundamentally altered by it and who first experienced its historical and spiritual impact. The Jewishness of Jesus' opponents should never be given more weight than the Jewishness of Jesus' disciples and those who first felt the power of the Christian revelation and proclaimed it to others. It was Jews who rejected and reviled Jesus; it was Jews whose lives were transformed by him, and it was a Jew who was reviled and revered in each case.

To think, as historical Christianity has sometimes allowed itself to think, that the responsibility for Jesus' death lies with the Jews is to entirely miss the meaning of the crucifixion. There is no better place to turn to disabuse ourselves of this notion than the Gospel whose language seems to have favored the notion in the first place, namely, the Gospel of John. The author of John's Gospel used the term "the Jews" often and in various ways, but the phrase is almost always used as a synonym for the religious authorities who oppose Jesus. Were we to substitute for the word "Jews" the word "religionists," we would be closer to the anthropological significance of the Gospel's reproach. Such a revision, however, would be both too narrow and too broad. Unless we identify it to some degree with Judaism, as many of the first Christians did, we cannot feel the pathos of Jewish opposition to Jesus. The most telling point to be made by indicating the Jewishness of Jesus' opposition is the point made in the prologue to John's Gospel, namely, that "he came to his own domain and *his own people* did not accept him" (John 1:11). Jesus was the victim of his *own people,* heirs as he was of the biblical revelation, but too blinded by a parochial understanding of that tradition to be able to recognize the living incarnation of its universality. Now that Jesus' own people are *Christians,* the moral weight of every New Testament reference to Jewish opposition to Jesus falls squarely on Christians.

John's Gospel provides the New Testament's most breathtaking vista on the universal meaning of the crucifixion and its eventual impact on the world. In far more detail than the synoptic evangelists (Mark, Matthew, and Luke), the Fourth Gospel explores the underlying forces that led to Jesus' death, and it provides the anthropological background for understanding the crucial role of the crowd. This is nowhere better demonstrated than in a passage in which the Johannine Jesus challenges "the Jews who believed in him." In John's Gospel, "belief" in Christ as the envoy of God is all important, but there are degrees of belief or faith, and many who believe-that-they-believe have in fact attained only very rudimentary forms of faith. So the fourth evangelist insists, for example, that those who believe in Jesus because of the miraculous signs he has performed, or because they are swept up in the enthusiasm of others, have yet to achieve the kind of faith that is decisive. Such a belief will not free the *mere believers* from the sacrificial predispositions by which their social and psychological lives are habitually ordered. As Rudolf Schnackenburg remarked, Jesus' call for faith "brings about a crisis" in which "all unbelief [is] unmasked."[5] There is an underlying "unbelief" of which "believers" are too often unaware. It is one that is too intractable to be eliminated by a mere change of conscious orientation. It is this unbelief that the Johannine Jesus is here "unmasking." To "the Jews who (merely) *believed* in him" Jesus said:

> If you make my word [*logos*] your *home*
> you will indeed be my *disciples,*
> you will learn the truth
> and the truth shall make you free.
> (John 8:31–32)

To dwell in the *Logos* of Christ, as the verses to follow explicitly show, is to transcend the parochial allegiances of conventional culture. It is to be emancipated from whatever culture-bound *logos* may have formerly served as one's mental and emotional envelope. As Paul so forcefully argued, by moral effort alone one cannot free oneself from the grip of the sacred and the logic of violence. The *logos* of conventional culture consists of so pervasive a web of conditioned reflexes that we remain largely oblivious of its influence. If we are to be freed from it, something from outside the cultural matrix must break in on us. Structurally and anthropologically speaking, there is only one thing truly outside of this matrix: the victim whose expulsion brought the system into being in the first place, the stone rejected by the builders of all culture, the Lamb slain since the foundation of the world.

What Jesus would accomplish by his death on the cross, and what he was already preaching in his public ministry, was the fulfillment of the great promise of universality that had been made to Abraham when, faithful to the biblical God, he initiated the long process of renouncing the sacrificial logic of the primitive sacred. Ironically, then, it was when Jesus reissued the call Abraham heard in his native Haran — to leave his father's house and take the journey of faith — that his listeners went deaf to the voice Abraham heard in the land of Moriah. More ironically still, their justification for doing so was that Abraham was their father. They insisted that *they* didn't need the truth that would set them free, for as children of Abraham their freedom was a foregone conclusion. As

Jesus' response to his interlocutors makes clear, however, he understands freedom to be freedom from sacrificial compulsions, for he proceeds to expose these sacrificial proclivities in the most explicit way. He says:

> I know that you are descended from Abraham;
> but in spite of that you want to kill me
> because my *logos* has not penetrated into you.
> What I, for my part, speak of
> is what I have seen with my Father;
> but you, you put into action
> the lessons learned from your father.
> (John 8:37–38)

Earlier I noted that the slightly divergent accounts of Jesus' wilderness temptations provided by Matthew and Luke form an interpretive diptych that allows us to appreciate the full anthropological implications of the story. In fact, it is when one approaches the New Testament with an anthropological sensibility that its central motifs become recognizable. Once these motifs have been recognized, all the evangelical discrepancies — so awkward and troubling when the texts are read as history, biography, or theology — have a unifying effect, inasmuch as they illuminate these central motifs from different angles. Another instance of this occurs in relation to the story of Jesus' baptism and has an important bearing on the passages in John's Gospel now under consideration. Whereas in Matthew's account of Jesus' baptism the words spoken from heaven are taken from Isaiah 42, in Luke's extremely brief allusion to the baptism the heavenly voice speaks the words of the Psalmist: "You are my son; today have I fathered you." This verse I think uniquely captures what was surely the constituting experience of Jesus' life, what some scholars call his "*Abba* experience." Jesus' public ministry was little more than a persevering effort to share with his contemporaries the liberating power and religious meaning of that experience. I mention this here because in the passages from John's Gospel we are now considering Jesus contrasts his life and message with the mounting sacrificial proclivities of his listeners in terms of the radically different *fathers* to whom each is being loyal. In the earlier passage, Jesus had told (mere) "believers" how they might become "disciples," namely, by making the *logos* of Jesus their home. The term *logos* now reappears in connection with the term "father," and it does so as Jesus begins to reveal the inner workings of the psychosocial complex we call culture.

The term "father" as the evangelist uses it here refers to a social law of gravity that predetermines the pattern (the *logos*) of social developments in the ordinary course of cultural history. No doubt first-century

Judaism was a patriarchal society, but the term "father" in these verses refers to the organizing principle of conventional culture regardless of its religious concepts or its peculiar form of social organization. What the Johannine Jesus calls the "father" — the father of lies and the murderer from the beginning — has virtually nothing to do with the male parent whom we call father.[6]

Jesus argues that those to whom he is speaking are neither the children of Abraham nor of God for, he says, "you want to kill me when I tell you the truth" (8:40). Those to whom Jesus is speaking have not been able to persevere in his *logos*. They have merely "believed" in him, while unwittingly remaining loyal to a "father" whom they mistakenly think is Abraham or God, but whom Jesus recognizes as a diabolical figure. The evidence for Jesus' claim that his listeners are in the grip of this diabolical figure consists of one thing: they want to kill him. It is this scapegoating predilection that Jesus is able to see when even those in whom it has begun to operate remain oblivious of it. And it is the existence of this scapegoating predisposition that proves that those in whom it exists have not made the *logos* of Christ their home. But their murderousness is not simply moral perversion. It is fundamental. It is anthropological. It is structural. It is the ordering principle of culture, "hidden since the foundation of the world."

"What you are doing," Jesus says, "is what your father does" (8:41). What they were doing at the moment these words were spoken was simply objecting to Jesus' annoying lack of interest in the religious pedigree upon which their social and psychological lives were premised. With nothing more on which to base a judgment than their irritation at having their descent from Abraham dismissed as irrelevant, Jesus extrapolates: soon they will want to kill him. How does the Jesus of John's Gospel know that they want to kill him? He has only one piece of evidence. When Jesus tried to invite them out of their cultural cocoon, they bristled and reasserted their ethnicity. The fact that they suddenly began to assert their ethnicity with indignation indicates that they have begun to sense the shattering effect Jesus and his preaching might have on their conventional religious and social orientation. Those to whom Jesus is speaking are right to sense that he is a threat to the conventional cultural and religious framework on which they depend, but his challenge to these things is neither gratuitous nor anti-Jewish. He is simply revealing a truth that is antithetical to conventional culture and the merely social self.

The Johannine Jesus uncovers the struggle between the *Logos* of Jesus (the *Logos* of love) and the *logos* of violence. These are the two ordering principles that confront one another in the Gospel, and especially in the passion story. Over each of these systems of *logic* there presides a *father.* In one of the New Testament's most anthropologically powerful passages, Jesus says:

> Do you know why you cannot take in what I say?
> It is because you are unable to understand my logos.
> The devil is your father,
> and you prefer to do
> what your father wants.
> He was a murderer from the beginning...
> he is a liar, and the father of lies. (John 8:43–44)

The *logos* under whose spell the world of conventional culture thrives is the *logos* of misrecognition, the *mythos,* "the father of lies," the "murderer from the beginning."

Son of the Father

Even when it is not explicit, the tension between Jesus' heavenly Father and the murderous father of lies hovers in the background of John's Gospel. One of the most vivid instances of the theme is also one of the most discrete. It occurs in the middle of the passion story. It was apparently customary for Roman authorities to indulge their Jewish subjects during the Passover celebration by releasing one of the Jewish prisoners held under Roman law. Those who might be released were probably somewhat comparable to what we would today call political prisoners, that is, Jewish nationalists whose zeal had led to their arrest by Roman authorities. As Roman authorities would have seen it, Jesus was such a figure. Hoping to placate the mob demanding a crucifixion, Pilate offers to release one prisoner. He offers them Jesus or Barabbas, apparently hoping they will take Jesus and assuming that they might. They choose Barabbas, of course.

The Aramaic name "Barabbas" means the "son of the father." Especially for the Johannine author, Jesus is the son of his "heavenly Father." In addition, some of the ancient texts give Barabbas's first name as Jesus. And so the mob is offered two men who are identical. The choice is between Jesus Barabbas (son of his father) and Jesus bar *Abba* (son of his Father). The theological irony is explicit. Barabbas, however, is identified as a "brigand." The Jewish historian Josephus uses this word, the Greek *lestes,* to refer to revolutionary Jewish nationalists. In New Testament times the term was probably a synonym for a guerrilla fighter, a Jewish revolutionary committed to overthrowing the Roman occupation. In Mark's Gospel, for instance, Barabbas is said to have been imprisoned for committing murder in an insurrection. In other words, Barabbas, the other "son of the father," was one for whom ethnicity was a holy cause and whose violence in the service of that cause he and many of his fellow Jews considered sacred.

Barabbas, abiding in the *logos* of violence, proposes to violently avenge the deaths of those whom he loves and to repay the violence of those whom he hates tit for tat. Whatever the historical circumstances that may have made their contempt for Rome understandable, Zealots such as Barabbas so hated their historical adversaries that they were willing to become morally indistinguishable from them in order to reciprocate the violence they had suffered. Barabbas's rival had become his model. In truth, the spiritual father of Barabbas the insurrectionist was the Roman tyrant — the murderer — whom he hoped to overthrow. It is in this sense that Barabbas's name is apt. He was the son of the father, and he, in turn, would surely become the father of the next son of the father. Barabbas was destined to extend history's violent reciprocities into the next generation and beyond ad infinitum.

Since mobs are products of mimetic contagion, and since by its very nature the mob is always and only eager for what excites its *esprit de corps* and focuses its vehemence, Jesus has nothing to offer the crowd. Should the mob demand his release, it would be tantamount to adjourning, and it has not gathered at the Roman praetorium in order to adjourn. In choosing Barabbas, the mob is choosing one of its own. He personifies the very sacrificial reflexes in the grip of which they are insisting that Jesus be put to death. And so the Barabbas episode is not a merely incidental feature of the passion story. It reverberates with the central issues of John's Gospel. It reveals the *logos* of Christ in obedience to the will of his heavenly Father in a decisive showdown with the *logos* of sacred violence and the father of lies.

Jesus' insistence that he recognized only God as his "father" implied a renunciation of the whole pattern of conventional allegiances for which the patriarchal system of first-century Judaism was by and large typical. In proclaiming that only God was his father, Jesus was repudiating the whole array of parochial loyalties that provided his contemporaries with their central organizing principle, their *logos*. Because we interpret the New Testament references to God as father in such silly and shallow ways, we mistake the Gospel's renunciation of patriarchy for another hackneyed expression of it. "Jesus neutralizes the absolute power of the earthly father by means of the claims of the heavenly Father," writes

Robert Hamerton-Kelly. "The fact that Jesus chose the 'father' symbol for this purpose suggests that he intended to direct his message especially at the patriarchy and to reorganize it by freeing people from its clutches."[7] To have God as one's "father" (or Christ as one's "Lord") is to have renounced or subordinated the patriarchies, patrons, and patriotisms on which conventional cultural life relies for its coherence.

As a result of the process — a historically inevitable one — by which the Christian gospel was domesticated and the Christian movement institutionalized, the revolutionary implication of Jesus' insistence that only God was his "father" receded into the background. During much of the Christian era, Jesus' appeal to the "Father" tended only to reinforce the kinds of social arrangements whose ultimate validity it undermines. If the patriarchal biases of earlier ages blinded them to the more radical implications of Jesus' invocation of God as his "father," modernity's contempt for patriarchy and its growing animus against any serious vestige of the paternal principle hardly qualify it for the task of rectifying the mistakes of the past. Two thousand years after the gospel proclaimed the provisional nature of cultural arrangements, we moderns decided that the Bible is patriarchy's charter document. With great fanfare and self-congratulations, we set to work dismantling the remnants of the patriarchal system. With vertiginous speed, we have made a joke out of the moral authority of fathers and all that they represented, but we have made little discernible effort to adhere to the will of a "heavenly Father," and signs of our continued bondage to "the father of lies, the murderer from the beginning" are everywhere. The *Logos* of Christ and the reign of Jesus' heavenly *Father,* on one hand, and, the *logos* of righteous violence and the reign of the murderous *father* of lies, on the other, represent two mental and spiritual horizons that are at war with one another throughout the Fourth Gospel. The evangelist's "dualism" is nothing more than his conviction that in the final analysis these two *logos* principles represent the only two options the human race has. According to this Gospel, the only viable alternative to living in witless complicity with the father of lies is to live in conscious conformity with the "heavenly Father," which Jesus' life made visible.

The Spirit

In John's Gospel, the crucifixion and the resurrection are the same thing. The Johannine Jesus had repeatedly said that when he was "lifted up" — meaning hung on the Cross — he would begin to draw all of humanity to himself. Whether some form of this claim goes back to the historical Jesus is, of course, uncertain, but even if the claim originates with the evangelist in the late first century, it is a bold, almost brazen claim. The striking and irrefutable fact is that history has borne it out. That is all the more reason to marvel at the prescience of the Fourth Gospel. Explicitly and with a calm assurance that in the hindsight of two thousand years is astonishing, the Gospel of John predicts that the crucifixion will have the most sweeping effects on human history.

The last words of the Johannine Jesus, spoken from the Cross, are: "It is accomplished." The verb used here, *telein,* means to bring to completion, but the deeper issue is not the predicate but the subject of the sentence. What is accomplished? What is brought to fulfillment? What is brought to an end?

In John's Gospel, Jesus pronounces the prologue to his own passion with these words:

> Now sentence is being passed on this world;
> now the prince of this world is to be overthrown.
> And when I am lifted up from the earth,
> I shall draw all men to myself. (John 12:31–32)

The crucifixion both "accomplishes" the decisive demystification of the demonic powers and inaugurates the historical epoch in which these powers — and the social and psychological structures based upon them — will undergo a progressive delegitimization, as the Crucified One gradually draws all of humanity to himself. As Rudolf Schnackenburg put it, "The ruler of the world encounters the final rejection, loses his sphere of influence, becomes powerless — over those who look up in faith to the crucified Jesus and let themselves be 'drawn' to him."[8]

According to the fourth evangelist, the spiritual and anthropological revolution set in motion by the crucifixion is a glacial process the driving force of which is the "Spirit of Truth" — the Paraclete. It was to be the task of this Spirit of Truth to gradually "accomplish" historically what was "accomplished" in the hearts of Jesus' disciples at the crucifixion and in the days that followed it. As I have said, the Greek word *Parakletos* means a "counselor" or "advocate." More precisely, it means one who defends the "accused one." The Paraclete is the planetary spirit who deconstructs the myths and mystifications spewed forth by Satan, the perennial "Accuser." Jesus, speaking of the Paraclete, said:

> ... unless I go,
> the Advocate will not come to you;
> but if I do go,
> I will send him to you.

> And when he comes,
> he will show the world how wrong it was,
> about sin,
> about who was in the right,
> and about judgment. (John 16:7–8)

The world would continue to hold itself together and make itself coherent by channeling its violence toward expendable victims. Cultures and subcultures in the grip of the "father of lies" would continue to drown out the victim's voice with myths and incantations and slogans. But from the moment of the crucifixion onward, the Paraclete would be at work in the world, slowly giving the victim's voice the ability, in the haunting words of Whittaker Chambers, to sweep away the logic of the mind, the logic of history, the logic of politics, and whatever contemporary myths might lend violence a momentary aura of righteousness. However formidable the structures of the sacrificial system might be, however beguilingly and discretely these structures might resort to their scapegoating mechanisms, relentlessly the Paraclete would "show the world how wrong it was," gradually leading humanity to "the complete truth" (John 16:8, 13).

Had not the crucifixion loosened the grip that the primitive sacred had on the human imagination, we would probably find Caiaphas's view on the matter far more intelligible than Paul's. Without the crucifixion we would still be living in one of the cultural subdivisions thoroughly under the spell of what the Fourth Gospel calls the father of lies and the murderer from the beginning. No doubt some amelioration of sacred violence would have occurred, but without something structurally equivalent to the Gospels, something with an anthropological and historical purview comparable to that which the Gospels have achieved, all critiques of the structures of sacred violence would be taking place from *within* these structures.

Once you show the world the picture of this planet taken from the moon, try as you may to resuscitate them, there are certain parochial myths that simply cannot be revived and sustained. The effect of the crucifixion is precisely the same, only with vastly greater anthropological significance. The gospel can neither be annihilated nor can its historical momentum be arrested because the process of arresting or annihilating it would be structurally identical to the crucifixion itself and would therefore have the effect of supplying the revelation with yet another proof of its historical pertinence. The Johannine Jesus said that once he was raised up on the Cross he would draw all humanity to himself, that gradually the sight of this innocent man on the gallows would become more compelling than all of conventional culture's techniques for making sanctioned violence morally respectable. By the time the biblical scholars finally succeed in disproving the "authenticity" of this saying and demonstrating beyond all scholarly doubt that it was never spoken by the historical Jesus, it will have been fulfilled in ways that the average ten-year-old will be able to recognize.

The Empty Tomb

As I have said, the author of the Fourth Gospel speaks of the source of human evil and delusion as the "father of lies" and the "murderer from the beginning." If this "father" is a father from the beginning, and if what he fathers is lies, then the first lie must also have taken place at the beginning. If he is a murderer from the beginning, then the beginning must have been a murder. The first lie took place at the site of the first event. The event was a collective murder; the lie was that it was not a murder but an act of religious devotion and zeal. The lie was the myth.

As it no doubt was at the beginning, so throughout history, it is at the graves of those slain by collective violence that the "grave" assurances of the "father of lies" have traditionally had their greatest appeal. The "father of lies" accounts for the collective violence in religious terms and converts the tomb of the slain one into a shrine where the camaraderie born of the murder can be revived and hallowed. By building a tomb and going there to perform solemn rites of *remembrance,* we humans *forget* our own responsibility for the deaths of those whom the grave purports to honor or those who will die in the violence required to avenge their deaths.

"Murder calls for the tomb," writes René Girard, "and the tomb is but the prolongation and perpetuation of murder."[9] The tomb of those who died violently is a myth in stone. Both the myths and the tombs relate the story of past violence and give it meaning. They exonerate those who fall under their mythic influence from moral responsibility for collective violence. They edify and unify the mourners. Tombs are the architectural components of rituals that, according to Elias Canetti, make it possible for those who have raged and murdered to feel themselves "aligned with the suffering" and free from "the accumulated guilt of killing."[10] The tomb is where the "father of lies" and the "murderer from the beginning" can be counted on to issue his solemn reassurances and conjure into existence another of the "kingdoms" of "this world" or revive a flagging one. "There is no culture without a tomb and no tomb without a culture," writes Girard; "in the end the tomb is the first and only cultural symbol."[11]

If speaking in these terms seems strange, one need only glance at the newspaper to see how casually and habitually the tombs of victims are turned into sacred justifications for more victimization. The July 8, 1992, edition of the *New York Times,* for instance, carried a story about the fierce ethnic fighting in the Nagorno-Karabakh enclave of Azerbaijan. The story begins by quoting a notice posted in a building in Armenia where assistance for the Nagorno-Karabakh partisans was organized. The notice read:

> All those who hold dear the graves of our ancestors, our churches and our holies, must sow terror on the foe. By day and by night, they must perish.

Whether one is living in the ancient world or the modern one, in order to "sow terror on the foe" night and day one must go mad. If the terror can be sanctified, if the violence can be experienced as holy, and if the *esprit de corps* of those sowing the terror can achieve religious intensity, then the madness can pass for lucidity itself. The "father of lies" of which the author of John's Gospel speaks is the force that converts the graves of those killed violently into the solemn obligation to unleash violence on others. To paraphrase Howard Nemerov, the tomb is where murders become memories and memories become the beautiful obligations.

One of the most graphic of the recent instances of this was ably recounted in Robert D. Kaplan's *Balkan Ghosts: A Journey through History.* Kaplan writes of the Serbian leader Slobodan Milosevic: "The only Eastern European Communist leader in the late 1980s who managed to save himself and his party from collapse did so by making a direct appeal to racial hatred."[12] Kaplan tries to explain why, but for a quick synopsis of his explanation, let me just quote the first two paragraphs of the Tina Rosenberg review of Kaplan's book that appeared in the March 28, 1993, edition of the *Washington Post Book World.* Rosenberg writes:

> On June 28, 1987, an ambitious Serbian Communist leader came to a field in Kosovo called Kosovo Polje, the Field of Black Birds, on the anniversary of the defeat there of a Serbian commander. "They'll never do this to you again," he pleaded to the crowd. "Never again will anyone defeat you." That was the moment, writes Robert D. Kaplan, when the Serbian revolt against the Yugoslav federation began. The speaker was Slobodan Milosevic. The defeat commemorated on that field took place in 1389.

> A year later, the coffin of the defeated Serb commander began a year-long pilgrimage through every village in Serbia, followed by multitudes of sobbing mourners dressed in black in each town. For many in Serbia, the year 1989 marked not the fall of communism, but the 600th anniversary of the defeat of Knez Lazar at Kosovo Polje.

If we now live outside the vortex of passion and ferocity that seized the Nagorno-Karabakh partisans and the Serbian nationalists, we are not immune to the seductive power the author of John's Gospel calls the "father of lies and murderer from the beginning." There is growing evidence that many unsatisfied with the utilitarian banalities of modern life are becoming nostalgic for the kind of pure conviction the "father of lies" dispenses often enough at the tomb. The American poet James Wright put it this way:

> Walking here lonely and strange now, I must find
> A grave to prod my wrath
> Back to its just devotions...[13]

Because culture begins, so to speak, at the grave site, tombs and graves have tended to provide existing cultures with an ideal venue for "prodding wrath toward its just devotions," and reviving cultural solidarity. The use of graves for deflecting moral responsibility for violence onto others is an explicit concern of the New Testament, and this concern sheds light on the structural significance of the empty tomb story. Jesus rebuked his religious opponents with these words:

> Alas for you, scribes and Pharisees, you hypocrites! You who build the sepulchers of the prophets and decorate the tombs of the holy men, saying, "We would never have joined in shedding the blood of the prophets, had we lived in our fathers' day." So! Your own evidence tells against you! You are the sons of those who murdered the prophets! Very well then, finish off the work that your fathers began. (Matt. 23:29–32)

Tombs have precisely the opposite effect that the crowing of the cock had on Peter in the passion story. The crowing cock made Peter *conscious* of the fact that he had been swept into the mimetic complicity with those who murdered Jesus. Tombs function to extinguish precisely that recognition of complicity. By decorating the tombs of past victims, those morally troubled by acts of collective violence can bemoan the violence and shift responsibility for it to others without having either to acknowledge or to renounce their own complicity in the violence. The interpretation becomes the next room of the dream, the dream from which Peter awoke upon hearing the cock crow.

According to the poetics of Matthew's Gospel, at the moment of Jesus' death "the tombs opened and the bodies of many holy ones rose from the dead," and all the evangelists indicate that shortly thereafter, when those closest to Jesus went to the tomb where his body was interred, they found that the tomb was empty. What actual historical event might be at the heart of the story of the empty tomb we cannot know. Paul, the earliest Christian source we have, never mentions the empty tomb. Like the story of tombs opening and the earthquake, the empty tomb may have been an interpretation in the form of a narrative detail. It may have been one of the several "events" in the passion story that exist to help the reader understand, not just what happened, but the meaning and significance of what happened. The story may have been based on an inability to find the corpse of Jesus, or the discovery that "he is not here" may have been a more profound discovery, one momentous enough to have been made even in the presence of a corpse. As I said, we can never know. What is important is what the Gospel texts tell us. The texts that speak of the empty tomb make it clear that it was originally a very troubling experience, with no positive connotations whatsoever. Those who had gone to the tomb to perform the anointing and mourning rituals were shocked and troubled to discover that Jesus was not there.

The empty tomb is essential for understanding the resurrection, not because it announced the resurrection, but because it deprived those who were later to experience the resurrection of a cathartic religious ritual that might have substituted for it. The discovery of the empty tomb meant that Jesus' corpse and its resting place could not be made into a shrine and become the locus for a new religious cult. Had Jesus' tomb not been empty, the explosive force that scattered the gospel revelation out beyond the culture-world in which it originated and broadcast it to the corners of the earth might have been offset by the gravitation pull of a central shrine. Had the tomb not been empty, what Paul feared might have happened. The Cross might have slowly moved to the margins of Christian awareness and the Christian message. Christianity might have become what some have recently declared it to be: a philosophical affair presided over by a Jeffersonian Jesus full of wise and occasionally ironic sayings.

Given the significance of the empty tomb, nothing symbolizes Christianity's apostasy in history as perfectly as do the Crusades, that cluster of sacrificial convulsions that essentially brought "Europe" as a cultural phenomenon into existence. Pope Urban II launched the First Crusade by passionately imploring European Christendom to arm for the task of reclaiming from the infidel the *sepulcher of Christ.* This sacred mission remained the supreme rallying cry for all the subsequent Crusades.

In other words, Christianity's most notorious revival of sacred violence involved a repudiation of the story of the empty tomb and a more or less spontaneous revival of the structures of sacred violence whose perversities the crucifixion had exposed.

The Resurrection

This is a book about the historical effects of the gospel, not about its theological or metaphysical meaning, but the first of these historical effects was the birth of a community of people whose lives make sense to us and would have made sense to them only in light of their experience of the resurrection. As the theologian John Macquarrie put it, "Only a belief in the resurrection provides anything like a sufficient reason for the rise of Christianity after the death of Jesus."[14] Paul stressed the point when he wrote, "If Christ has not been raised then our preaching is useless and your believing in it is useless" (1 Cor. 15:14). The resurrection is a historical event. Christianity would not exist without it. But Christianity came into existence with the *proclamation* of the resurrection, a declaration of its supreme significance. Furthermore, it is clear from the New Testament that for those who first experienced it the resurrection coincided with an act of recognition and was accompanied by the awakening of a new kind of mental clarity.

The proclamation of the resurrection was and is: Christ *is risen*. It is a proclamation that can be convincingly made only in the present tense and only by those who have experienced it. Moreover, it is always a post-crucifixion experience. The rending of the Temple veil, the quaking earth, and the opening tombs are the poetic images that the evangelists use to express the profound emancipation that the crucifixion brought about and made possible. So radical is this emancipation that it cannot even be imagined from inside the mental bunkers from which it liberates us. Even those who believe in the resurrection as an act of faith in the church's teaching are able to do so because the emancipating power of the Cross has begun to sweep away the mythological, ideological, and rationalistic clutter that stands in the way of that belief.

Primitive myth, and the ideological pseudo-myths and rationalistic counter-myths that are its modern residue, exists to keep the revelation of the Cross from breaking in on us. If successful, the bulwarks against truth that mythological superstition, ideological *idées fixes,* and Procrustean rationalism erect prevent what happened to Saul on the road to Damascus from happening (Acts 9:1–19). But they also prevent from happening what happened to the two disciples on the road to Emmaus, when the truth of the resurrection began to slowly break in on them (Luke 24:13–35). Just as the Risen Christ in Luke's Gospel remained unrecognizable until he sat at table and broke bread with his companions, so the resurrection remains a historical enigma and an object of theological speculation until — at the breaking of bread, or while at prayer, or in the giving or receiving of unearned love — everything is suffused with the light of the resurrection. At that moment, one feels what Paul must have felt when he said: "Death, where is thy sting?"

Chapter 13

"Where Are the Philosophers Now?"

> Since the attempt to understand religion on the basis of philosophy has failed, we ought to try the reverse method and read philosophy in the light of religion.[1]
>
> René Girard

> The word of the Cross is, therefore, the kind of blunt and honest talk about the violence that religion and philosophy cover over with ritual, myth, and rhetoric, even and especially the myth and rhetoric of nonviolent rationality.[2]
>
> Robert Hamerton-Kelly

> It is not enough to cover the rock with leaves.
> We must be cured of it by a cure of the ground
> Or a cure of ourselves, that is equal to a cure
> Of the ground, a cure beyond forgetfulness.[3]
>
> Wallace Stevens, "The Rock"

The New Testament was written by people who were reeling from the revelation of the Cross and trying at the same time to find the words and concepts with which to express its spiritual and historical significance. They made claims that remain baffling until the gospel begins to produce the mental clarity it takes to recognize the nature of the claims and to appreciate the extent to which history is validating them. One such claim is the one made by Paul in his first letter to the Christians at Corinth, where he says that in light of the Christian revelation philosophy has become irrelevant:

> As scripture says: "I shall destroy the wisdom of the wise and bring to nothing all the learning of the learned. Where are the philosophers now?

> Where are the scribes?" Where are any of our thinkers today? Do you see how God has shown up the foolishness of human wisdom? (1 Cor. 1:19–20)

On the rare occasions when the New Testament deigns even to mention philosophy, it treats it as a garrulous Greek exercise that must not be allowed to distract the serious-minded from discovering the truth-telling power of the gospel. In the letter to the Colossians we find this: "Make sure that no one traps you and deprives you of your freedom by some secondhand, empty, rational philosophy based on the principles of this world instead of on Christ" (Col. 2:8). Paul stressed that the gospel could not be expressed philosophically and that efforts to do so would have the effect of emptying the Cross of its revelatory power (1 Cor. 1:17).

The rapprochement between philosophical thought and the early Christian sensibility was not the marriage-made-in-heaven it has sometimes been thought to have been. It was not until Origen wrote *First Principles* in the third century that the wedding of the two achieved a kind of canonical status. It may not be simply coincidental, however, that the man who played such a seminal role in launching the Christian philosophical tradition was also influential in defining the church as a sacred structure analogous to the secular political state, wherein power and absolute authority resided exclusively in the hierarchs. It is difficult to imagine how the church could have survived the trials of the second and third centuries and those of the dark ages without these hints of sacralization, but it is more difficult still to reconcile them with the teachings of Jesus and the freedom of which Paul wrote.

Paul's insight that the Cross superseded the philosophical tradition as a path to truth is as serious a proposal as his more concerted argument that the Cross had replaced the Jewish Law. As complex as it is, Paul's position on the relationship between the Jewish Torah and the Christian gospel is a well-documented one that has received considerable attention. Had Paul's earlier life been as deeply committed to the philosophical tradition as it had been to Pharisaical Judaism, the references in his letters to the superiority of the gospel revelation over the speculation of philosophers would doubtless have been more numerous, more explicit, and more carefully worked out. Nevertheless, there is warrant, I feel, for taking up Paul's challenge to the philosophical tradition.

As European Christianity developed, it borrowed as much from Hellenistic philosophy as it did from biblical Judaism. And while Christianity, like all other cultural institutions, is in crisis in our day, it is perhaps philosophical Christianity that is in the deepest crisis. There has always been something slightly oxymoronic about the effort to make the salvific claims of the New Testament philosophically plausible, but this is especially so now that the world has grown so contemptuous of those claims and philosophy has gradually defined itself out of existence.

Its venerable age and former prestige notwithstanding, philosophy is an intellectually spent force in our world. In its day it served as a formidable and respectable bastion against ignorance and religious excesses. A synthesis of classical philosophy and Christianity was for a long time at the center of European intellectual life. Given this long and distinguished history, no doubt something calling itself philosophy will carry on into the future. It is perfectly clear, however, that philosophy is no longer able to supervise — and reluctant even to chaperon — humanity's moral and intellectual adventure. Hegel's notion of philosophy as an intellectual court of last resort seems almost quaint in a world where philosophy is rapidly becoming a minor branch of linguistics. Claims such as Hegel's were once plausible in part because the alliance with Christian doctrine in the Middle Ages endowed philosophical speculation with a stateliness and substantiality that have eluded its post-modern practitioners. During the last two centuries, philosophy has returned to its more ancient role as an intellectual alternative to prophetic religion. From Hegel to Nietzsche to Heidegger to Derrida, philosophy has become the intellectual Bermuda Triangle for the Western mind. Something intriguing seems to be taking place in its vicinity, but whatever it is forever eludes the existing methods of detection. Reconnaissance missions set out on a regular basis to discover more, but the mystery is never solved. And now that "writing off" philosophy has become philosophy's most intellectually stimulating undertaking, perhaps it is time for those who take seriously the New Testament's claim about the epistemological superiority of the Cross to try to make that claim intelligible.

The Precious Error and the Radical Past

In 1943, the Spanish philosopher José Ortega y Gasset undertook what he thought would be a modest epilogue to Julián Marías's *History of Philosophy.* As his little project developed, however, Ortega found himself increasingly intrigued by the issues he faced. Like his German contemporary Martin Heidegger — who was to have so much influence on twentieth-century intellectual life — Ortega returned to the origins of philosophy in his search for its unifying principle. As these origins came more clearly into focus for him, he sensed that he was embarked on a more momentous task than he had at first realized. Astronomers can predict the location and dimensions of a black hole that they cannot see by observing its gravitational effects on other objects that they can see. In the same way, Ortega's essay circles around a revelation that it never manages to make explicit, but it serves as a marvelous prologue to the explication. He wrote:

> Without attempting now to formalize an opinion on this matter, I wish to suggest the possibility that what we are now beginning to engage in under the traditional aegis of philosophy is not another philosophy but something new and different from all philosophy.[4]

Ortega points out that there was nothing inevitable about the emergence of the philosophical tradition. It was born of certain historical and cultural circumstances. Philosophy, as we have come to know it, says Ortega, "came about one fine day in Greece and has indeed come down to us, with no guarantee, however, of its perpetuation."[5] The greatest single factor in the emergence of philosophy was the rejection of conventional religious cults by those who were to leave their mark on the philosophical tradition. "During the sixth century," Ortega writes, "among certain enclaves in colonial Greece, religion ceased to be a possible way of life and consequently a new position toward the changed existence had to be devised in opposition to religious existence."[6] Signs of this waning of conventional religious sensibility are found in the pre-Socratic philosophers, in whose writings so many modern thinkers have renewed an interest. Speaking of those of his contemporaries who still participated in religious practices, Heraclitus, one of the most important of the pre-Socratics, wrote: "They pray to statues like a man chattering to his own house, knowing nothing of gods or heroes or what they are."[7]

The first to engage in philosophical speculation, Ortega says, were those who "had abandoned religious belief, and feeling lost in a world whose traditional foundations were severed, felt compelled to seek through intellectual free choice a new foundation."[8] In other words, the first philosophers tried to do what religion had theretofore done, but to do it without having to resort to religion. As we moderns now have reason to realize, however, wrenching oneself free of religious superstition is no easy task. The prospect of achieving such a liberation "through intellectual free choice" is, shall we say, vastly overrated.

Once it was inaugurated, Ortega notes, the philosophical tradition never fundamentally altered, despite the contentiousness of even the earliest philosophical debates. The first dilemma Ortega faced, therefore, was how to reconcile this notorious lack of consensus with philosophy's strange and haunting homogeneity. Philosophy itself had begun, as Ortega puts it, "with an onrush of invective," as the first pre-Socratic thinkers denounced the religious superstitions of the pious and the errors of their philosophical rivals. Philosophy was born in polemic, and it thrived on polemics. According to Ortega, "each new philosophy began with a denunciation of its predecessor, and,...by its formal recognition of the latter's invalidity, it identified itself as another philosophy."[9] In spite of the efforts each new philosophy made to dis-identify itself with its philosophical forerunners, an inscrutable sameness pervaded the philosophical discourses. The incessant philosophical jousting was accompanied by great fanfare, but all these intellectual tournaments were being played on the same deeply rutted fields. The philosophers, writes Josef Pieper, "deal with the same topics all the time." They "discuss perpetually the same problems."[10] Ortega makes the point more emphatically:

> One fact that ought to be more startling to us than it ordinarily is, is that once the profession of philosophy exists formally, no philosophy appears to begin anew, but all emerge from their predecessors, and — after a certain point — one can say, from all prior ones. Nothing seemingly would be more "natural" in the history of philosophy than if now and then some appeared that bore no precedent to others, but that were spontaneous and *a nihilo*. But this has never happened.[11]

Whether it was religion or a preexisting philosophy that was being repudiated, there seemed to be something in the very process of trying to break with the past that prevented new philosophies from fully breaking with it. Ortega failed to understand the full implications of this, but he made it easier for others to do so by distinguishing between philosophy's "relative past" and its "radical past." For Ortega, philosophy's "radical past" is enshrouded in a more profound and mysterious obscurity than its ordinary or relative past. What distinguished the "radical past" from the "relative past," however, was not just the greater antiquity of the former. The term "radical past" meant for Ortega something that was "*par excellence*...absent" from philosophical discourse.[12] In other words, what the widely varying philosophies had in common was not something they *all shared,* but something that they *each lacked,* and whatever it was that they lacked, it had been absent since the beginning of philosophy.

Echoing Ortega's idea of philosophy's "radical past," Josef Pieper points out that philosophy is a "process resembling the illumination of something already vaguely and darkly known, the conquest of something almost lost in oblivion, indeed the regaining of what had been forgotten, which is called 'remembrance.'"[13] Since philosophy never really accomplishes this remembrance, Pieper concedes that the idea of philosophical progress makes little sense. He likens philosophy to an "unending trail."[14] Intuitively, Pieper seems to share Ortega's suspicion that something at the center of philosophy's inquiry is par excellence absent from its explicit discourse. Philosophy is necessarily inconclusive because its continued existence depends upon what Ortega calls philosophy's "precious error."[15]

As vigorously as each new philosophy tries to eliminate the errors of its predecessors, says Ortega, all it manages to do is to *resuscitate* "all the yesterdays of philosophy."[16] He concludes: "The efficacy of old ideas is perpetually restored in us and becomes *everlasting*" (emphasis added). Here Ortega employs one of his priceless metaphors for the philosophical enterprise. He likens the historical business of philosophizing to "a long, long road that must be traversed century after century, but a road that in the process winds upon itself, and becomes a load on the traveler's back — it is transformed from a road into luggage."[17] Though he never succeeded in doing so himself, Ortega clearly feels that the time has come to unpack the luggage. But that is precisely what philosophy cannot do and remain what it has always been. To unpack the luggage that philosophy has been carrying on its back for twenty-five hundred years would be to arrive at where it started and to know the place for the first time.

What Ortega could not quite see is that philosophy would never arrive at the truth around which it has always been in orbit because that truth was identical with philosophy's "radical past," its "precious error." What is it that philosophy has failed to retrieve precisely because it always revives its determination to retrieve it by condemning those who have failed to retrieve it? In pondering these things, Ortega uses a word over which he suddenly seems to lose control. The word seems to take on a life of its own and pull Ortega's essay momentarily off course. This occurs while he is discussing the way new philosophies establish themselves by refuting their philosophical predecessors. The word "refutation" seems to stop Ortega's thinking in its tracks. He italicizes *refutation* and remarks on what a ghastly word it is. Alas, he says, it is the most appropriate term for what he is trying to discuss, but he clearly finds the word's darker implications disturbing. Then, almost as though he is blurting out some half-formed thought, Ortega says that the endless process of philosophical refutation "is not at all similar to an *electrocution!*" However, he says, the phonetics of the term *refutation* "would seem to promise no less awesome a spectacle."[18] Ortega is suddenly made morally uncomfortable by the fact that no philosophy can come into its own until it has performed this "ghastly" act of *refutation* on its predecessor.

The "precious error" hidden in the "radical past" is the victim. Philosophy was as incapable of discovering the truth of the victim as was conventional religion and as reluctant to trespass on the sacred ground where it might come upon it unawares. In fact, philosophy's intellectual contests function in somewhat the same way ritual sacrifices function in the world of primitive religion. They reproduce stylized versions of the founding violence. By expelling the philosophical error of the "relative past" philosophers replicate the "precious error" of the "radical past" without having to reckon with it directly. It is in light of this strange process that Jesus' rebuke to the Pharisees, which I mentioned in the last chapter, takes on its real significance. "Alas for you, scribes and Pharisees," he scolded, "you hypocrites!"

> You who build the sepulchers of the prophets and decorate the tombs of the holy men, saying "We would never have joined in shedding the blood of the prophets, had we lived in our fathers' day." So! Your own evidence tells against you! You are the sons of those who murdered the prophets! (Matt. 23:29–31)

The question, of course, is how could the behavior of the Pharisees—decorating the tombs of those their fathers murdered and proclaiming their own innocence—*prove* that they, too, are murderers? Once again, Jesus has seen patterns that those caught up in these patterns cannot see. Structurally, there is no difference between what the fathers of the Pharisees did — namely, scapegoat the prophets — and what the Pharisees do — namely, scapegoat their fathers. By decorating the tombs of past victims, those who have grown morally troubled by evidence of structural violence can bemoan the violence of their predecessors without having to account for their own continued complicity in those same structures. Without fully realizing it, Ortega is grappling with the philosophical version of precisely this same structure. Speaking of the process of philosophical *refutation,* he writes: "Let us recognize that the *defective* idea, *convicted of error, disappears* within the new intellectual creation."[19] Again, the diction here suggests that a latent insight more radical and profound than Ortega's explicit one is straining to declare itself. By refuting their philosophical predecessors, philosophers reenact — albeit in the most genteel way — the sacrificial motif that is the primary generator of human ignorance, philosophy's official *bête noire.*

The ignorance induced by this sacrificial motif is not stupidity. It is the unconscious act of *ignoring* how much one's philosophical conviction depends on the ritual expulsion that brought it about. This is why the "defective idea" that philosophy incessantly struggles to extrude is forever being abolished *and* preserved. If the ignorance that philosophy is forever trying to expel is reborn in the act of expulsion, then the moral and intellectual exhaustion of contemporary philosophy begins to make sense.

The Logic of Violence

Like others, Ortega felt that in order to understand what philosophy is one had to return to its origins. Especially was this so for Ortega, because he argued that, once it began, philosophy never fundamentally altered. Again, like others, Ortega returned to the pre-Socratic thinkers, and especially Heraclitus and Parmenides, whom he declared to be the two most important "proto-philosophers." Following Ortega's lead, therefore, let me now turn to Heraclitus. Heraclitus offered a theory of cultural origins strikingly different from the myths of creation that were a familiar feature of the pagan cults and the mystery religions of his time. For him, the "world" did not originate with the conniving schemes of Gaia, Uranus, Cronus, and their peevish, incestuous, and parricidal Olympian intrigues. It began with human violence, albeit a violence structured by some mysterious organizing principle. Heraclitus sensed that violence behaved in accord with an enigmatic logic of its own, which he called its *logos.* This *logos* or logic of violence made it possible for violence to both create and destroy. Heraclitus wrote:

> War [*polemos*] is the father and king of all things; he has shown some to be gods and some mortals, he has made some slaves and others free.... Everything originates in strife.... Strife is justice; and all things both come to pass and perish through strife.[20]

For Heraclitus, the *logos* of violence was an ordering principle that was generated by disorder itself. Once in play, this *logos* turned chaotic and destructive violence into socially stable and hierarchically differentiated social systems. Heraclitus saw that however random and lawless it is, collective violence nevertheless develops according to certain recognizable patterns, patterns that could not be traced to any cause or any conscious intent on the part of those participating in the violence. Furthermore, he appears to have seen that it is violence of the most lawless and random kind that is the most likely to conform to the mysterious ordering principle he termed the *logos*. In his history of the French Revolution, H. G. Wells provides what amounts to an illustration of Heraclitus's notion of the *logos*. Wells writes:

> The National Convention met on September 21st, 1792, and immediately proclaimed a republic. The trial and execution of the king followed *with a sort of logical necessity* upon these things.[21]

What made it *logically necessary* for the founders of the Republic to behead the king was the *logos* of violence, first formulated in nonmythological language by Heraclitus. Heraclitus's idea of the *logos* extols the same phenomenon extolled by primitive religion. It is a conceptual synonym for the *mythos* of the primitive sacred. For Heraclitus, the *logos* functions as culture's mysterious law of gravity. As inscrutable and mysterious as it is, the *logos* of Heraclitus is a philosophical concept, not a myth, but it *functions mythologically* within the philosophical tradition.

The significance of this last observation comes to the fore when we realize how pivotal Heraclitus's concept of the *logos* became in the history of philosophy. In his study of the pre-Socratic philosophers, Milton Nahm points out that Heraclitus's concept of *logos* lies "at the core of Alexandrian speculation."[22] Even more to the point is Nahm's observation that with his concept of the *logos,* Heraclitus "begins the differentiation of systems of language from the events to which the words refer,"[23] a differentiation that was to become the defining characteristic of the philosophical enterprise. The business of myth has always been to generate a system of language removed from, but not entirely separated from, the events to which the words refer. Heraclitus was contemptuous of conventional religion and its myths, but his major achievement was to use a kind of oracular, quasi-mythic, quasi-rational concept for the purpose of doing what myth had theretofore done, namely, to put a screen between the words and the events to which they referred. It was that screen that made it possible for philosophical discourse to proceed for twenty-five hundred years without ever having to come to grips with the "precious error" that made it all possible.

Heraclitus saw that violence (*polemos*) was the origin of both disorder and order, and he gave the name *logos* to the mysterious "logic" by which destructive violence was able to become ordering or constructive violence. It was precisely this near-revelation that may have functioned as philosophy's germinating insight. Or rather, it was the fact that this insight came so close to exposing—without of course morally condemning—the mechanism of founding violence that it provoked reactions, much like an invading disease triggers the body's antibodies in response. Soon philosophy would have to invent itself and give itself to the task of isolating Heraclitus's impious indiscretion and healing the tiny rift he had opened in the mythological world view.

With a fierce relish somewhat reminiscent of the nineteenth-century Nietzsche, Heraclitus threw his doctrine of strife and the *logos* of violence at the heads of his shocked and pious contemporaries. Since for the most part these heads were still safely filled with conventional religious and mythic preconceptions, most were only bemused or mildly irritated. One who seemed to sense the significance of what Heraclitus had done and who reacted to it with intense hostility was Parmenides.[24] He seems to have realized what kind of fire Heraclitus was playing with. He passionately denounced any attempt to proffer philosophical opinions on the subject of origins. He insisted that nothing could be known of the origin of things because there was no origin. Either something is or it is not. Nothing is generated.

> What *is* is without beginning.... Whence and how could it have grown? I will not let you say or think that it was from what is not; for it cannot be said or thought that anything is not. What need made it arise at one time rather than another, if it arose out of nothing and grew thence? So it must either be entirely, or not at all.... How then could that which *is* be about to be? How could it come into being? For if it has come to pass or is about to be, then it is now.[25]

Parmenides may have understood the implications of the Heraclitan breakthrough better than did Heraclitus. What his attack on Heraclitus amounts to is philosophy's first decisive act of self-preservation. At issue was whether the philosophical tradition was to regard either violence or culture as legitimate objects of scrutiny. Parmenides' pseudo-mythological doctrine of *being* served to deflect inquiry away from the subject of generative violence, just as Heraclitus's oracular utterances on the violent nature of the *logos* served to muddle his own remarkable insight into culture-founding violence. In other words, philosophy's first two thinkers quarreled over how best to deal with what Ortega called the "radical past." Dealing with it had theretofore always been the business of religion. As the conceptual stepchild of religion, philosophy operates with fewer mythological resources, and it manipulates them more clumsily. Its steadfast reluctance to scrutinize the "precious error" at its origin, however, and its genius for setting up a screen between its "systems of language" and "the events to which the words refer" have allowed it to accomplish astonishing feats of logical dexterity and rational ingenuity without seriously jeopardizing that which archaic religion existed to keep from jeopardizing.

Philosophical Reflection

It was in the teachings of Socrates and the writings of Plato that philosophy's incipient wariness of generative violence was raised to the status of principle and made a permanent feature of the philosophical *modus operandi.* In Plato's *Phaedo,* for instance, as he faces his death and looks back on his life, Socrates says:

> I thought that as I had failed in the contemplation of true existence, I ought to be careful that I did not lose the eye of my soul; as people may injure their bodily eye by observing and gazing on the sun during an eclipse, unless they take the precaution of only looking at the image *reflected* in the water, or in some similar medium. That occurred to me, and I was afraid that my soul might be blinded altogether if I looked at things with my eyes or tried by the help of the senses to apprehend them. And I thought that I had better have recourse to *ideas,* and seek in them the truth of existence.[26]

In light of my previous comments about the ambiguous relationship between religion and philosophy, it is illuminating to note that Socrates is talking about a quite unusual and unique situation, namely, a solar eclipse. Under ordinary circumstances — that is to say, when the world and its inhabitants remained within the mythological envelope of primitive religion — there is little danger that the sun might cause damage to the eyes. So dazzling is the solar (sacred) radiance that involuntary reflexes prevent its rays from blinding those who might cast a careless glance toward it. It is when the sun is in partial eclipse, with the waning of religious sensibilities, that the dangers arise. Socrates is therefore describing precisely the dangers that he and the philosophical tradition faced at precisely the moment when they began facing them. To those for whom philosophical speculation had begun to replace ritual religion as the prism through which to view the world, the aureole of the primitive sacred dimmed and *seemed* less harmful to look upon. But, as Socrates here notes, it is especially at this moment, when an inadvertent glance toward the solar (sacred) realm would be unimpeded by natural reflexes, that such a glance would be the most devastating. Like Parmenides, Socrates knew when and where to exercise philosophical discretion.

What Socrates' comment makes clear is that part of the purpose of philosophical *re*flection is to *de*flect truths that must not be directly encountered. However helpful philosophy might be for arranging certain observations and conceptualizing certain relationships, in the first instance philosophical reflection is a precaution taken to *avoid* a discovery that is philosophically *unthinkable*. For Socrates at least, the precaution involves a conscious shift from the actual world to the world of *ideas*.

Idea is the Platonic notion par excellence. The Greek word *eidos* means "image" or "appearance." Credit goes to Heidegger for realizing that by directing philosophical attention toward *ideas* Plato provided the reality behind the idea — what Heidegger calls the "original world-making power" — with a more congenial facade, "a front, a surface,...an appearance to be looked at."[27] One cannot look at the sun except by blocking most of its rays with one's hand. Likewise, one cannot think about violent origins or speak about conventional culture's dependence on sacred violence until the *unthinkable* and *unspeakable* aspects of these things have been diffused or veiled. The myths of primitive religion eclipsed these things, but philosophy begins with the repudiation of myth and religion. What characterized the proto-philosophical age, the age of Heraclitus and Parmenides, was a kind of thrashing about for something that would perform for philosophy the mediating function that myth had performed for religion. Plato's elevation of the idea of the *idea* finally provided that mediation. As Socrates notes in the passage quoted, philosophical *ideas* made it possible to consider under a more benign aspect certain *glaring* and *unspeakable* realities that would have left their observers blind and speechless had they been encountered directly. Clearly, those setting off on philosophy's highly touted search for truth were reluctant to look for it where Peter and Paul found it.

The "Death" of Socrates

In this regard, a word is in order about how the death of Socrates and Plato's account of it epitomizes philosophy's characteristic reticence regarding the victimage mechanism. The writings of Plato represent Western philosophy's *locus classicus*. Plato launched the philosophical enterprise in part because, as Helmut Koester put it, "the historical Socrates could no longer explain the world that had radically changed because of his death."[28] Likewise, as Koester notes, for the disciples of Jesus, "his execution implied a denial of all values of a world order that had made Jesus its victim."[29] In other words, Western philosophy and Christianity came into existence as a result of remarkably similar provocations. If, as Jacques Derrida states, Plato wrote "out of the death of Socrates," it is likewise true that Paul wrote out of the crucifixion of Jesus. The differences immediately begin to leap out. Plato wrote of a wise and philosophical Socrates who calmly accepted his death, while Paul wrote of a *crucified* Christ, and the evangelists of a Jesus anguishing over his approaching *victimization.* What the New Testament gives us is the passion of Christ and his Cross. What Plato and the philosophical tradition gives us is the dispassion of Socrates, his wisdom and serenity, *sans* blood, *sans* mob, *sans* everything. However profound an experience it was for Plato and his other disciples, as far as the philosophical tradition was concerned, the "death" of Socrates was merely incidental to the wisdom of Socrates, whereas for Christianity everything Jesus said or did becomes fully significant only in the light of his public execution. The Cross stands at the center and not to one side of Christian revelation. Given the parallels between the origins of philosophy and of Christianity, the question is: Is one of them better suited than the other for the task of revealing truth? Since *truth* means unforgetting, does philosophy or Christianity have the greater potential for revealing our "radical past" and for curing us of our "precious error"?

In 399 B.C.E. Socrates was convicted of corrupting the youth of Athens with religious heresy. Once sentence was passed, Socrates refused to be part of any plan to flee Athens. It was his duty as a citizen, he maintained, to obey the laws of the state. As Plato describes Socrates' death in the *Phaedo,* the condemned man is surrounded by his loving disciples. Discoursing with his disciples calmly and at great length about the soul's immortality, Socrates' approach to his death stands in the sharpest possible contrast to that other death—the crucifixion of Jesus. The two "deaths" were as profoundly different as were their historical, spiritual, and epistemological consequences. When the appropriate time came, Socrates drank the poison "readily and cheerfully." When he saw his sympathizers weeping, he reproached them and told them that he wanted only to die in peace. Those who were to set Western philosophy on its course saw a condemned man stoically embrace his fate. Jesus, by contrast, died as a despised outcast, abandoned by *all* his disciples, a wretched loser jeered at by his executioners and passersby.

Socrates was condemned by a vote of 280 to 220. Jesus was unanimously condemned not only by the mob but by both the political (Roman) and the religious (Jewish) authorities. The unanimity-minus-one structure of the crucifixion is highlighted and made explicit in the story of Peter denying his association with Jesus even after he had emphatically announced he would never abandon him. There is something almost humorous, but at the same time deeply significant, about the role played by the cock in the death of Socrates and in the passion story, respectively. In both accounts, the cock appears at the end of the story, and, of course, in both contexts, the cock was associated with awakening and the dawning of new light. In the passion story the cock crows, shocking Peter out of his complicity with the mob that murdered Jesus, making him contrite, and giving rise eventually, not to philosophy's timid epistemology, but to a truth (*a-letheia*) that had real liberating power. By stark contrast, the cock appears in the story of Socrates' death as an animal to be sacrificed in fulfillment of a religious duty to a Greek god. As the hemlock began to have its effect, Socrates spoke his last words. "Crito," he said, "I owe a cock to Asclepius; will you remember to pay the debt?" There is no crowing cock. There is a matter-of-fact decision to sacrifice one to a pagan god. Socrates dies making sure at the end that his religious affairs are in order. If it is true that Plato more than anyone else gave the philosophical enterprise its charter documents, and if Jacques Derrida was right when he said that Plato wrote "out of the death of Socrates," then perhaps the final judgment on philosophy might be that an unexamined death is not worth philosophizing.

What's in a Name?

Socrates was not the only philosopher to suffer the scorn of the conventional and the pious. As soon as the proto-philosophers began to have influence, a backlash against them set in. Ortega says they were attacked because they "knew too much."[30] From the beginning, Ortega observes, philosophers had to take precautions against "the ire of the *demos*" — the people. One of the most important precautions concerned what name would be given to these thinkers and their new style of thinking. Ortega says that several terms were used to designate this new activity before the term "philosophy" was finally settled upon. At first, the word *historia* was used. According to Guthrie, the word simply carried the connotation of "inquiry."[31] In addition to this term, the early philosophers also used the word *aletheia*, the Greek word for "truth." Apparently, neither of these terms successfully accomplished what it was intended to accomplish, namely, to specify what philosophers did while mollifying those who might take offense at what they were doing. Finally, therefore, these early terms for the new form of conceptualizing gave way to the word "philosophy," a term simply meaning "the love of the goddess of wisdom." The vagueness and quasi-religious tone of this term were surely not merely fortuitous. As Ortega puts it, "the illustrious discipline in all likelihood received its name primarily out of defensive reasons, as a precaution the 'thinker' had to take against the wrath of his fellow-citizens who still clung to a religious position."[32] The word *philosophy* "barely denoted anything," Ortega writes. "Its meaning consisted rather in saying nothing precise, and in fact the only precise thing about it was its evasive meaning."[33]

As I have tried to show, this evasiveness is not a coincidental feature of philosophy. Josef Pieper points out that philosophy "is primarily a negative term, explicitly expressing the *absence* of wisdom."[34] One would, therefore, better translate the word "philosophy" to mean, not *loving* the goddess of wisdom, but *yearning* for her in her perpetual absence. In fact, Pieper argues, "to persist in spite of the awareness that the ultimate, finally satisfying answer remains ever elusive: this precisely would mark the true philosopher!"[35] In the modern world there has been a tendency to turn the philosophical "quest" into a kind of intellectual fetish, an aimless aim. As it became ever clearer that philosophy was circling certain fundamental problems rather than making "progress," there was a growing tendency to turn philosophy's penchant for uncertainty and ambiguity into its chief virtue.

According to Heidegger, for instance, the business of philosophy is not so much to uncover truth but rather to "endure" with heroic determination the "absolute questioning" that was philosophy's special calling.[36] It was this endurance, and not its intellectual accomplishments, that was for Heidegger "the highest form of knowledge." Pieper notices the obvious. "For Heidegger," he writes, " 'questioning' seems to mean the absolute exclusion and rejection of any possible answer (which answer, in fact, would infringe on the purity of questioning itself.)"[37] One would have thought that a more diffident attitude toward truth would never be found, but, alas, Pieper was writing before Derrida, Heidegger's former student, invented philosophical deconstruction and brought things to their logical inconclusion.

It is in Derrida's post-philosophical writings that philosophy's penchant for evasiveness and ambivalence openly declares itself. In an interview, Derrida spoke of his writing as a "meaning-to-say-nothing," the act of "carrying off each concept into an interminable chain of differences, surrounding or confusing itself with so many precautions, references, notes, citations...."[38] As deftly enigmatic as Derrida is, he remains the philosophical legatee of Nietzsche and Heidegger. He is as prone as they to getting caught on the updraft of his own rhetorical whirlwinds. In *Writing and Difference,* he speaks of the "joyous affirmation of the play of the world and of the innocence of becoming, the affirmation of signs without fault, without truth, and without *origin* which is offered to an active interpretation."[39] The cheapest way to restore innocence, of course, is to eliminate the moral standards by comparison with which doubt might be cast on one's innocence. Similarly, the deconstructionist recipe for retaining philosophical and literary innocence is "the affirmation of signs *without fault, without truth,* and *without origin.*" The deconstructionists have rightly seen the problem of violence at the heart of philosophy, but their response to it has been to perform what amounts to intellectual purification rituals. Just as all moral misgivings about sanctioned violence dissolve in the mythic and ritual routines of primitive religion, so in the world of philosophical deconstruction, moral quandaries are eclipsed by textual ones. By despairing of ever knowing the reality to which the text might refer or from which it might emanate, deconstruction clings to its innocence, but it also abandons its responsibility for truth-telling. Today, the truth about victims is unavoidable, and the same historical force that has unearthed that truth is at this moment unearthing the underlying truth about generative violence. Despite its ingenuity, the attempt to take refuge from these truths in textuality and to issue cryptic communiqués about undecidability cannot last much longer. Eventually, we will have to abandon "the innocence of becoming, the affirmation of signs without fault, without truth, and without *origin*" and discover *origin, fault,* and *truth*. The venue for that discovery is the Cross.

The irony is that the closer philosophy has gotten to discovering the truth that it has been skillfully orbiting for twenty-five hundred years, the readier it has been to dismiss this truth in favor of a (blessedly) endless truth-seeking activity. Sooner or later, someone was bound to blow the whistle. Girard has. "Philosophical concepts," writes Girard, "serve to shield from sight the tragic conflict of human antagonisms."[40]

The Walls Come Tumbling Down

Equivocating about culture-founding, language-forming, and thought-provoking violence was philosophy's part of its Faustian bargain. As the biblical revelation increasingly forced evidence of founding violence to the surface, it became more and more difficult for philosophers to exercise their intellectual genius to the highest degree while at the same time avoiding the revelation that would put an end to philosophy. In this regard, there is an especially relevant passage in Ortega's essay. There

Ortega uses a metaphor that is interesting in part because it was so inherently uninteresting. So prosaic is his analogy, in fact, one suspects it might have been chosen for its reliable banality. Ortega seems to have sensed something beginning to slip, and, as a precaution against losing control, he took care to employ a metaphor with no moving parts. He likens the business of philosophy to an observer looking at a wall. With each additional glance, or as his casual attention becomes more focused, the philosophical observer sees that "specks, shapes, little cracks, slight spots, shadings of color, at first unseen, are at second glance *revealed* ('revealed' being employed here in its photographic sense)."[41] Always, however, greater clarity about one of the wall's aspects is acquired at the cost of having another of its aspects go out of focus. So far, then, this wall is behaving like the prosaic metaphor that it is. Abruptly, however, as though suddenly in the presence of something that doesn't love a wall, Ortega speaks as though the wall conceals or contains something more interesting than itself. His metaphor gets away from him. He writes:

> And with each glance cast by the eye, the wall, *wounded to the core,* allowed fresh aspects of itself to *escape.* However, even if our eye had not wandered, the same thing would have happened, because *the wall, too, makes our attention wander.*[42]

I want to comment briefly on two aspects of Ortega's metaphor. First, I want to ask about the function of metaphors, and, second, I want to ask whether there is anything to be learned from a closer look at just how and why the metaphor Ortega chose breaks down at the critical moment.

Robert Frost said that poetry is talking about one thing in terms of another, but he didn't try to explain why it was necessary to do so or what might have given rise to the metaphorical impulse in the first place. No doubt metaphorical language can be used in a truth-seeking way, but there is no compelling reason to believe that such was its original purpose. In his well-known essay "The Dehumanization of Art," Ortega himself expressed opinions on the subject of metaphor that are intriguing in light of the present discussion. The metaphor, he says there, furnishes an *escape* from "the realm of the real."[43] He continues:

> A strange thing, indeed, the existence in man of this mental activity which substitutes one thing for another—from an urge not so much to get at the first as to get rid of the second. The metaphor disposes of an object by having it masquerade as something else. Such a procedure would make no sense if we did not discern beneath it an instinctive avoidance of certain realities.[44]

Ortega refers to a study by Heinz Werner: "In his search for the origin of the metaphor a psychologist recently discovered to his surprise that one of its roots lies in the spirit of taboo."[45] He gives an example. When Polynesians, who must not call by name anything belonging to the king, see the torches lighted in the royal hut, they will say: "The lightning shines in the clouds of heaven."[46]

Metaphor is born, Ortega speculates, in a world where humans felt an overwhelming compulsion "to keep clear of certain realities which, on the other hand, could not be entirely avoided."[47] It is with the help of metaphors, Ortega says, that primitives were able to avoid a direct and unwanted encounter with the sacred.[48] The metaphor made it possible, he says, for the primitive to "get around a reality" considered too sacred and taboo to be directly confronted. The primitive human being, says Ortega, "finds it impossible to name the awful object on which a taboo has fallen." "Such an object has to be alluded to by a word denoting something else and thus appears in speech vicariously and surreptitiously." If the *original* function of metaphor was to "keep clear of certain realities," then a close look would be in order.

In trying to locate the haunting power of the most compelling poetry, the Spanish poet Federico García Lorca used the word *duende,* the Spanish word for demonic possession. He said that Goethe had virtually defined *duende* when he described the effect of Paganini's music as "a mysterious power that all may feel and no philosophy can explain." García Lorca only adds: "This 'mysterious power that all may feel and no philosophy can explain' is, in sum, the earth-force, the same *duende* that fired the heart of Nietzsche."[49] "The *duende* I speak of," García Lorca goes on to say, "is a descendant of that benignest *daimon* of Socrates, ... who scratched the master angrily the day he drank the hemlock." This is a particularly striking example of what Cesáreo Bandera has described as "poetry trying to displace philosophy as the guardian of the sacred, just as philosophy had once been invented to displace poetry from that same role."[50] Clearly, the violence at the heart of the sacred — long veiled by primitive religion, or by the shamanic voice of poet-prophet-priest, or by philosophy's discrete preference for platonic *ideas* — is being unveiled. Under the circumstances, García Lorca knew where to turn for fortification for the onerous work at hand. He leaned over the tripod and inhaled the heady fumes that "fired the heart of Nietzsche."

Few modern poets have wrestled with the dilemma underlying their vocation more persistently than Czeslaw Milosz, the Polish-born American writer who received the 1980 Nobel Prize for literature. Some of his meditations on this dilemma are strikingly reminiscent of the story, to which I referred in chapter 1, of the German diplomat who heard screams in Moscow. Milosz's formative experience during the period of great crisis in Europe caused him to harbor suspicions about the poetic Muse. He seems to sense that however uplifting the Muse's lyrical strains, there is at least a chance that they are making something else inaudible. "The very act of writing a poem is an act of faith," Milosz wrote, "yet if screams of the tortured are audible in the poet's room, is not his activity an offense to human suffering?"[51] Later, Milosz was to return to this theme in *The Captive Mind;* there he is even more explicit, and his comments are even more reminiscent of those of the German diplomat. "Human sufferings are drowned in the trumpet-blare: the orchestra in the concentration camp; and I, as a poet, had my place already marked out for me among the first violins." In Ortega's essay on the dehumanization of art, he seems similarly troubled by the potential of metaphor for *keeping clear of certain realities that could not be entirely avoided.*

Once put on notice about the role metaphors potentially play in obfuscating the sacred and deferring to its taboos, we can return to the metaphor that so ingloriously collapsed under the weight of Ortega's own ponderings: the wall that suddenly revealed itself to be "wounded to the core." Jesus had told those who wanted to silence his followers that if they were silenced the very stones themselves would cry out. Suddenly, Ortega's wall begins to behave as though under just that sort of compulsion. But then, just as suddenly and unexpectedly, the wall, now revealed as wounded to the core, "makes our attention wander." Even as it is being shorn of its religious mystifications, the sacred retains enough bedeviling power to distract.

Here we have a parable, far more significant than the one Ortega intended. It is not a parable about the philosophical method, but about the philosophical *crisis,* a crisis of dis-covery for which the philosophical enterprise is unprepared. The walls themselves have begun to cry out. If the first immediate effect of the crucifixion was that the curtain of the Jerusalem Temple was rent from top to bottom, it was only because that Temple and the sacrificial cult it epitomized lay so near the epicenter of the revelation of the Cross. As the revelation moved into the Greek world it would only be a matter of time — a long time to be sure — before the philosophical walls would come tumbling down. The crucifixion's effect on sacrificial religion works at every level. To the extent that the conceptual pseudo-myths of the philosophical tradition — from the *logos* of Heraclitus to the *Being* of Heidegger — provided an intellectually respectable haven for the primitive sacred, the revelation that rent the Temple curtain would eventually have a comparable effect on philosophical walls.

As Ortega said, "The wall, too, makes our attention wander." As soon as the wall reveals something "wounded to the core," Ortega himself grows suddenly reticent. He begins to speak of the inconclusiveness of the philosophical task and the virtue of not insisting on clarity. He suggests that due to some undeciphered element in its make-up, philosophy will always perform its labors in the midst of confusion, and that assaults on the confusion should be discrete lest they have unwelcome consequences. The philosophers must not, he says, let their philosophical poise be destroyed by "some snob sense of urgency."

It would be foolish to dismiss Ortega's forebodings. There are colossal dangers involved in unveiling and dismantling the sacrificial system in a world still dependent upon it for cultural coherence. One cannot recognize these dangers, however, without calling into question the morality of trying to avoid them. For both historical and moral reasons, therefore, we can no longer avoid the perils involved in continuing to dismantle the sacrificial system and continuing to deconstruct its nimbus of mythic and quasi-mythic justifications. It is not, after all, *we* who are doing any of this; it is the gospel itself, and it is useless, as Paul said, to kick against the goad.

In a footnote Ortega explains his sudden sense of wariness. Caution and circumspection should be the philosophical watchword, he says. The encounter between the philosophers and that which has forever eluded their comprehension must be a discrete one. One must be suspicious, he says, of encounters that are "immediate, clear, and precise." An "immediate, clear, and precise" encounter with philosophy's central enigmas, Ortega warns, can lead to "a strange sudden crisis." Depending on a number of unmentioned factors this crisis can result in "conversion," "sudden ecstasy," or "bewilderment."[52]

Our world in general and the philosophical world in particular seem to be divided between these three responses: bewilderment, ecstasy, and conversion. It is no doubt a little too facile, but it is generally correct to say that contemporary philosophy is in a state of bewilderment and that philosophical deconstruction has bestowed on that bewilderment honors once reserved for those things that *overcame* bewilderment. It is, however, the more "ecstatic" forms of philosophical discourse that deserve our greatest attention. It is these philosophies that constitute at once the most sinister recrudescence of the primitive sacred and the most beguiling exposition of its seductive power. The philosopher, wrote Nietzsche in *Ecce Homo,* is a "*concealed* priest."[53] Nietzsche, of course, personifies philosophy's return to ecstasy, and perhaps Ortega had Nietzsche in mind when he issued his warnings against testing the limits of philosophical discourse. It was Nietzsche, after all, who had scoffed at the merely sane among the philosophers and who predicted that these timid remnants of philosophy's bygone age would soon be shoved aside by the throng of ecstatic Dionysiac revelers with no qualms about delivering a *coup de grâce* to the philosophical tradition. Nietzsche's influence in this regard has been both profound and catastrophic, but it is to the writings of his intellectual successor, Martin Heidegger, that we must look to find a more systematic revival of philosophical ecstasy. Heidegger's enigmatic ponderings constituted a lifelong effort to turn the philosophical apparatus into a distillery for brewing one final flask of the ancient sacrificial elixir.

Drawn into the Withdrawal: Martin Heidegger

Heidegger wrote largely in reaction against the shallowness of Enlightenment positivism and the superficiality of the modern world, whose loss of authentic existence he deeply lamented. By insulating the world from the fructifying power of primordial *Being,* Heidegger felt conventional philosophy shared responsibility for the regrettable banality of the modern world. His philosophical instinct was to rediscover philosophy's robust beginnings and, once and for all, to put an end to all the philosophical equivocation. For Heidegger, as for Ortega and others, philosophy begins with Heraclitus and Parmenides. Whereas Ortega regarded these two figures as personifications of philosophy's perennial ambivalence, for Heidegger there was ultimately no discrepancy between them. Heraclitus had tried to understand the world by reckoning its *origins,* and Parmenides had tried to understand it by speculating about its *essences.* For Heidegger, it was in following the footprints of both Heraclitus and Parmenides that philosophy might finally rediscover authentic *Being.* He equates this notion of authentic *Being* with the Greek term *physis,* which he defines as "the original world-making power." And he defined the Heraclitan *logos* as "the primal gathering principle." In pursuing his quest for primal and authentic *Being,* therefore, Heidegger uncovers the rudiments of generative violence toward which philosophy had exhibited so much ambivalence since its beginnings in Heraclitus and Parmenides.

Heidegger understood that conventional philosophy was finished, and he felt that if humanity was to recover its valor and restore its greatness it would have to break the unwritten taboo and vouch again, as Heraclitus had, for "the original world-making power" and "the primal gathering principle." Nietzsche had undertaken this task with perhaps a greater genius, but with a decomposing mind. If Heidegger's genius suffered a deterioration, it was not an intellectual one. Perhaps Heidegger's sturdier mental constitution was due, in part, to the fact that by the time he was writing the toxins Nietzsche concocted in his lonely garret had leached into the cultural water table and were having their historical repercussions. The heady revival of "the primal gathering principle" in Germany of the 1930s seems to have provided an agreeable intellectual environment for Heidegger's conspicuously esoteric philosophical musings. As the Nazi program was reassembling the cogs and gears of the sacrificial machine, Heidegger was rediscovering the necessary link between authentic being, historical greatness, and violence. As Hitler gave the mob its vocabulary and its moral sanction, Heidegger was brooding over the dark necessities demanded of those "embarked on the great and long venture of demolishing a world that has grown old and of rebuilding it authentically anew."[54]

This was the historical setting for the famous series of lectures Heidegger gave at the University of Freiburg in 1935. In these lectures, he interpreted Heraclitus's assertion that violence, or *polemos,* is the father and king of all things. He argued that Heraclitus was right. Conflict or strife, Heidegger insisted, involves "a binding-together," a "*logos.*" "Logos," he said, "must... signify the (human) act of violence, by which being is gathered in its togetherness."[55] In other words, violence, behaving in accord with its own internal "logic," produces togetherness.

The key, according to Heidegger, is the *logos,* "the primal gathering principle." The *logos* "requires violence."[56] "We can hear [the *logos*] truly only if we are followers," he says. "The man who is no longer a follower is removed and excluded from the *logos* from the start."[57] When Heidegger laments modernity's reluctance to exercise the "will to mastery," it should be remembered that his lament is being expressed in a University of Freiburg lecture hall in 1935, at the height of Germany's Nazi frenzy. Given that historical setting, how is one to assess Heidegger's grandiloquence, delivered to those whose ears were ringing with the bombast of Hitler's rally speeches? We must place Heidegger's Olympian prose in precisely this setting in order to feel its darker implications. "The *violent one,* the creative man," writes Heidegger, "must risk dispersion, in-stability, disorder, mischief."[58] The "violent one knows no kindness and conciliation."[59] Like Nietzsche before him, Heidegger sensed how dependent humanity has always been on the structures of sacred violence, and, like Nietzsche, he felt that a return to these structures was imperative and that it was the biblical tradition that stood in the way of this important revival.

What is missing in Heidegger's subtle and evocative discourse is the suffering of the victims who are at the receiving end of all this culture-rejuvenating violence. For someone of Heidegger's genius, this oversight is not likely to have been inadvertent. He was, after all, retailing Nietzsche's will-to-power to the world, and everything depended on the ability of the superman to override the moral misgivings with which the Judeo-Christian tradition had burdened him. The age in which it was still possible to completely eliminate these misgivings was, alas, gone. The only alternative to the elimination of the violence that produced the misgivings was to subordinate the moral qualms to the iron will of those who recognized the necessity of violence. "The true is not for every man but only for the strong."[60] When all the metaphysical mists fade away, at the heart of the Nietzschean and Heideggerian project is the hardening of the human heart.

Heidegger's genius is morally tainted but not intellectually diminished by the perversity of its philosophical proposals. If the essential element in the decommissioning of the sacrificial system is exposing its workings to the light of day, then the contribution Heidegger made is not to be scoffed at. Like Nietzsche, it is not for what he saw that he should be faulted, but for his moral and intellectual response to what he saw. What he saw was more or less what St. Paul had seen on the road to Damascus and more or less what René Girard has seen in his literary, anthropological, and biblical studies. One can learn from Heidegger in the same way that one can learn from myths or from accounts of Salem witch trials. If Heidegger found in the Heraclitan furnace the white-hot core of generative violence, he studied it through the cobalt-blue lenses of Parmenidean *essence.* This was his one concession to philosophical reticence, and yet there was always the itch to dispense with the metaphysical vagaries and look directly at the thing itself. In the fall and winter of 1951–52, he delivered a series of lectures entitled "What Calls for Thinking?" In these remarkable lectures, Heidegger declared: "*Most thought-provoking in our thought-provoking time is that we are still not thinking.*"[61] In order to understand the dimensions of this fact, he said, we must disabuse ourselves of "the stubborn illusion that we are thinking just because we are incessantly 'philosophizing.' "[62] That philosophy has failed to think about what is most thought-provoking is only in part due to philosophical timidity. In part it is due to the fact that, as Heidegger says, what is to be thought turns away from our thoughts. He writes: "That which really gives us food for thought did not turn away from man at some time or other which can be fixed in history — no, what really must be thought keeps itself turned away from man since the beginning."[63] Humanity remains incapable of thinking, said Heidegger, "as long as that which must be thought about withdraws." *Withdraws,* what an innocent sounding word.

Were one to substitute for the words "withdraws" and "withdrawal" the words "expelled" and "expulsion" — or even the term "the victim" — Heidegger's otherwise murky and darkly romantic argument would take on an almost revelatory depth and significance. What if Heidegger had said that we will remain incapable of thinking "as long as that which must be thought about is the one whose expulsion gave rise to thought"? What philosophy cannot see is that it is the victim through whom the world of the victimizers came into existence, the very world about which philosophy wants to say wise things. What philosophy could only vaguely glimpse on its deathbed is what the Gospel of John saw clearly at its outset:

> He was in the world
> that had its being through him,
> and the world did not know him.
> He came to his own domain
> and his own people did not accept him.
> (John 1:10–11)

With his discussion of the soul's immortality still hanging in the air and the hemlock slowly having its narcotic and poisonous effect, the peaceful Socrates must have seemed to his disciples to be "withdrawing." By waxing melancholy about how what must be thought about is forever "withdrawing," Heidegger, the anti-philosopher, performs a quintessentially philosophical gesture. He alludes to the central truth: namely, that when it comes to knowing the human condition and gaining real historical and anthropological knowledge, there is nothing left to think about except the victim. But he only alludes to this truth. There isn't the slightest hint that this "withdrawal" was a bloody affair. In one sense, however, the term "withdrawal" is felicitous. Like Ortega's wall, it is innocuous enough to lull the wary philosopher into dropping his defenses a little. As he toys with the rhetorical and semantic possibilities, Heidegger is slowly *drawn* toward that which has forever *with*-drawn from philosophy's gaze. He says:

> Once we are drawn into the withdrawal, we are, somewhat like migratory birds, but in an entirely different way, caught in the pull of what draws, attracts us by its withdrawal. And once we, being so attracted, are drawing toward what draws us, our essential being already bears the stamp of that "pull."[64]

These may be the most important two sentences Heidegger ever wrote. It would take another book the size of this one to do them justice. When, for instance, Heidegger says that being pulled by that which has withdrawn involves "an essential and therefore constant pointing toward what withdraws," he fairly defines Western civilization. Suffice it to say that Heidegger has simply reformulated the words of Jesus in John's Gospel:

> "Now sentence is being passed on this world:
> now the prince of this world is to be overthrown.
> And when I am lifted up from the earth,
> I shall draw all men to myself." (John 12:31–32)

The whole world is, in Heidegger's words, "caught in the pull of what draws," and each of us "bears the stamp of that 'pull.' "

Peering into the sacrificial machinery as Heidegger did is structurally equivalent to standing at the foot of the Cross. All that is required is that one hear the cock crowing, or, as Paul did on the road to Damascus, hear the voice of the Victim calling one's name. One cannot, I feel, read Heidegger's melancholy lines about being drawn by what withdraws without sensing how close he must have been as he wrote these lines to a Christian conversion. Far closer, no doubt, than he himself realized.

Radical Demystification

"Our rationality cannot reach the founding role of mimetic victimage because it remains tainted with it," writes Girard.[65] The philosophical tradition is at this moment exhausting the last of its intellectual resources in an effort to account for its intellectual exhaustion. The question remains: Where is the truth that will set us free? Where might we find an interpretive tool capable of countering the manifold powers of mystification that are still at work in our world? And where might we find the inspiration to live in the light of the truth that counters them?

"What is it," Heidegger asks, "that calls us into thinking?"[66] "What is it that claims us so that we must think?"[67] Here Heidegger comes as close as he was ever to come to completing his philosophical journey and correcting at last what Ortega termed philosophy's "precious error." The one remaining step — which he apparently never took — would have landed him at the foot of the Cross and freed him at last from the philosophical maze. If Heidegger did not take that step, he left evidence enough that it is the only one left to take. The reasons for taking it are not exclusively religious. The world in which we live is in the grip of an anthropological crisis of unimaginable proportions. If we hope to fully comprehend this challenge and to respond to it intelligently and gracefully, then in the words of René Girard, we must try to take advantage of the incredible interpretive power "that is bestowed on humankind by the Passion of Christ."[68]

"What calls on us to think" says Heidegger, is that which is "thought-provoking *per se.*"[69] Is there a basis, then, for an intellectually rigorous post-philosophical epistemology? Simone Weil spoke a truth whose validity we and our descendants will come to appreciate exactly to the degree that the truth itself frees us from forms of rationality whose task it has been to prevent its recognition. "The Cross of Christ," she wrote, "is the only gateway to knowledge."[70]

Chapter 14

The Voice from La Cruz

What we call evil is only the directionless plunging and storming of the sparks in need of redemption.

MARTIN BUBER

Things are going to slide in all directions
Won't be nothing
Nothing you can measure anymore
The blizzard of the world
has crossed the threshold
and it has overturned
the order of the soul
When they said REPENT
I wonder what they meant[1]

LEONARD COHEN, "THE FUTURE"

"What is called thinking?" We are playing with the verb "to call." One might ask, for instance: "What do you call that village up there on the hill?"[2]

MARTIN HEIDEGGER

Ancient Israel's scapegoating ritual was a rite performed annually on the solemn day of Atonement. The high priest, "lest he should die," had to perform elaborate ritual procedures when he entered the sanctuary beyond the curtain that otherwise veiled the sacred and protected both priests and community from the violence that contact with the sacred might all too easily provoke. Since the effect of the veil is to shroud the sacred and to ward off the violence that an unmediated exposure to it could entail, once the high priest no longer had the veil for protection, other precautions had to be taken. Following the instructions in the book of Leviticus, the high priest had to light a censer and fill the sacred precinct with a cloud of incense. Clearly, the smoking incense was designed to reproduce as much as possible the aura, mystery, and obscurity that the veil provided more concretely. All of this, I think, is a perfect analogue for what Martin Heidegger did with respect to the generative violence of the Heraclitan *logos* that had remained veiled in philosophical discourse for twenty-five hundred years. Heidegger removed the veil that the philosophical priesthood had long and solemnly maintained. He then proceeded to envelop the primitive sacred with the metaphysical haze that made it possible for both himself and his intellectual franchisees to deconstruct philosophy *philosophically.*

In many ways, what René Girard has discovered is what Nietzsche and Heidegger discovered, though the moral and religious conclusions he draws are exactly opposite of theirs. Of course, the history of ideas in which these three thinkers take their place is an extremely complex one. But neither can this intellectual history entirely be explained in terms of the thinking and thinkers that participated in it. Rather, Nietzsche, Heidegger, Girard, and others are the intellectual beneficiaries of the gradual unveiling of the sacred that has been taking place since "the veil of the Temple was rent in two from top to bottom." (Of the three, only Girard recognized that this was the case.) Furthermore, as radically different as their conclusions are, in one way or another all three of these thinkers realized that a revival of sacred violence under nonbiblical religious auspices is ultimately the only alternative to the anthropological revolution the Christian revelation set in motion.

There is more to history than the history of ideas, however. While Nietzsche and Heidegger were working on a philosophical blueprint for the revival of sacrificial efficacy, there were countless others who were tinkering with whatever combination of religious paraphernalia and social circumstance they had at hand toward the same end. If Heidegger's philosophical enterprise functioned in a way analogous to the way the high priest's censer functioned in the cultic rituals of ancient Israel, there have been a great number of less highbrow analogues, driven by social rather than philosophical fascinations. One of the most conspicuous of these is the rise of what I suppose we could call cultic nationalism. The most conspicuous and horrendous of these, it is worth noting in passing, was the German National Socialism that found Heideggerian thought so intellectually convenient. As Heidegger was toying with the metaphysical nuances of the Heraclitan notion that violence creates togetherness, the Nazi ideologists were trying to put the principle to work in history. And they were not the last to try to do so.

As a historical phenomenon, nationalism may be vast and complex, but as a concept it is familiar and reassuring. It sounds like something we know about. The word "nationalism" is one of the familiar terms we use today in an effort to fit certain troubling events into categories that are intelligible to us. To think that what happened in Croatia was "nationalism" is as reassuring as to think that what happened in Rwanda was a "civil war." Terms such as these are the workaday language of the system of meaning I have referred to as "history." As the explanatory power of this system fails, the inadequacy of its terminology becomes more apparent. Supplementing and qualifying terms are added, "ethnic cleansing" being one of the most recent and disturbing ones. What, then, are we finally to make of all the stories that tell us of *nationalism, civil war,* and *ethnic cleansing?* What are we to make of Auschwitz? What are we to make of the following passage from the May 16, 1994, *Time* magazine cover story about Rwanda?

> First come the corpses of men and older boys, slain trying to protect their sisters and mothers. Then come the women and girls, flushed out from their hiding places and cut down. Last are the babies, who may bear no wounds: they are tossed alive into the water, to drown on their way downstream. The bodies, or pieces of them, glide by for half an hour or so, the time it takes to wipe out a community, carry the victims to the banks and dump them in. Then the water runs clear for awhile, until men and older boys drift into view again, then women, then babies, reuniting in the shallows as the river becomes the grave.

In many of the contexts in which they are now being used, words like "nationalism," "civil war," and even "ethnic cleansing" are words for trying to talk about the recrudescence of the primitive sacred as though it were something less ominous and significant than it is. What is happening in various degrees of severity — within our own culture as well as more catastrophically in less privileged and structured societies — is what Girard calls the crisis of distinctions or the sacrificial crisis. Anthropologically it is a *religious* phenomenon. It involves spasms of violence of the kind that we humans were once able to endow with religious meaning and whose cathartic climax we were once able to convert into reasonably durable cultural structures. Being the result of mimetic meltdowns, these "sacrificial crises" continue to occur whenever mimetic passions overwhelm those cultural structures designed to restrain them.

How, in light of this, are we to understand the resurgence of "the new nationalism" about which we have begun to hear so much? To begin with, as I have said, we should regard it anthropologically and not just politically. And to see things anthropologically is to see them religiously. Of course, in virtually all of the "new nationalisms," religious issues are either explicitly in play or just beneath the surface, but, in the West at least, the religious issues tend to remain subordinated to nationalist ones. People caught up in the scandals and frenzy of a sacrificial crisis are prone to believe almost anything that will allow them to unleash their scapegoating violence with moral impunity. In Christianized cultures, however, attempts to claim such moral immunity by appealing to Christianity have been increasingly less successful. The moral blindness a sacrificial crisis induces in those who get caught up in it is incredibly powerful. Speaking both etymologically and biblically, it is nothing less than the power of Satan (the accuser). But its power is not unlimited, and Christian confidence in history is based on the faith (and experience) that at the crucifixion the stranglehold of this power was broken. And so gradually, but ineluctably, when thrown into a sacrificial crisis, those whose only explicit religious appeal would have to be to the authority of the gospel have tended to look elsewhere for their "religious" justification. They have tended to endow something else — race, ethnicity, nationality, ideology — with religious significance rather than trying to establish the righteousness of their collective violence by invoking the name of the one who died at the hands of a self-righteous mob.

To a far less extent, even societies with little direct contact with the biblical tradition face milder forms of this awkward dilemma. This is so because the secularism that these societies are trying either to foster or slough off is a thoroughly Western phenomenon, suffused with biblical moral sensibilities, both those it repudiates and those it claims to have invented. Since, then, Western secularism carries the biblical virus it eschews, by the time a society has been affected by it enough to either embrace it or react against it, it has already been infected to some degree with these biblical sensibilities. To exactly that degree, its sacrificial apparatus will be destabilized and its justifying myths will be undermined.

Nationalism is an enormously complex phenomenon, and I do not mean to oversimplify, but to treat the current upsurge in nationalist sentiment as a purely political event is, I think, to miss its deepest significance. According to Tony Judt, professor of European Studies at New York University, for more and more people, "nationalism tells the most convincing story about their condition."[3] If this is so, it is not because nationalism tells a particularly compelling story, but for two intertwined reasons. First, because it provides a kind of social transcendence that fosters camaraderie, and, second, because it can be fairly easily invoked to justify the kind of violence those caught in a sacrificial crisis are disposed to commit. In other words, radical nationalism — blood-and-soil nationalism and its ideological variants—provides those living in a world that is both secularized and residually or inchoately Christianized with a facsimile of the sacred. It is a resurgence of *this* that is taking place in our world. This is not to say that the "new nationalism" has no valid historical rationale, but rather to point out that, once engulfed in a sacrificial crisis, such rationale can easily be exploited in ways that unleash the irrational forces of sacred violence.

The point I am trying to make is that the resurgence of "nationalism" we are witnessing is a symptom of a religious crisis. More specifically, it amounts to a crude and sometimes violent cry for *transcendence.* It has been said that humanity in the twenty-first century will be religious or it will not be. I would paraphrase that to say that we human beings *are* religious, and we will not forever tolerate a life devoid of religious transcendence, no matter how materially comfortable it is. And no matter the cost in material terms, sooner or later, we will either discover the experience of genuine religious transcendence or we will fashion out of our own social and spiritual confusions something that simulates it.

Divided Consciousness

In March of 1994, *Harper's* magazine published excerpts of Michael Ignatieff's *Blood and Belonging: Journeys into the New Nationalism,* a chronicle of his travels in Croatia, Serbia, Ukraine, Kurdistan, Northern Ireland, and elsewhere. The piece reads like that of a modern-day Captain Cook reporting on his visit to cultures in the throes of a sacrificial crisis, having witnessed their violent rituals without benefit of the moral Novocaine their justifying myths provide. As a cultural outsider, Ignatieff found the rituals as morally baffling as Cook found those he witnessed in Polynesia. They differed from the Tahitian rituals in two ways, however. First, those performing them did not think of them as religious rituals, but rather as rational historical events, and, second, they consumed a vastly greater number of victims. In the end, Ignatieff summarized and anticipated the moral shock that so many have felt over the last few years. He wrote:

> After you have been to the wastelands of the new world order, particularly to those fields of graves marked with numberless wooden crosses, you feel stunned into silence by a deficit of moral explanation.[4]

Like Captain Cook more than two hundred years earlier, Ignatieff sensed the relationship between the violent rituals of the new nationalism and the social solidarity of those who participated in them and condoned them.

> I have been to places where belonging is so strong, so intense, that I now recoil from it in fear. The rational core of such fear is that there is a deep connection between violence and belonging.... You can't have this intensity of belonging without violence.[5]

The most remarkable thing about Ignatieff's report, however, and what makes it so valuable, is that he was able to get beyond the surface vehemence and to recognize how fragile were the myths that unleashed all the violence and endowed it with moral legitimacy. He explained:

> In his 1959 essay, "What Does Coming to Terms with the Past Mean?" Theodor Adorno says, in passing, "Nationalism no longer quite believes in itself." Everywhere I went, there was a bewildering insincerity and inauthenticity to nationalist rhetoric, as if the people who mouthed nationalist slogans were aware, somewhere inside, of the implausibility of their own words. Serbs who, in one breath, would tell you that all Croats were Ustashe beasts would, in the next, recall the happy days when they lived with them in peace. In this divided consciousness, the plane of abstract fantasy and the plane of direct experience were never allowed to intersect.[6]

The "divided consciousness" Ignatieff mentions brings us back to a theme that I discussed briefly in the first chapter. There I quoted the remark by *Time* magazine essayist Lance Morrow to the effect that the conduct of foreign policy requires that one use "a different part of the brain from the one engaged by horrifying images." The "divided consciousness" that allows one to switch from the part of the brain where direct experience is both rationally and morally assessed to "a different part of the brain" where abstract fantasies and foreign policies are formed — that is the *real* "unconscious." The world's most trenchant analysis of it remains those words spoken by Jesus as he looked down on his persecutors from the Cross: "Forgive them for they know not what they do." The moment these words were spoken, the delusion to which they refer was exposed, and shortly thereafter the paramount power of the delusional system that produced it was undermined. And shortly after that, Peter heard the cock crow.

When Ignatieff observes that nationalism no longer believes in itself, he is saying that not even the new nationalism's most fanatical and mind-numbing frenzies can drown out the crowing of the cock. This means that those who might have otherwise fallen completely under the spell of the justifying myth hear, instead, the crowing of the cock, and by trying to shout above its crowing their shrill voices betray "a bewildering insincerity and inauthenticity." It means that the more the spokesmen for the justifying myth try to be convincing, the less convincing they will be to those not directly under the spell of the myth they espouse. Ignatieff observes:

> Nationalism is a form of speech that shouts, not merely so that it will be heard but so that it will believe itself. It is almost as if the quotient of crude historical fiction, violent moral exaggeration, ludicrous caricature of the enemy is in direct proportion to the degree to which the speaker is himself aware that it is all really a pack of lies.[7]

In the Gospel of John, we are told that "the prince of this world is already condemned." This *kosmokrator* is the personification of the Heraclitan *logos,* the mystifying force that endows violence with religious meaning and thereby makes it culturally invigorating. What Ignatieff has noticed is that even its most vehement and violent manifestations are losing their mythological power. Unfortunately, as Ignatieff's astute observation suggests, the need to override vague moral uncertainties can lead to "violent moral exaggeration," as its adherents try to suppress the growing realization that "it is all really a pack of lies." This paradox is a miniature version of the logic of the New Testament notion of apocalyptic violence. The weaker the sacrificial myths and rituals become, the less completely we fall under their spell and the more rapacious the mad attempt to turn violence into the "wrath of God."

There is an even more powerful reminder of these things in Mark Danner's report on the massacre of 767 people, many of them women and children, by the Salvadoran military in 1981.[8] Danner's book contains two passages that, grim as they are, speak volumes about the ultimate religious and anthropological struggle that is taking place in the world today. In the first, he quotes the reported remarks of one of the officers under whose command the massacre took place. It is best, I think, to ponder the officer's words in light of Ignatieff's observation about the "violent moral exaggeration" with which those charged with dispensing the new nationalist rhetoric mouthed slogans, as if struggling to suppress a moral truth that was overtaking them. The Salvadoran officer reportedly said:

> "What we did yesterday, and the day before, this is called war. This is what war is. War is hell....Now, I don't want to hear that, afterward, while you're out drinking...you're whining and complaining about this, about how terrible it was. I don't want to hear that. Because what we did yesterday, what we've been doing on this operation — this is war, gentlemen. This is what war is."[9]

As I said, as a historical fact, "war" is a terrible and devastating phenomenon, but, as a concept, it is — as is "nationalism" — familiar. War has been so ardently valorized for so long that an aura of primitive religious prestige has clung to it. In the above quotation, there can be no doubt that it is being used precisely in order to exploit its mythic power. When the Salvadoran officer tries to convince the soldiers under him that what he ordered them to do the day before was "war," he is trying to provide them, and himself, with the justifying myth that will relieve the moral burden that his words strongly suggest both he and they have begun to feel.

Again, we must try to see such things not only politically and historically, but anthropologically and religiously. The myth that justifies scapegoating or sacrificial violence is a product of the primitive *sacred.* Religion is the final arbiter of violence in cultural life. As I said, the term "war" carries some of the vestigial power of the sacred, but why did not the Salvadoran officer make a direct appeal to religion? What would have been more convincing than to convince his soldiers what the vast majority of their counterparts down through history were convinced of, namely, that their violence was God's will. When he launched the First Crusade, for instance, Pope Urban II was able to admonish his eager listeners with the words: "Let the army of the Lord, when it rushes upon his enemies, shout but that one cry, '*Dieu le veult! Dieu le veult!*' "[10] "God wants it!" In the eleventh century, these words had an effect on their hearers that the Salvadoran officer could not dream of having on his by using only the word "war" to justify his and their violence. Why did he not follow Urban II's example and tell his troops that they had performed God's work the day before? It would be difficult to argue that the officer and his troops were morally superior to Urban II and those who assembled at the Council of Clermont to hear him. On the other hand, there is little evidence that our officer is an enlightenment rationalist, though I suppose that cannot be ruled out. Clearly, however, he did not avail himself of this obviously superior rationale because he knew that he could bring neither himself nor his soldiers to believe that the Christian God had wanted them to do what they had done.

So much for what he could not do. How about what he did? How about his effort to use the "war" to lend moral sanction to the massacre? Does his use of this word carry any religious overtones? In this regard, Christopher Lehmann-Haupt, who reviewed Danner's book for the *New York Times,* made a telling comment. After referring to the officer's admonition to his subordinates, Lehmann-Haupt remarked that "you can only stare in dumbfounded horror. There is no one to blame but the gods of war."[11] The reason I am calling attention to this grim story is because, for all its horror, it is a vivid parable about the anthropological and religious struggle that is now taking place in our world. It is a world in which the Salvadoran officer, and all those who try to do what he tried to do, are reduced to using bland, generic, and religiously attenuated terms like "war" to veil acts of sacrificial or scapegoating violence for which they cannot use Christian justification without doing their moral credibility more damage than good. Obviously, this would not have been the case, or it would have been much less the case, had the events in need of religious justification occurred in a cultural setting less influenced by the gospel revelation. There are religious cultures where the idea of God's holy savagery is still a viable one, and, as the story of the massacre at El Mozote shows, the gospel invalidation of that concept can be overridden even in cultures where the gospel has taken root. But there can be no doubt that the effect of the gospel is to invalidate such notions and that those who would perpetuate them face a formidable task in trying to formulate a myth that will override the gospel.

What I am suggesting is what I have stressed throughout this book, that in our world a struggle is taking place between the power of the sacrificial and scapegoating myths and the gospel's deconstruction of them. When one speaks of the moral, epistemological, and historical power of the gospel revelation, it is proper to ask: Where is the power? Can it be seen? Is it merely metaphysical? This brings me to the primary reason I have chosen to refer to Danner's account of the massacre at El Mozote in bringing our discussion of the unveiling of violence to a conclusion. In one of the most heartrending and poignant passages in his book, Danner tells of one of the victims of the El Mozote massacre, and I want to pause briefly to reflect on it.

Before and during the massacre, the government soldiers had plundered the village and raped many of its women. There was one girl, Danner says, that the soldiers could not get out of their minds, a girl whom they had raped many times during the course of the afternoon. All during her torture, this girl, an evangelical Christian, had sung hymns.

> She had kept right on singing, too, even after they had done what had to be done, and shot her in the chest. She had lain there on La Cruz with the blood flowing from her chest, and had kept on singing — a bit weaker than before, but still singing. And the soldiers, stupefied, had watched and pointed. Then they had grown tired of the game and shot her again, and she sang still, and their wonder began to turn to fear — until finally

> they had unsheathed their machetes and hacked through her neck, and at last the singing had stopped.[12]

La Cruz was the name of a hill where the soldiers raped and murdered. The name, of course, means "The Cross." "*On La Cruz,* soldiers were raping the young girls...." The young girl whose song would not die "had lain there *on La Cruz* with blood flowing from her chest..." (my emphasis). The crucifixion of Christ was, and is, a ghastly thing. The question is, when will we stop it? We will not do so by fleeing from the Cross and its ghastliness, but by recognizing its universal meaning.

Her Song and His War

To see the larger significance of this terrible story, we must place this girl's muted song alongside the officer's rhetoric about "war" and its implacable necessity. This, I think, is an extreme but apt representation of the spiritual contest that is taking place in history between the intoxicating power of sacred violence and the *unforgettable* power of the gospel revelation. And what is happening in history is that the intoxicating power of the sacred is wearing off, a moral hangover is setting in, which some are trying to fend off, as addicts do, by drinking to the dregs what's left in the flask.

The crucifixion of Jesus took place on a lonely hill outside the city, all his friends and followers having fled. If someone at the time had suggested that his death would be the most remembered death in human history, it would have seemed completely absurd. The massacre at El Mozote occurred in a remote village, and all but a very few of those who might have told the truth of it were killed there. And yet this girl's faint voice has survived. The officer's invocation of the grim necessity of "war" provides a dark background for it, against which it stands out even more vividly. The light shines in the darkness and the darkness cannot overcome it. If the soldiers who murdered her could not forget this haunting figure, neither should we, for in more profound ways than even Danner supposes, we share responsibility for it. Even should we want to forget this girl's voice, however, it would difficult to do so. The *Times* reviewer was obviously haunted by it. He said that after reading Danner's account of this girl's death, he kept "straining hopelessly to hear the sound of that singing." As Michael Ignatieff's report makes clear, it is easy enough to get so caught up in the scandals and cycles of violence that one strains, instead, to hear a myth such as the Salvadoran officer espoused. But as terrible as they are, not even the dark omens of our time should make us doubt for one moment that the world is awakening *to* that girl's song and *from* the officer's myth.

However shrill and bombastic the voices of the victors and victimizers may grow, there is now something at work in history that endows the faintest gestures of the victim with a *lasting* moral power that will sooner or later be all the world remembers (*aletheia*). The story of the girl *on La Cruz,* of course, is a striking example of this, but there are many, many others, and I would like to mention in passing one of them. It is a note, scratched on a piece of scrap paper by someone who was killed in the German death camp at Buchenwald. It reads as follows:

> Peace to all men of evil will! Let there be an end to all vengeance, to all demands for punishment and retribution. There are too many martyrs.... Lay not their sufferings to the torturer's charge to exact a terrible reckoning from them, Lord. Instead, put down in favor of all men of evil will, the courage, humility, dignity, love and spiritual strength of the others. Let it be laid before Thee for the forgiveness of sins.... And may we remain in your enemies' memory not as their victims... not as haunting spectres, but as helpers in their striving to destroy the fury of their criminal passions. There is nothing more that we want for them.[13]

Besides the obvious ones, there is an important similarity between the girl on La Cruz who died singing a hymn and the anonymous Jew at Buchenwald who wrote this amazing note. Both were at prayer. And both were murdered by those who had thrown into the furnace of their fury every moral restraint in a mad effort to forge their violence into something that simulates real religious transcendence. There, in all its stark contrast, is the ultimate choice we face. We are innately religious beings, and, as Augustine said, we are restless until we rest in God. And if we cannot find rest there, we will eventually turn our restlessness into some shabby semblance of transcendence, a transcendence that is either born of violence or the prelude to it. When Jesus taught his disciples how to pray, he taught them this: "Lead us not into temptation." Most of us, therefore, can thank God that we live in the vast middle ground of history, where the choice between sanctity and savagery is never this stark. But, ultimately, we live in a world that will be ordered and made coherent by one or the other of the two forms of religious transcendence that struggled with one another so pitiably on *La Cruz.*

The Glory of God

A perfect analogue for the contest between these two orders of reality—premised on two radically different forms of religious experience—is the story of the stoning of Stephen in the Acts of the Apostles. Speaking as the next victim of the mob of religious zealots, and speaking on behalf of the mob's last victim, Jesus, Stephen made explicit what was implicit in the prayer of the Buchenwald victim and the song of the girl from La Cruz: "In spite of being given the Law through angels, you have not kept it." Upon hearing this, the response of the mob caught in its spasm of righteous zeal was not long in coming:

> They were infuriated when they heard this, and ground their teeth at him. But Stephen, filled with the Holy Spirit, gazed into heaven and saw the glory of God, and Jesus standing at God's right hand. "Look! I can see heaven thrown open," he said, "and the Son of man standing at the right hand of God." All the members of the council shouted out and stopped their ears with their hands; then they made a concerted rush at him, thrust him out of the city and stoned him. (Acts 7:54–58)

At its zenith of frenzy, violence provides — for its perpetrators and enthusiastic spectators — a semblance of religious transcendence. The naive assumptions of Enlightenment rationalism to the contrary notwithstanding, unless we discover or rediscover more authentic forms of religious transcendence, the prospects for eliminating such violence or calming the social passions that lead to it are nil. To some, shifting from the question of violence to the question of authentic religious transcendence may seem too abrupt, perhaps confounding. I hope the foregoing pages will have made it less so, but there is, and always has been, and always will be, something *inherently confounding* about the "solution" to the human dilemma that the biblical tradition offers. The God we glimpse in biblical literature and whom we see most vividly in and through the life of Christ is not a God who exists to put an end to humanity's historical tribulations. Rather, the light shines *in* the darkness. The question is not: will things get better and better? Some may, most won't. The question is: do we have a prayer? We do if there is both a reason to pray and One to whom a prayer might be addressed. We are no more likely to eliminate the kinds of personal and historical tribulations that so often lead to prayer than we are to discover a God so objectively provable that prayer will cease to be an act of faith.

Historical tribulations are as inherently a part of human existence as are matter and death. It isn't, finally, a question of whether we humans have what we need to solve our problems or survive our crises. Finally, it's a question of whether or not we have what we need to transform the materiality, mortality, and occasional madness of existence into a love that neither madness nor mortality can destroy. As strange as it may seem, therefore, there is scriptural warrant for turning from the dreadful accounts of the Buchenwald death camp and the girl murdered *on La Cruz* — contemporary versions of the crucifixion — to a passage that may seem at first totally unrelated. It is Jesus' reply to a Pharisee who asked what was the greatest commandment. Jesus told him:

> You must love the Lord your God with all your heart, with all your soul, and with all your mind. This is the greatest and the first commandment. The second resembles it: You must love your neighbor as yourself. (Matt. 22:37–39)

The Jesus of Matthew's Gospel did not say that the greatest commandment was to *believe* in God and love humanity. He did not say that we should be nice to one another because that's the way God would like us to behave. He said the first and most essential thing is to *love God* with a paramount love. It is the most hackneyed notion in the world, but once or twice in a lifetime its dulling familiarity vanishes, and one feels for a moment the unfathomable significance and centrality of Jesus' suggestion for breaking the grip of sin and death: to *love* God. Partly due to the humanists' romantic idea of basic human benevolence and partly to the rationalistic "where-there's-a-will-there's-a-way" spirit of the Enlightenment, the modern world came to believe that it could fulfill the requirements of the second commandment without having to bother with the first. We moderns came to believe, in effect, that, by itself, the second commandment was a civilizing force sufficient to the task at hand. The creaking and groaning, indeed, the shouting and shooting, that we now hear all around us is coming from the collapse of that assumption. If we need an epitaph for it, this from Girard will serve:

> In reality, no purely intellectual process and no experience of a purely philosophical nature can secure the individual the slightest victory over mimetic desire and its victimage delusions. Intellection can achieve only displacement and substitution, though these may give individuals the sense of having achieved a victory. For there to be even the slightest degree of progress, the victimage delusion must be vanquished on the most intimate level of experience.[14]

Epilogue

Redeem the Time

> I would so like to believe that the "childhood" of Christendom is over, that it is breaking away from ideology and legalism, no longer emphasizing concepts — the Western representation of things — tearing down its doctrinal scaffolding, or at least keeping it at a distance, something for specialists, and becoming at once more feeble and more strong, more apt to express itself in terms of our common anthropological foundation.[1]
>
> JEAN SULIVAN

> It is not for us to prophesy the day (though the day will come) when men will once more be called so to utter the Word of God that the world will be changed and renewed by it. It will be a new language, perhaps quite non-religious, but liberating and redeeming — as was Jesus' language; it will shock people and yet overcome them by its power.[2]
>
> DIETRICH BONHOEFFER

According to the synoptic Gospels, it was Peter who first recognized the messianic scope of Jesus' message and mission, and it was Peter who immediately thereafter urged Jesus to act with an eye to the success and longevity of his ministry. It was Peter whom Jesus thereupon called a Satan and a stumbling block. It was Peter who resorted to violence at the arrest of Jesus. At Jesus' arraignment before the High Priest, it was Peter who denied his relationship with him in order to huddle in safety with the minor religious functionaries, begging, in effect, to be admitted to membership in the kind of sacrificial community whose binding power the crucifixion was about to destroy. And, of course, it was Peter whom Jesus in Matthew's Gospel designated as the rock on which the church would be built. As Jean Sulivan points out:

> The Aramaic word kephas, Peter, has the same meaning as Caiaphas. The history of twenty centuries is there in embryo. Peter and the Church with him — faithful, loving and betraying at the same time, unable to avoid betrayal because of their conception of things.[3]

We have only just begun to understand how deeply the Caiaphas principle is embedded in all our social and psychological reflexes. To be human, to be part of what Paul termed "the old humanity," is to betray the gospel revelation. I have no doubt betrayed it dozens of times in the preceding pages. To be Christian is to betray the gospel revelation *and* to try not to. To make matters even more perplexing, some of the most perverse betrayals of the gospel have resulted from fanatical efforts to prevent betrayal at all cost. Hyper-scrupulous adherence to received doctrine has led to distortions of the gospel spirit at least as often as has doctrinal carelessness. One of the many paradoxes with which Christians must wrestle is the fact that, by its very nature, a "pro-Christian" position is antithetical to the spirit of the gospel. Precisely because the Cross is indistinguishable from the sacrificial violence it reveals and repudiates, the revelations that flow from it are peculiarly susceptible to perversion. As G. K. Chesterton noted, the church is announcing to the world "terrible ideas and devouring doctrines, each one of them strong enough to turn to a false religion and lay waste the world."[4] He cautioned that "if some small mistake were made in doctrine, huge blunders might be made in human happiness." On the other hand, of course, Jesus was crucified by people who were afraid that doctrinal mistakes were being made and that some false religion was going to lay waste the world. "Few were as careless of orthodox formulas as Jesus," wrote C. K. Barrett, "and there is something more than a little precious in affecting a greater concern for orthodoxy than his."[5]

Perhaps the *anthropological* role of the Christian church in human history might be oversimplified as follows: To undermine the structures of sacred violence by making it impossible to forget how Jesus *died* and to show the world how to live without such structures by making it impossible to forget how Jesus *lived.* In both life and death, Jesus was opposed by the most respected institutions of his world. Not surprisingly, therefore, the prospects of institutionalizing either the Sermon on the Mount or the revelation of the Cross are not great. "The Church," wrote Karl Barth, "sets fire to a charge that blows up every sacred edifice which men ever erected or can erect in its vicinity."[6] In every instance, the institution in closest proximity to the gospel's explosive charge is the institution we call the church. As Andrew McKenna puts it, "The breakdown of institutional Christianity is the legacy of the crucifixion narrative, which is one with the Hebrew Bible's denunciation of overtly sacrificial institutions, indeed, of all forms of victimization."[7] Fortunately, however, the breakdown of institutional Christianity is not the *only* legacy of the crucifixion narrative. Peter's Aramaic name should be a perpetual reminder of the lingering lure of sacrificial thinking in Christian history, but it should not obscure the fact that the name means "rock" and that, especially in a world as radically destabilized as the one in which we live, we should not casually dispense with the few forms of stability that survive. The church, like Peter, is both a stumbling block and a cornerstone. It is the latter only when it is consciously contrite for being, and having been, the former. The inherent contradiction with which institutional Christianity is always faced was perhaps best summed up by T. S. Eliot in his poem *Ash Wednesday,* where he wrote:

> Redeem
> The time. Redeem
> The unread vision in the higher dream
> While jewelled unicorns draw by the gilded hearse.[8]

The gilded hearse drawn by jewelled unicorns is Eliot's Dantesque image for the ridiculous pageant of Christian pomp that has sometimes been the only access people living under the weight of history have had to the unread vision of the gospel revelation. Lampooning the pomposities and hypocrisy of the gaudy pageant has its place, but in light of the present urgencies such things hardly deserve top priority. The real challenge is to redeem the time and to do so by redeeming the unread vision in the higher dream. Jesus, we're told, was born in a squalid little barn. The institutions that bear the Christian revelation through history are as seemingly inadequate to the task they've been given as was the feeding trough in which the newborn Christ was laid. The fact that we are less offended by the smelly manger than by the "jewelled unicorns" and "gilded hearse" is proof that the latter haven't prevented the spirit of the gospel from having its effect on us after all.

This began as a book about the present anthropological, cultural, and historical crisis, analyzed in the light of the remarkable work of René Girard. At the outset, I had no intention of ending it, as I have, on such a confessional note. It has ended that way because writing it has drawn me ever deeper into the mysterious power of the Christian revelation, and it would be silly to put on a wooden face and pretend otherwise. While one needn't wear one's faith on one's sleeve, neither is there reason to equivocate. In writing this book, I have grown ever more aware of how great is my intellectual debt to René Girard. More importantly, however, I have come to realize the degree to which his groundbreaking work is part of what Andrew McKenna has called "the legacy of the crucifixion narrative." Mediated as it is through the example, work, and thought of others, I now believe that legacy to be the world's wellspring of moral and religious truth and its ultimate guarantor of intellectual clarity.

Grateful for his inspiration and friendship, I want to give the concluding word to René Girard, for he summarizes best the work he so profoundly inspired:

> Beyond the misunderstandings, calumnies and encroachments of which it is the object, beyond the historical reversals and even the disasters that result, and beyond all that disfigures it in our eyes, the truth of the victim that we at last possess is the greatest, most fortunate event in the history of religion and the whole of humanity.[9]

Notes

Introduction: The Hole in the Parlor Floor

1. Richard Wilbur, "A Hole in the Floor," *The Poems of Richard Wilbur* (New York: Harcourt, Brace & World, n.d.), 15.

2. Girard is Andrew B. Hammond Professor of French Language, Literature and Civilization at Stanford University, where he is also Professor of Religious Studies and Comparative Literature.

3. *Le Monde,* October 27, 1972, quoted by Raymund Schwager, S.J., *Must There Be Scapegoats?* (San Francisco, Harper & Row, 1987), xi.

4. Sandor Goodhart, "'I Am Joseph': René Girard and the Prophetic Law," in Paul Dumouchel, ed., *Violence and Truth* (Stanford, Calif.: Stanford University Press, 1988), 53.

5. Dumouchel, *Violence and Truth,* 23.

6. Robert Hamerton-Kelly, "A Religious Theory of Ethno-Nationalist Violence" (draft), 5.

7. The term "scapegoat" is central to Girard's important analysis of cultural process. The term comes from the atonement ritual described in the Hebrew Bible (Leviticus 16). In a later section of this book I will discuss the term at greater length. The term has come into common usage in Western culture in the last few centuries to refer to a spontaneous social phenomenon. I use it here, as elsewhere, in its conventional sense, referring to the process whereby a society revives its sense of both social solidarity and moral righteousness by uniting against one regarded as a source of evil, one whose selection is more arbitrary than the persecuting crowd is able to realize.

8. Robert G. Hamerton-Kelly, *Sacred Violence: Paul's Hermeneutic of the Cross* (Minneapolis: Fortress, 1992), 59.

Chapter 1: "A Sort of Surreal Confusion"

1. H. G. Wells, *The Outline of History* (Garden City, N.Y.: Garden City Books, 1961), 2:725.

2. Joseph Brodsky, "The Post-communist Nightmare: An Exchange," *New York Review of Books,* February 17, 1994.

3. Johann Baptist Metz, *The Emergent Church,* trans. Peter Mann (New York: Crossroad, 1987), 18.

4. John Lukacs, *Historical Consciousness* (New York: Schocken Books, 1985), 15.

5. Charles S. Maier, *The Unmasterable Past: History, Holocaust and German National Identity* (Cambridge: Harvard University Press, 1988), 100;

quoted in Andrew J. McKenna, *Violence and Difference* (Urbana: University of Illinois Press, 1992), 128.

6. Lukacs, *Historical Consciousness,* 23.

7. Henri de Lubac, *Paradoxes of Faith* (San Francisco: Ignatius Press, 1987), 145.

8. Northrop Frye, *The Great Code: The Bible and Literature* (New York: Harcourt Brace Jovanovich, 1982), 136.

9. Cesáreo Bandera, *The Sacred Game* (University Park: Pennsylvania State University Press, 1994), 147.

10. Frye, *The Great Code,* 136.

11. Ibid.

12. René Girard, *A Theater of Envy* (New York: Oxford University Press, 1991), 282. By "a desacralized and sacrificially unprotected world" what Girard means is a world in which, increasingly, those who participate in collective violence are unable, and those against whom it is perpetrated are unwilling, to regard the violence as "God's violence."

13. René Girard, *Violence and the Sacred,* trans. Patrick Gregory (Baltimore: Johns Hopkins University Press, 1979), 240.

14. Ibid.

15. Wendy Haminer, "I'm Dysfunctional, You're Dysfunctional," *Image Magazine* (*Sunday Examiner-Chronicle*), June 28, 1992, 12.

16. *New York Times,* Sunday, November 24, 1991.

17. McKenna, *Violence and Difference,* 164.

18. Edward Schillebeeckx, *Christ: The Experience of Jesus as Lord* (New York: Crossroad, 1983), 650.

19. This essay subsequently appeared in Hughes's book, *Culture of Complaint* (New York: Oxford University Press, 1993).

20. In the *Collected Poems,* edited by Edward Mendelson, the term "New Age" has been changed to "New Tragedy."

21. René Girard, *Job: The Victim of His People* (Stanford: Stanford University Press, 1987), 35.

22. *The Portable Nietzsche,* ed. and trans. Walter Kaufmann (New York: Penguin, 1968), 655.

23. Ibid., 572.

Chapter 2: "Jesus Thrown Everything Off . . ."

1. René Girard, *The Scapegoat,* trans. Yvonne Freccero (Baltimore: Johns Hopkins University Press, 1986), 166.

2. John W. Dixon, Jr., *The Physiology of Faith* (San Francisco: Harper & Row, 1979), 253.

3. Aeschylus, *The Oresteian Trilogy,* trans. Philip Vellacott (New York: Viking Penguin, 1986).

4. René Girard, *Violence and the Sacred,* trans. Patrick Gregory (Baltimore: Johns Hopkins University Press, 1979), 66–67. To anticipate a later discussion, the tragic spirit leaves no "Paraclete" behind.

5. René Girard, *Things Hidden since the Foundation of the World* (Stanford, Calif.: Stanford University Press, 1987), 256.

6. Aeschylus, *The Oresteian Trilogy,* 47.

7. Gustave Le Bon, *The Crowd* (London: Ernest Benn, 1947), 187–88.

8. Whittaker Chambers, *Witness* (New York: Random House, 1952), 14.

9. Ibid.

10. Masao Yamaguchi, "Towards a Poetics of the Scapegoat," in Paul Dumouchel, ed., *Violence and Truth* (Stanford, Calif.: Stanford University Press, 1988), 179.

11. Flannery O'Connor, "A Good Man Is Hard to Find," *The Complete Stories* (New York: Farrar, Straus and Giroux, 1973), 131.

12. René Girard, *Violent Origins,* ed. Robert G. Hamerton-Kelly (Stanford, Calif.: Stanford University Press, 1987), 141.

13. Victor White, *God the Unknown and Other Essays* (London: Harvill Press, 1956), 102.

14. Leszek Kolakowski, *Modernity on Endless Trial* (Chicago: University of Chicago Press, 1990), 18.

Chapter 3: "The Ceremony of Innocence Is Drowned"

1. M. L. Rosenthal, ed., *Selected Poems and Two Plays of William Butler Yeats* (New York: Collier, 1966), 91.

2. Eric Gans, "The Victim as Subject: The Esthetico-Ethical System of Rousseau's *Rêveries,*" *Studies in Romanticism* 21, no. 1 (Spring 1982): 4.

3. René Girard, *Things Hidden since the Foundation of the World* (Stanford, Calif.: Stanford University Press, 1987), 256.

4. *Christian Science Monitor,* July 24, 1991.

5. Bob Spichen, "A Riot by Any Other Name...," *Los Angeles Times,* August 3, 1992, A1.

6. Milton C. Nahm, ed., *Selections from Early Greek Philosophy* (New York: Appleton-Century-Crofts, 1964), 71–72.

7. Bill Keller, "Bullied by Its Children, a Township Is Festering," *New York Times,* July 31, 1992, A4.

8. Léon Bing, *Do or Die* (New York: HarperCollins, 1991).

9. The Los Angeles gangs at the time were divided into two major clans: the Crips and the Bloods.

10. Freeman Dyson, *Weapons and Hope* (New York: Harper & Row, 1985), 7, quoted by Andrew J. McKenna, *Violence and Difference* (Urbana: University of Illinois Press, 1992), 150.

11. Bing, *Do or Die,* 13.

12. William Golding, *Lord of the Flies* (New York: Putnam, 1954), 182.

13. Ibid., 186.

14. Robert G. Hamerton-Kelly, *Sacred Violence: Paul's Hermeneutic of the Cross* (Minneapolis: Fortress, 1992), 39.

Chapter 4: Shaken Witnesses

1. René Girard, *A Theater of Envy* (New York: Oxford University Press, 1991), 283.

2. *A Voyage to the Pacific Ocean, Undertaken by the Command of His Majesty, for Making Discoveries in the Northern Hemisphere, to Determine the Position and Extent of the West Side of North America; Its Distance from Asia; and the Practicability of a Northern Passage to Europe. Performed under the Direction of Captains Cook, Clerke, and Gore, in His Majesty's Ships the "Resolution" and "Discovery." In the years 1776, 1777, 1778, 1779, and 1780,.* 2:27ff. My attention was first called to Cook's account by references to it in Joseph Campbell's *The Mythic Image* (Princeton, N.J.: Princeton University Press, 1974), 439ff.

3. The decision, for instance, by California officials to hold the state executions at San Quentin prison at three o'clock in the morning to discourage protesting crowds is a strikingly similar development. The misgivings felt two hundred years ago in Tahiti are clearly being felt in Marin County, California, today.

4. Quoted by Anthony Lewis in a column on the *New York Times* Op-Ed page, May 20, 1991.

5. *Santa Rosa Press Democrat,* April 19, 1992.

6. Joseph T. Shipley, *Dictionary of Word Origins* (Ames, Iowa: Littlefield, Adams, 1955), 149.

7. René Girard, *Things Hidden since the Foundation of the World* (Stanford, Calif.: Stanford University Press, 1987), 218.

8. Cesáreo Bandera, "From Mythical Bees to Medieval Anti-Semitism," in Paul Dumouchel, ed., *Violence and Truth* (Stanford, Calif.: Stanford University Press, 1988), 218; emphasis added.

9. Coventry Patmore, "A London Fête," *The Harper Anthology of Poetry,* ed. John Frederick Nims (New York: Harper & Row, 1981), 413–14.

10. Andrew J. McKenna, *Violence and Difference* (Urbana: University of Illinois Press, 1992), 85.

11. Girard, *A Theater of Envy* (New York: Oxford University Press, 1991), 220.

12. See René Girard, *Violence and the Sacred,* trans. Patrick Gregory (Baltimore: Johns Hopkins University Press, 1979), 94–98.

13. *Napa Register,* June 19, 1992.

14. Søren Kierkegaard, *The Present Age,* trans. Alexander Dru (New York: Harper & Row, 1962), 54–55.

15. R. G. Hamerton-Kelly, "Violent Epiphany: Nuclear Deterrence and the Sacred," *Journal of the American Academy of Religion* 59, no. 3 (1991): 485. Let me here acknowledge a debt to Robert Hamerton-Kelly not only for the material in this citation, but for so many illuminating insights gleaned from his writings and from conversations with him at the Center for International Security and Arms Control at Stanford University, where he is Senior Research Scholar.

Chapter 5: A Land of Mirrors

1. Paul Dumouchel, ed., *Violence and Truth* (Stanford, Calif.: Stanford University Press, 1988), 13.

2. Christian anti-Semitism had always been an attempt to find scapegoats whom Christians could for a while distinguish from the Scapegoated Jew whom they called their Lord. The implausibility of that attempt is as striking as is the historical fact that Christians desperate for scapegoats found it plausible for as long as they (we) did.

3. W. H. Auden, "Diaspora," *Collected Poems,* ed. Edward Mendelson (New York: Random House, 1979), 234–35.

4. Rudolf Otto, *The Idea of the Holy* (London: Oxford University Press, 1958), 31. Otto's essay is flawed and dated, but he occasionally touches on profundities. His analysis of them remains murky, but, when read in the light of Girard's mimetic theory, tremendous insights can be gleaned from Otto's work.

5. *New York Times,* May 16, 1991.

6. René Girard, *Things Hidden since the Foundation of the World* (Stanford, Calif.: Stanford University Press, 1987), 288.

Chapter 6: "To Know the Place for the First Time"

1. Letter to W. S. Smith, November 13, 1787.

2. René Girard, *A Theater of Envy* (New York: Oxford University Press, 1991), 210.

3. "Little Gidding," T. S. Eliot, *The Complete Poems and Plays, 1909–1950* (New York: Harcourt, Brace and World, 1971), 145.

4. René Girard, *Deceit, Desire, and the Novel,* trans. Yvonne Freccero (Baltimore: Johns Hopkins University Press, 1965).

5. René Girard, *Things Hidden since the Foundation of the World* (Stanford, Calif.: Stanford University Press, 1987), 288.

6. See René Girard, *Violence and the Sacred,* trans. Patrick Gregory (Baltimore: Johns Hopkins University Press, 1979).

7. Andrew J. McKenna, *Violence and Difference* (Urbana: University of Illinois Press, 1992), 133.

8. René Girard, *The Scapegoat,* trans. Yvonne Freccero (Baltimore: Johns Hopkins University Press, 1986), 110.

9. In fact, mass-production market economies function precisely this way. After advertising has awakened mimetic desire, the assembly lines keep these desires from turning into warfare between the haves and the have-nots by making reasonably similar facsimiles reasonably available. The problem with this system, of course, is that mimetic desires are always insatiable while natural resources are not. The moment the society that relies on mass production can no longer provide facsimiles, both commodities and comity will become scarce at the same time.

10. My inspiration for this play on words is Andrew J. McKenna, *Violence and Difference* (Urbana: University of Illinois Press, 1992), 153.

11. A. O. Hirschman, *Shifting Involvements: Private Interests and Public Action* (Princeton, N.J.: Princeton University Press, 1982), 21, quoted by André Orléan, "Money and Mimetic Speculation," *Violence and Truth* (Stanford, Calif.: Stanford University Press, 1988), 101.
12. Aristotle, *Poetics,* 4:2.
13. Girard, *Violence and the Sacred,* 161.
14. Rudolf Otto, *The Idea of the Holy* (London: Oxford University Press, 1958), 31.
15. McKenna, *Violence and Difference,* 167.
16. Girard, *Violence and the Sacred,* 107.
17. P. Du Chaillu, *Explorations and Adventures in Equatorial Africa* (London, 1861), 18ff, quoted in Elias Canetti, *Crowds and Power* (New York: Farrar, Straus and Giroux, 1984), 411–12.
18. Canetti, *Crowds and Power,* 418
19. Monteil, *Les Bambara du Ségou* (Paris, 1924), 305, quoted in Canetti, *Crowds and Power,* 418.
20. Simon Simonse, *Kings of Disaster* (Leiden: E. J. Brill, 1992), 396.
21. Canetti, *Crowds and Power,* 414.
22. Joseph Campbell, *The Masks of God: Creative Mythology* (New York: Viking Press, 1968), 406; emphasis added.
23. Ibid., 26.
24. *The Collected Poems of Howard Nemerov* (Chicago: University of Chicago, 1977), 237.

Chapter 7: A Text in Travail

1. René Girard, *Job: The Victim of His People* (Stanford University Press, 1987), 38.
2. Martin Buber, *On the Bible: Eighteen Studies by Martin Buber* (New York: Schocken Books, 1968), 5.
3. For a more detailed exposition of many of the points I will be making, see Raymond Schwager, S.J., *Must There Be Scapegoats?* (San Francisco: Harper & Row, 1987); James G. Williams, *The Bible, Violence, and the Sacred* (San Francisco: HarperSanFrancisco, 1991).
4. Eric Gans, *The End of Culture* (Berkeley: University of California Press, 1985), 203.
5. Andrew J. McKenna, *Violence and Difference* (Urbana: University of Illinois Press, 1992), 201.
6. René Girard, *Violent Origins,* ed. Robert G. Hamerton-Kelly (Stanford, Calif.: Stanford University Press, 1987), 141.
7. For a related discussion, see Robert G. Hamerton-Kelly, *Sacred Violence: Paul's Hermeneutic of the Cross* (Minneapolis: Fortress, 1992), 88–119, and Gans, *The End of Culture,* 190–202.
8. For a discussion of the individual commandments and for a much more thorough examination of many of the related issues, see Williams, *The Bible, Violence, and the Sacred.*

9. H. L. Ellison, *Exodus,* The Daily Study Bible Series, ed. John C. L. Gibson (Philadelphia: Westminster Press, 1982), 115; emphasis added.

10. C. K. Barrett, *A Commentary on the Epistle to the Romans* (New York: Harper & Row, 1957), 141.

11. This second code is widely regarded as older than the code in Exodus 20 (with Martin Buber dissenting from that view). I don't necessarily dispute this, but the comparative dates of the respective literary fragments should not completely eclipse the fact that the present arrangement of the two texts better accords with what seems to me at least to have been Moses' initial lack of interest in cultic matters.

12. Roland J. Faley, *Jerome Biblical Commentary,* ed. Raymond E. Brown, S.S., Joseph A. Fitzmyer, S.J., and Roland E. Murphy, O.Carm. (Englewood Cliffs, N.J.: Prentice-Hall, 1990), 67.

Chapter 8: Crossing the Jordan Opposite Jericho

1. René Girard, *A Theater of Envy* (New York: Oxford University Press, 1991), 224.

2. See, however, James G. Williams, "History-Writing as Protest: Kingship and the Beginning of Historical Narrative," *Contagion: Journal of Violence, Mimesis, and Culture* 1 (Spring 1994): 91–110.

3. *New York Times,* July 31, 1992.

4. Elias Canetti, *Crowds and Power* (New York: Farrar, Straus and Giroux, 1984), 63.

5. Gerhard von Rad, *Studies in Deuteronomy,* trans. D. Stalker (London: SCM Press, 1953), 58.

6. Ibid., 59; emphasis added.

7. von Rad, *Studies in Deuteronomy,* 45.

Chapter 9: The Prophets

1. Eric Gans, *The End of Culture* (Berkeley: University of California Press, 1985), 205.

2. Sandor Goodhart, "'I Am Joseph': René Girard and the Prophetic Law," in Paul Dumouchel, ed., *Violence and Truth* (Stanford, Calif.: Stanford University Press, 1988), 57–58.

3. Gerhard von Rad, *The Message of the Prophets* (New York: Harper & Row, 1965), 35, 37.

4. Ibid., 34.

5. Samuel Sandmel, *The Hebrew Scriptures* (New York: Oxford University Press, 1978), 150.

6. *Semeia* 33, 4, 1985.

Chapter 10: Repenting of the Violence of Our Justice

1. Robert G. Hamerton-Kelly, *The Gospel and the Sacred* (Minneapolis: Fortress, 1994), 126.

2. Jean-Michel Oughourlian, quoted in René Girard, *Things Hidden since the Foundation of the World* (Stanford, Calif.: Stanford University Press, 1987), 288.

3. Robert Hamerton-Kelly, "Violent Epiphany: Nuclear Deterrence and the Sacred," *Journal of the American Academy of Religion* 59, no. 3 (1991): 486.

4. Quoted by Frans Jozef van Beeck, S.J., *Loving the Torah More Than God?* (Chicago: Loyola University Press, 1989), 32ff.

5. Ibid., 81.

Chapter 11: "His Snares Are Broke"

1. Max Picard, *The World of Silence* (Washington, D.C.: Regnery Gateway, 1988), 89.

2. Edward Schillebeeckx, *Jesus: An Experiment in Christology* (New York: Random House, 1981), 134.

3. In pointing these things out, I am not trying to burden the reader with the minutiae of exegesis. I am simply trying to highlight one of the structures of meaning buried in the temptation accounts.

4. Marcus J. Borg, *Jesus: A New Vision* (San Francisco: HarperSanFrancisco, 1991), 114 (Borg's emphasis).

5. Ibid., 116.

6. For a related discussion, see David McCracken, *The Scandal of the Gospels: Jesus, Story, and Offense* (New York: Oxford University Press, 1994).

7. Ibid., 132.

8. Geza Vermes, *Jesus the Jew* (New York: Macmillan, 1973), 224; cited by Borg, *Jesus: A New Vision,* 145n.

9. Borg, *Jesus: A New Vision,* 139.

10. Elias Canetti, *Crowds and Power* (New York: Farrar, Straus and Giroux, 1984), 49.

Chapter 12: "It Is Accomplished"

1. Paul Johnson, *A History of Christianity* (New York: Macmillan, 1976), 29.

2. Eric Gans, "The Victim as Subject: The Esthetico-Ethical System of Rousseau's *Rêveries,*" *Studies in Romanticism* 21, no. 1 (Spring 1982): 27.

3. René Girard, *Things Hidden since the Foundation of the World* (Stanford, Calif.: Stanford University Press, 1987), 204.

4. Johnson, *A History of Christianity,* 29.

5. Rudolf Schnackenburg, *The Gospel according to St. John* (New York: Crossroad, 1990), 1:571.

6. Alas, our world has become so completely preoccupied with matters of gender that the analysis of anything expressed in gender-specific terms is increasingly likely to get stuck there.

7. Robert Hamerton-Kelly, *God the Father* (Philadelphia: Fortress Press, 1979), 102–3.

8. Schnackenburg, *The Gospel according to St. John,* 2:392.

9. Girard, *Things Hidden since the Foundation of the World,* 164.

10. Elias Canetti, *Crowds and Power* (New York: Farrar, Straus and Giroux, 1984), 145.

11. Girard, *Things Hidden since the Foundation of the World,* 83.

12. Robert D. Kaplan, *Balkan Ghosts: A Journey through History* (New York: St. Martin's Press, 1993), 39.

13. Quoted in Richard Howard, *Alone with America* (New York: Atheneum, 1969), 578.

14. John Macquarrie, *Jesus Christ in Modern Thought* (Philadelphia: Trinity Press International, 1990), 406.

Chapter 13: "Where Are the Philosophers Now?"

1. René Girard, *Things Hidden since the Foundation of the World* (Stanford, Calif.: Stanford University Press, 1987), 15.

2. Robert G. Hamerton-Kelly, *Sacred Violence: Paul's Hermeneutic of the Cross* (Minneapolis: Fortress, 1992), 84.

3. From "The Rock," in *Poems by Wallace Stevens,* ed. Samuel French Morse (New York: Vintage Books, Random House, 1959), 155.

4. José Ortega y Gasset, *The Origin of Philosophy* (New York: W. W. Norton, 1967), 76–77.

5. Ibid., 8.

6. Ibid., 106.

7. Milton C. Nahm, ed., *Selections from Early Greek Philosophy* (New York: Appleton-Century-Crofts, 1964), 75.

8. Ortega y Gasset, *The Origin of Philosophy,* 105.

9. Ibid., 18.

10. Josef Pieper, *In Defense of Philosophy,* trans. Lothar Krauth (San Francisco: Ignatius Press, 1992), 92.

11. Ortega, y Gasset, *The Origin of Philosophy,* 18n.

12. Ibid., 56.

13. Pieper, *In Defense of Philosophy,* 91.

14. Ibid., 85.

15. Ortega y Gasset, *The Origin of Philosophy,* 25.

16. Ibid., 29.

17. Ibid.

18. Ibid., 25. I am not trying to psychologize Ortega, but I am trying to read his essay carefully, and in my view a careful reading leads one to suspect that the author was being surprised by the drift of his own thought.

19. Ibid., 26.

20. Nahm, *Selections from Early Greek Philosophy,* 71–72.

21. H. G. Wells, *The Outline of History* (New York: Doubleday, 1961), 2:723; emphasis added.

22. Nahm, *Selections from Early Greek Philosophy,* 62.

23. Ibid.

24. Though dissenters such as Heidegger can be found, most still agree that Parmenides' invective against those who would try to account for the origins and the processes of change was directed specifically at Heraclitus.

25. Nahm, *Selections from Early Greek Philosophy,* 93.

26. Plato, *The Republic and Other Works,* trans. B. Jowett (New York: Doubleday, n.d.), 533.

27. Martin Heidegger, *An Introduction to Metaphysics* (New Haven: Yale University Press, 1959), 180f.

28. Helmut Koester, "Jesus the Victim," *Journal of Biblical Literature* 3, no. 1 (Spring 1992): 8.

29. Ibid., 8–9.

30. Ortega y Gasset, *The Origin of Philosophy,* 114.

31. W. K. C. Guthrie, *A History of Greek Philosophy* (Cambridge: Cambridge University Press, 1962), 1:417.

32. Ortega y Gasset, *The Origin of Philosophy,* 122.

33. Ibid., 123.

34. Pieper, *In Defense of Philosophy,* 72.

35. Ibid.

36. M. Heidegger, *Die Selbstbehauptung der deutschen Universität* (Breslau, 1933), 12f; quoted in Pieper, *In Defense of Philosophy,* 115.

37. Ibid.

38. Quoted in Louis A. Sass, *Madness and Modernism* (New York: Basic Books, 1992), 534.

39. Jacques Derrida, *Writing and Difference* (Chicago: University of Chicago Press, 1978), 292.

40. René Girard, *Violence and the Sacred,* trans. Patrick Gregory (Baltimore: Johns Hopkins University Press, 1979), 204.

41. Ortega y Gasset, *The Origin of Philosophy,* 38.

42. Ibid., 39. The emphasis in the last sentence is Ortega's; the earlier italic emphases are mine.

43. José Ortega y Gasset, *The Dehumanization of Art and Other Essays on Art, Culture, and Literature* (Princeton: Princeton University Press, 1972), 36.

44. Ibid., 33.

45. Ibid.

46. Ibid., 34.

47. Ibid., 33.

48. Ibid., 33–34.

49. Federico García Lorca, "The Duende: Theory and Divertissement," *The Poet's Work,* ed. Reginald Gibbons (Boston: Houghton Mifflin, 1979), 28ff.

50. Cesáreo Bandera, *The Sacred Game* (University Park: Pennsylvania State University Press, 1994), 126.

51. Czeslaw Milosz, *The History of Polish Literature* (Berkeley: University of California Press, 1983), 458; quoted in Leonard Nathan and Arthur Quinn, *The Poet's Work* (Cambridge: Harvard University Press, 1991), 24–25.

52. Ortega y Gasset, *The Origin of Philosophy,* 52n.

53. Friedrich Nietzsche, *Ecce Homo* (London: Penguin, 1992), 96.
54. Heidegger, *An Introduction to Metaphysics,* 126.
55. Ibid., 169.
56. Ibid., 174.
57. Ibid., 129.
58. Ibid., 161.
59. Ibid., 163.
60. Ibid., 133.
61. Ibid., 347; Heidegger's emphasis.
62. Ibid.
63. Ibid., 348–49.
64. Ibid., 350.
65. René Girard, *A Theater of Envy* (New York: Oxford University Press, 1991), 208.
66. Heidegger, *An Introduction to Metaphysics,* 360.
67. Ibid., 364.
68. Girard, *Things Hidden since the Foundation of the World,* 278.
69. Heidegger, *An Introduction to Metaphysics,* 367.
70. Simone Weil, *Gravity and Grace* (London: Routledge and Kegan Paul, 1972), 51.

Chapter 14: The Voice from La Cruz

1. "The Future," *Stranger Music* (New York: Pantheon Books, 1993), 370.
2. Martin Heidegger, *Basic Writings,* ed. David Farrell Krell (San Francisco: Harper San Francisco, 1977), 362.
3. Tony Judt, "The New Old Nationalism," *New York Review of Books,* May 26, 1994, 51.
4. Michael Ignatieff, "Blood and Belonging: Journeys into the New Nationalism" (excerpts), *Harper's,* March 1994, 18.
5. Ibid., 20.
6. Ibid., 18.
7. Ibid.
8. Mark Danner, *The Massacre at El Mozote* (New York: Vintage, 1994).
9. Ibid., 82.
10. Charles Mackay, *Extraordinary Popular Delusions and the Madness of Crowds* (New York: Farrar, Straus and Giroux, 1932), 365.
11. *New York Times,* May 9, 1994, B-2.
12. Danner, *The Massacre at El Mozote,* 78–79.
13. Quoted in Marjorie J. Thompson, "Obedience: The Deepest Passion of Love," *Weavings* 3, no. 3 (May–June 1988): 31.
14. René Girard, *Things Hidden since the Foundation of the World* (Stanford, Calif.: Stanford University Press, 1987), 399.

Epilogue: Redeem the Time

1. Jean Sulivan, *Morning Light,* trans. Joseph Cunneen and Patrick Gormally (New York: Paulist Press, 1988), 127.

2. Dietrich Bonhoeffer, *Letters and Papers from Prison* (New York: Macmillan, 1967), 300.

3. Sulivan, *Morning Light,* 74.

4. G. K. Chesterton, *Orthodoxy* (Garden City, N.Y.: Doubleday, 1959), 100.

5. C. K. Barrett, *The Signs of an Apostle* (1970), 88, quoted in James D. G. Dunn, "Rediscovering the Spirit" *Expository Times* 84 (1972–73): 44.

6. Karl Barth, *The Epistle to the Romans,* trans. E. C. Hoskins (Oxford, 1933), 375.

7. Andrew J. McKenna, *Violence and Difference* (Urbana: University of Illinois Press, 1992), 110.

8. T. S. Eliot, "Ash Wednesday," *The Complete Poems and Plays, 1909–1950* (New York: Harcourt, Brace & World, 1971), 64.

9. René Girard, *Job: The Victim of His People* (Stanford, Calif.: Stanford University Press, 1987), 108.

Index